HIMAVAT

Diary Leaves

Portrait of Nicholas Roerich by Svetoslav Roerich

HIMAVAT

NICHOLAS ROERICH

DIARY LEAVES

NICHOLAS ROERICH MUSEUM

NEW YORK   MMXVII

Nicholas Roerich Museum
319 West 107th Street
New York NY 10025
www.roerich.org

© 1946 by Nicholas Roerich.
© 2017 by Nicholas Roerich Museum.
First edition published in 1946. Second edition 2017.

Cover illustration: Nicholas Roerich. *Guru Guri Dhar.* 1931

FOREWORD TO THE FIRST EDITION

HIMAVAT is devoted basically to the concept of Culture. With his usual versatility and deep understanding, Nicholas Roerich extols the concepts of evolution, beauty, peace, and knowledge. In his address as President of the League of Culture, Roerich says:

"Culture is the reverence of Light. Culture is the love of humanity. Culture is fragrance, the unity of life, and beauty. Culture is the synthesis of uplifting and sensitive attainments. Culture is the armor of light. Culture is salvation. Culture is the moving force. Culture is the Heart.

"If we gather all the definitions of Culture, we find the synthesis of active Bliss, the altar of enlightenment, and constructive beauty."

The present volume should be truly a friend of each student and teacher. In these tenets of creative labor and vitality are generously spread out the fruits of the all-embracing artistic and philosophic thought of Roerich, who has been justly recognized by the public opinion of many countries, not only as the mighty creator in the field of art but also as the Leader of Culture. As the Hon. George Gordon Battle rightly affirmed: "Nicholas Roerich is unquestionably one of the greatest leaders of history." Combined with his extraordinary breadth of mind, there is a sublime sympathy with the opinions of, and tolerance for, the prejudices of others. He has a marvelous equipment to be the leader of an international movement. He has power not only to plan but to act. He can translate his dreams into action."

Great Russian Artist, Nicholas Roerich is a great friend of India.

India will always recall these blessed words of Roerich: "O Bharata, all-beautiful, let me send thee my heartfelt admiration for all the greatness and inspiration which fill thy ancient cities and temples, thy meadows, thy deobans, thy sacred rivers, and the Himalayas."

CONTENTS

CONTENTS

I

HIMAVAT

HIMAVAT

ATHANASIUS Nikitin Tveritin, a Moscovite of the fifteenth century, after his journey to India, exclaimed:
"And I, out of the midst of many troubles went to India."

The most excellent Hali, the Arabian, mentioned by
Paracelsus, said: *Vade, filii, ad Montes Indiae et ad cavernas suas,
et accipe ex cis lapides honoratos!* "Go, my son, to the mountains
of India, and to their quarries, and take from there those
precious stones!"—Let us go to the mountains of India!

From all parts of the world, people want to know
about the Himalayas. The best people are striving in heart
toward this jewel of India. They ask to send at least a small
sketch, or a snapshot, which they can keep on their desk
for inspiration. In all ages, there was this attraction to the
Himalayas. People know that when anyone seeks spiritual
upliftment, he has to look toward the Himalayas.

Many expeditions are striving to conquer the gorgeous
peaks of the Himalayas. Severely the unconquered giants
meet the daring intruders. Again Everest refused to welcome the newcomers. And Nanga Parbat does not facilitate
matters in the attempted conquest. And the Kinchanjunga
peak is not even contested. And yet from all sides, various
nations aspire to reach the resplendent Himalayan summits. Such a procession turns into an homage of pilgrims
to the highest of the world.

The local Lamas smile mysteriously when they hear
that yet another attempt was defeated. If they have confidence in you, they will tell you in whispers some ancient
prophecies that assert that certain sacred summits will
never be defiled. Not long ago, a well-known Lama, who

is now dead, told us: "Curious people are the Pelings. Why do they undertake such dangers in the physical body, when we can visit these summits and do so in our subtle body?"

Indeed, in every striving to the summits, in every ascent, is contained an untold joy. An inner impulse irresistibly calls people toward the heights.

If someone would begin to trace historically these aspirations, having the Himalayas as their goal, an unusually significant study would result. Truly, if one could trace back the force of attraction of these heights for a thousand years, one could readily see why the Himalayas have been called "incomparable." Since times immemorial innumerable tokens of divinity have been connected with this country of mountains. Even in the dark middle ages, remote countries dreamed of beautiful India, which was epitomized in the imagination of people by the mysterious sacred snowy giants.

Let us mentally compare all these beautiful legends, which could only be conceived in the Himalayas. First of all, we will be astonished at the amazing diversity of this heritage. It is true that this wealth of legends has originated in the accumulations of many tribes, becoming more bounteous through the grateful contributions of many millenniums, and is crowned by the achievements of great seekers after truth. All this is so. But for such supreme achievements a magnificent environ is necessary, and what could be more majestic than the unconquered mountains with all their inexpressible radiance and all their exquisite variations of forms.

It would be a rather unfortunate and feeble effort to compare the Himalayas with any of the other splendid mountain ranges of the world. The Andes, the Caucasus, the Alps, the Altai—all the most beautiful heights will appear to be but single peaks when compared with the supreme mountain ranges of the Himalayas.

What does it not encompass, this multiform Beauty? Tropical approaches, Alpine slopes and, finally, all the incalculable glaciers, powdered with meteoric dust. No one describes the Himalayas as overwhelming; no one would dare to call them gloomy portals, nor mention the word monotony, in thinking of the Himalayas. Truly, a great part of the human vocabulary must be forgotten when you enter the realm of the Himalayan Snow—the part of one's vocabulary comprising its sinister and effete expressions.

The human spirit, seeking to overcome all obstacles, is filled with a yearning, which irresistibly impels one onward toward the conquest of these summits. And the very difficulties that at times loom so dangerously become only the most necessary and the most desired steps of ascent, overcoming earthly conventionality. All the dangerous bamboo bridges over the thundering mountain torrents; all the slippery steps on the age-old glaciers over perilous precipices; all the unavoidable inclines before each successive ascent; and the storms, thunder and cold and heat are surmounted when the chalice of achievement is full.

Not the feelings of ambition nor boastfulness alone could inspire so many travelers and searchers to go to the Himalayas. Other difficult peaks could be found for competition and contests. But, above all, thoughts of competition and contests is a yearning toward these world magnets, an ineffable holy aspiration of which heroes are born.

The true magnets are not competitive laurels of contests nor the fleeting front pages of books and newspapers, but the attraction to this surpassing grandeur which sustains the spirit; and in such striving there can be no harm.

"Is this another tribute to the Himalayas?" one may ask.

But does the solemn grandeur of the Himalayas need any tributes?

Of course, in this case tributes are out of place; and any of them, even the most excellent, can be but feeble echoes. But then, why does one think of the Himalayas? Why are we seemingly compelled to think of them, remember them, and strive toward them?

Because even mental communion with their solemn

grandeur provides one of the best tonics. Everything is impelled toward the beautiful in its own way. Everyone thinks about beauty, and he will feel an impulse to say something or other about it. The thought of Beauty is so powerful and moving that man cannot contain it silently within himself, but always tries to clothe it in words. Perhaps in song or in some other expression of his being, man must manifest and record his thought of the Beautiful.

From the tiniest flower, from the wing of the butterfly, from the glow of a crystal and on, further and higher, through beautiful human forms, through the mysterious sublime touch, man wants to fortify himself by the immutably Beautiful. Wherever on earth there have been beautiful creations of human hands, the pilgrim will come to them. He will find calm under their created vaults and in the radiance of their frescoes and stained glass. And if the pilgrim is captivated by mirages of nature's far- off horizons, he will set out toward them. And if, at last, he becomes aware of these loftiest peaks shining far off, he will be drawn to them, and in this very striving he will become stronger, purer, and will be inspired to achievements for the good, for beauty, and for ascent.

The pilgrim is always listened to with special attention near the campfire or at a gathering of men. And not only in ancient chronicles does one read of the respect accorded to those who came from afar. Even now, despite all the speedy ways of communication, when the world has already become small, when people strive into higher strata or down toward the center of the planet, even now, the narrative of the pilgrim still remains the highlight of every gathering.

"Are the Himalayas truly so beautiful?"

"Are they really incomparable?"

"Tell us something about the Himalayas and whether anything unusual is to be found there!"

People expect something unusual in every narrative of a pilgrim. Customs, habits, immovability due to attachments depress even the coarsest heart. Even a depressed spirit strives toward movement. After all, no one thinks of movement as directed downward only.

I recall the story that a traveler once related having begun the descent of the Grand Canyon in Arizona: surrounded by most beautiful colors, he was oppressed by the very thought of such endless descent: "We descended lower and lower, and this thought of descending even prevented our admitting the country."

Of course, exaltation and transport is primarily connected with ascent. During ascent there is the urgent desire to look beyond the snow peaks that soar before you. But when you descend, each parting summit pronounces a sad "goodbye." Therefore, it is so joyous not only to ascend a summit, but at least to follow the ways of ascent in thought. When we hear of new travelers to the Himalayas, we are thankful even for that, for they remind us of the summits of the call ever beautiful and ever necessary.

Himalayas, let me send once more my heartfelt admiration!

Likewise, India, all beautiful, let me send thee another greeting for all the greatness and inspiration, which fill thy meadows, thy ancient cities and sacred rivers!

Kailasa, Manasarowar, Badrinath, Kedarnath, Trilokinath, Ravalsar—these glorious gems of the Highest always fill the heart with special blissful tremor. When we were within a day's journey from Manasarowar, the entire caravan already became uplifted—thus far around does the aura of a holy ashram act.

Another vivid recollection arises from the path to Trilokinath. A long line of Sadhus and Lamas stretches along this road—the old sanctuary, the site of pilgrimage and prayer. These pilgrims have met here from many different roads. Some already completing their spiritual journeyings, are walking along with a trident; some carry bamboo staves; others are without anything, even without clothing. And the snow of the Rotang Pass is no impediment to them.

The pilgrims proceed, knowing that the Rishis and the Pandavas dwelt here. Here is the Beas of Vyasa; here is Vyasakund—the place of the fulfillment of all wishes. Here Vyasa Rishi compiled the Mahabharata.

Not in legend alone, but in reality, did the great Rishis live here. Their presence breathes life into the cliffs that are crowned with glaciers, into the emerald pastures where the yaks graze, and into the caves and the roaring torrents. From here were sent forth those spiritual calls of which humanity has heard through all ages. These calls are taught in schools; they have been translated into many languages—and this crystal of acquisitions has been stratified on the cliffs of the Himalayas.

"Where can one find words with which to praise the Creator after seeing the incomparable beauty of the Himalayas?" sings the Hindu. Along the paths of the Guru, along the peaks of the Rishi, along the mountain paths of the pilgrims of the spirit, lies that treasure, which no torrent of rain can wear away, nor any lightning turn to ashes. He who walks toward the Good is blessed on all paths. How touching are all the narratives which tell of the meeting of the righteous ones of various nations! The tops of the deodars in the forest touch each other in the wind. Thus, everything that is of the highest meets without injury and harm. Time was when quarrels were settled by single combat, and decisions were reached by a conference of chiefs. So do the deodars discuss matters between themselves. What a meaningful word: deodar—the gift of God. And this significant name is not without reason: for the resin of the deodar has healing powers. Deodar, musk, valerian, roses, and other similar substances comprise the beneficent medicines of the Rishis. Some have wanted to do away with these medicines by substituting an invasion of new discoveries; however, humanity again reverts to the foundations.

Here is a photograph of a man who walks through fire without harming himself. This is not a fiction. Witnesses will tell you of the same trials by fire in Madras, Lucknow,

Benares. And not only does the Sadhu walk harmlessly on the flaming coals, but he leads behind him those who desire to follow him and hold on to him.

In Benares a Sadhu sits in sacred posture upon the water of the Ganges. His crossed legs are covered by the brim of the water. The people flock to the banks, amazed at the holy man.

Still another Sadhu has been buried alive for many days; another swallows various poisons without any harm. Here is a Lama, who can levitate himself; another Lama by means of *tumo* can generate his own heat, thus protecting himself against snow and mountain glaciers; there a Lama can give the death stroke with his "deadly eye" to a mad dog. A venerated Lama from Bhutan relates, how during his stay in the Tzang district in Tibet, a Lama asked the ferryman to take him across from Tzampo free of charge, but the cunning man replied: "I will gladly take you over, if you can prove that you are a great Lama. A mad dog is running about here, doing great harm—kill it." The Lama said nothing; but looking at the dog, he raised his hand and said a few words, and the dog fell dead! The Bhutanese Lama saw this himself. One hears frequently in Tibet and in India of the same "deadly eye" and the "eye of Kapila." And on a map of the seventeenth century printed in Antwerp, by authority of the Catholic clergy, is mentioned the name of the country, Shambhala.

If one can walk through fire, and another can sit on water, and a third remain suspended in the air, and a fourth repose on nails, and a fifth swallow poison, and a sixth kill with a glance, and a seventh lie buried without harm, then one may collect all those grains of knowledge in himself. And thus the obstacles of lower matter can be transmuted! Not in a remote age, but now, right here, where Millikan's cosmic rays, Rhine's thought-transference, and the reality of finest psychic energy are also being studied and affirmed.

Every Rishi pronounced in his own language the sacred

pledge for the construction of a revived, refined, and beautiful world!

For the sake of a single righteous being, a whole city was saved. As beacons, lightning rods, and citadels of God stood the Rishis of various nations, of various creeds, of various ages, yet one in the spirit of salvation and ascension for all!

Whether the Rishi came upon fire, whether he arrived home upon a stone, whether he came upon the whirlwind, he always hastened for the general good. Whether he prayed on mountain summits, or on a steep riverbank, or in a hidden cave, he always sent out his prayers for the unknown, for the stranger, for the laborers, for the sick and the crippled.

Whether the Rishi sent out white horses to save the unknown pilgrims, or whether he blessed unknown seafarers, or guarded a city by night, he always stood as a pillar of light for all, without condemnation and without extinguishing the flame.

Without condemnation, without mutual suspicion, without weakening each other, ever upwards, the Rishis ascended the eternal Mount Meru.

Before us is the road to Kailas. There rises one of the fifteen wonders described in Tibetan books: The Mount of the Bell! Along sharp ridges one climbs to its summit. It stands higher than the last junipers, higher than the last yellow and white mountain ranges. There Padma Sambhava once walked—this is recorded in the ancient monastery Gandola. It is exactly here that the caves of Milarepa are situated. And not one but many have been sanctified with the name of the hermit who hearkened before dawn to the voices of the Devas. Not far away are also legends which surround Pahari Baba. Here also are the spiritual strongholds of Gautama Rishi. Many Rishis walked here. And he who gave the mountain its enticing name, "Mount of the Bell," also thought of the call of the Bell for all, of helping all, of the Universal Good!

Here Rishis lived for Universal Good!

When Rishis meet on the mountain paths, they do not ask each other: "From where do you come? Is it from the East, or West, or South, or North?" This is quite apparent: that they come from the Good and go to the Good. An exalted, refined flaming heart knows where is the Good and, in it, what can be found.

Some of the travelers in our caravan were once discussing the qualities of the various Rishis, but a gray-haired pilgrim, pointing to snowy peaks, effulgent in their complete beauty, said:

"Are we to judge the qualities of these summits? We can but bow in admiration before their unattainable splendor!

Satyam, Shivam, Sundaram.

The Upanishads affirm: "There is no joy without infiniteness. There is no joy in the finite. Joy is infinity. But it is needful to wish to cognize infinity."

The lofty spiritual mood in which a Hindu recites the words of the sacred tradition is something not easily forgotten. The great poet Tagore, whose sensitive heart is a storehouse of these great rhythms, knows how to evoke all their beauties.

In India, when the verses of the Mahabharata, the Upanishads, and the Puranas are being recited, then there is joy, despite all troubles; and even if the modernization of India is inevitable, the beauty of such sacred poetry will live on forever.

This inner joy of the heart is something that we have to cultivate and learn how to retain so that it takes up its abode in the heart, and this beneficent joy of the heart becomes a lasting power to disperse all the forces of darkness.

Whether we think of those sublime temples of southern India, of the grandeur of Chittur and Gwalior, and the great strongholds of Rajputana, or the solemn spirit of the Himalayas, everywhere we shall find the joy of great thoughts.

On the moonlit Ganges, in the mystery of Benares

seen at night, and in the great cadences of the Himalayan waterfalls, we shall find the same lofty sense of joy.

In the repetition of such ancient names as Manu, Rama, Vyasa, Arjuna, Krishna, of the Pandavas, Rishis, heroes, creators, and great constructors, we recognize a loving respect for the past.

From the Mother of the World, from the Queen of Peace, we receive this delicate flowerlike joy of the heart.

Marvelous India! Splendid in outer beauty, most beautiful in its secret inner life.

Beautiful, beloved India!

INDIA

DURING the days of the present Armageddon, I have been asked to send my message to several art exhibitions in India. My message was: "Art should be protected by all means. Armageddon is roaring. Art and Knowledge are the cornerstones of Evolution. Art and Science are needed always; but in our days of Armageddon, they must be especially guarded by all the powers of our hearts. It is a great mistake to think that during troubled times culture can be disregarded. On the contrary, the need of culture is especially felt in times of war and human misunderstandings. Outside of Art, Religion is inaccessible; outside of Art, the spirit of Nationality is lost; outside of Art, Science is dark. This is not a utopia. The history of humanity gives innumerable examples of Art being a great beacon of light in times of calamity. Scientists assert that color and sound are a panacea. By beauty and harmony even wild beasts were tamed. Let the sacred flute of Sri Krishna resound again. Let us visualize that peace in which the majestic frescoes of Ajanta were created. In times of war, let us think of future peace, affirmed by creativeness, labor, and beauty.

"Traveling through blessed India we once passed along a road in the shadow of mighty chinars. Our guide told us: 'The great emperor Akbar thought of the future travelers who will be sheltered by these beautiful trees. He looked into the future.' 'To regard the beautiful means to improve," said Plato. 'Man becomes that of which he thinks,' preordained the Upanishads.

"A renaissance of art is the evidence of the renaissance

of a nation. In a declining country, art becomes only an abstract luxury. But when a country is in its full progress, art becomes the real motive power of its people. Let us imagine the history of humanity without the treasure of beauty. We will then readily realize that the epochs are left meaningless, denuded of their soul. Without a manifestation of the spirit of the beautiful, we shall remain amid the ugliness of death. And when we proclaim that beauty–art is life–we speak about the coming evolution of beauty. Everything accomplished for art is an attainment for evolution. Every coworker in this field is already a hero.

It is a great praise to this country that the roll of its creative workers cannot be expressed in one list but merits an entire great series, even with the briefest appreciation. We are happy to feel what a vast material is before us, and what a joy it is to show to the young generation the brilliant legion that has constructed the most beautiful achievements. Wherever art and knowledge flourish, we may be enthusiasts. And in this joyful enthusiasm we may greet the true creative forces of the nation. An exhibition is not only a monument to the creator, the worker, but it is the best evocation for the youth to come. I am happy to greet the brilliant artists, to hail the essence of beautiful creative thought, and to salute the young generation to which this creative thought brings its coming happiness."

O Bharata, all-beautiful, let me send thee my heartfelt admiration for all the greatness and inspiration that fill thy ancient cities and temples, thy meadows, thy *deobans*, thy sacred rivers and the Himalayas.

FRIENDS OF THE EAST

Y OUR letter came just at a time when I was finishing my essay, *Tolerance,* with the following passage:
"Let us remember the instructive from a Chinese. Legend: A famous artist was invited to the Court of the Chinese Emperor in order to paint his best possible painting. The expenses connected with remuneration and traveling of the artist were great, but the Emperor—the Protector of Art—wanted to have the best masterpiece, and spared no effort to give the artist the best conditions. The artist agreed to complete the picture within a year. Special apartments were allotted to him. Here he spent day after day in contemplative thinking, so that everyone became worried as to when after all he would begin to paint. All material was long ready, but the artist apparently had no intention to start work on the canvas. Finally they decided to ask the artist, in view of the approach of the term, but he merely replied: 'Don't disturb me.' And two days before the expiration of the year, he got up, and with precise touches of the brush accomplished his best masterpiece, stating afterward: 'To make does not take long, but one has to visualize first what one wants to make.'"

It seems that sufficient time has elapsed for humanity to realize the impracticability, the baseness, and meanness of intolerance. Let us hope that past centuries have already taught us to see and realize the harm which is continuously done. Let us hope that in accordance with the saying of the wise Chinese artist: "To visualize takes a long time, but to do takes little."

Is it not a happy coincidence that just at the time of

receipt of your letter, I was mentioning three important principles: Chinese wisdom; The Ruler as a protector of Art; and striving toward achievement. If I wouldn't have written this article at a time, I still would have had to mention these three basic points. And I may also quote in addition the following passage from Agni Yoga: "According to ancient wisdom, patience is a gift of Heaven." And no doubt you have read in my book *Altai-Himalaya*, my quotation from the Tao-Te-Ching about the distinctions of a sage, which closes with the phrase: "He who possesses the quality of Tao is like a child—the venomous insects will not sting him; wild animals will not attack him; birds of prey will not strike him!" The great wisdom of Tao is also reflected on the great ancient Chinese Art. What a wonderful example for the future this unfading wisdom can give! The perfection of quality, if once already attained can always be easily renewed. How wonderful are all the teachings of the East, revealing the power of the heart with all mighty flames and achievements.

It is so gratifying to see that also in our times such great conceptions are obtained, and they can transmute the dull twilight into radiance of the future.

And Agni Yoga indicates again: "We do everything, and we exist only for the future." How beautiful is it to realize our great responsibility in face of the future. First of all, this responsibility should express itself in safeguarding the great treasures of Culture. This is a heavy task but we should rejoice at being entrusted to accomplish something great. Numerous are the obstacles on the great Path. But by these we learn, through them we ascend and develop in us vigilance, resourcefulness, and creative abilities. In everything, from the smallest to the largest, we have to affirm untiringly this glorious call: create, create, create! May this call be transformed into an imperative stimulus of life. Bringing into existence these virile commandments, let us not forget the young generation, for whom it is our duty to prepare the path of ascent.

Thus, gathering all the best treasures of the past and

creating a new image of heroism, achievement, and spiritual beauty, we shall point out to the young ones where are the true treasures, where lies the Great Reality, and where the human spirit is to find its justification.

"Verily, verily, Beauty is Brahman. Art is Brahman. Science is Brahman. Every Glory, every Magnificence, every Greatness is Brahman."

Thus exclaimed the Hindu saint coming back from the greatest *samadhi.* A new path of beauty and wisdom shall come.

And we are not alone in our struggle. The great Swami Vivekananda tells us: "Don't you see I am above all a poet. That man cannot be truly religious, who has not the faculty of feeling the beauty and grandeur of art. Non-appreciation of art is gross ignorance."

"Illumine yourself with the light of knowledge." (Hosea, 10–12)

"Man has to become the co-worker of heaven and earth."

"All beings nourish each other."

"Consciousness, Humanness, and courage are the three universal qualities, but sincerity is needed to apply them."

"Does there not exist a panacea for everything that exists? Is it not love to humanity? Do not do unto others that which you do not wish done unto you."

"If man would know how to govern himself, what difficulty could he encounter in governing a state?"

"An ignoramus proud of his knowledge, a nonentity excessively desirous of freedom, a man who returns to ancient customs are subject to unavoidable calamities." (Confucius)

"It is not better in the world." Verily it is so! The world structure is cracking. But where there are pilgrims, where there are stonemasons, where there are creators, there hope itself is being transmuted into straight-knowledge. This knowledge speaks of the undeferrableness of the hour. Let us hasten and be not afraid.

Rabindranath Tagore finishes his book (*What Is Art*)

with such words: "In Art the person in us is sending its answer to the Supreme Person, who reveals Himself to us in a world of endless beauty across the lightless world of facts."

There is no other way. O friends scattered! May my call penetrate to you. Let us join ourselves by the invisible threads of the Beautiful. I turn to you, I call to you: in the name of Beauty and Wisdom, let us combine for struggle and work.

During days of Armageddon let us ponder on Eternal Values, which are the cornerstones of Evolution.

In the name of Culture I send you from the Himalayas my heartiest greetings!

SCRIPTURES OF ASIA

IN the torn and yellow manuscripts of Turfan, we find hymns to "The God of Light," "To the Sun," "To the Eternal Living Soul." We find prayers of peace and quiet and ascension, where the word peace is often repeated.

Besides an immense collection of Buddhist texts, discoveries were also made of many Chinese, Manichean, Nestorian, Tibetan, Iranian, and other Central Asian manuscripts.

The deserted temples are now in ruins, and the vestiges of towers and ramparts buried beneath the sands, indicate the sites of flourishing cities. The frescoes have gone, the libraries have been scattered, and all their treasures ransacked. The traveler today, who goes by another route, no longer sees those brilliant colors, that shining metalware, but only darkness.

These manuscripts have suffered as much from the hands of vandals as from dampness and decay, and yet their mildewed pages still remind us that these dark and deserted ruins were at one time the abode of clean and luminous thought. The soul of many an ancient scribe is still enshrined in lofty messages.

A recent translation from one of the Turfan hymns reads thus: (Omissions shown by . . .)

"A hymn to the Living Soul . . . all the sins, all the hesitations, internal and external, all the thoughts, all that has been thought and said mixture of good and evil thoughts, unconsciousness. 'Know Thyself,' the pure word that leads to the soul. Through the soul understand all the wicked words of the Master of Evil, which are likely to lead you toward the eternal Darkness.

"As a judge, weigh every word that is said and manifested. Understand the transmigration of the soul and behold the depths of hell where the souls suffer torments.

"Preserve the purity of your soul and the treasures of the Word. . . .

"O devouring fire of Man! And you luminous-winged Free Soul.

"Predestination and transmigration defend your heart and thought from all wicked impulses.

"Go to the land of Light by the road of Peace. . . .

"I sing Thee O God omnipotent, O Living Soul, O gift of the Father.

"By the saintly path return to thy home. O Power so generously dispensing happiness.

"Wisdom . . . all . . . Herself . . . Trembling . . . hearing . . . peace . . . you the Son of the Almighty.

"All the persecutions, all the torments and poverty and need which you have assumed, who could endure them? Thou art the Luminous One, the Gracious One, the Blessed One, the Powerful and Noble Master. . . .

"Proceeding from the Light, from God, I have lost my native land, I have been exiled.

"Be blessed he who will deliver my soul from torments. . . .

"You will receive Eternal Life.

"Purify your luminous soul, and she will liberate you.

"Sing beautifully and rejoice in the thought: 'O Luminous Guide of the Soul'!

"Sing that beautiful hymn, the hymn of Good for peace, for confidence.

"With the trumpet declare with joy: 'Guide our souls in unity toward salvation.'

"To the call of the trumpet the sons of God will joyfully respond.

"Say Holy! Holy! Holy! Say Amen, Amen!

"Sing O Luminous Wisdom: Repeat the pure saying,

'The Living word of Truth will liberate the prisoners from their chains.' Glorify the Truth.

"Sing 'Be ardent in the fear of God; unite in the commandments. . . . Light . . . call . . . the herald . . . the great peace, treasures, which the souls, the eyes, the ears . . . Invite the Son of God to the Divine Banquet, decorate the beloved groves, show the way to the Light.'

"Group your members in numbers of five, seven, twelve. There they are the seven glittering noble stones on which the world is based. Through their power the worlds and all beings live. It is like a lamp in the house shining in darkness. . . .

"Do not strike him who has struck you. Do not be revenged on him who takes revenge. Do not seduce those who try to seduce you.

"Receive in a friendly way those who come to you in anger. Do not do unto others what you would not they do to you. Suffer offenses from those higher than yourself, from your equals, and from those inferior.

"Do not let the elephant be bound by the flowers that are thrown at him. Let not the stone be dissolved by drops of water. Offences and calumnies will not shake the long-suffering ones. The long-suffering One will stand like Mount Sumeru.

"The long-suffering will know how to appear at times as a disciple, at times as a master, at others as a slave, or as a lord. . . .

"There is the path, there is the mystery, there is the great commandment and the gates of liberation!

"Let Thy will be done. Let Thy magnificence protect me, and let my patience, righteousness, and fear of God be increased. Thy voice and my ear . . .

"Happy is he who in your purity and justice O God knows the variety, the multiformity, the charitableness, the miracle. . . .

"Here is a disciple of righteous heart and one who loves his master. He follows his master, he honors his name and cherishes him

"Receive those brothers who come to you. If they would draw from thy wisdom then teach them as if they were your own children. . . .

"I like the Lord who takes off his armor and lays aside his weapons to put on his royal robes. Thus the envoy of light sets aside his militant character, and sits in light and in his divine aspect, with a shining crown, with a beautiful crown. And in great joy the luminous Ones hurry to him from right and left singing a hymn of joy. They all gather around the divine miracle like flashes of lightning. . . .

"The noble Lord has kept his promise. I shall sit on high, at the predestined hour, I shall send you help."

So say these moldy manuscripts. In these Pehlevi and Uigur scriptures have been kept the voices from distant lands.

In the frescoes the characteristics of various nations combine harmoniously, and both in imagery and technique you will find the outlines of the Chinese, Iranian, and Hindu genius. Luminous great-eyed figures surrounded by various symbols send up their prayers for peace.

"And from beyond the Himalayas resound the prayers of the ancient Vedas.

"Let all the pain of the world bring us peace. Let God be witness to it.

"Let peace be one and let it reign everywhere.

"Let peace come unto us."

In the midst of the whirlwinds of the West, Dante in his immortal way tells us:

"O Man, what tempests must strike thee, what losses thou must suffer, what shipwreck and loss must ensue, while you strive like a many-headed monster toward evil. You are sick in your consciousness, you are sick in sentiment. Insoluble reasoning will not help your consciousness. The clearest proofs will not convince your low understanding.

"Even sweet and divine clearness does not attract you, though it breathes through the harmonies of the Holy

Spirit. Remember brother how well and agreeable it is to live in unity."

Asia prayed for peace, and the great souls of the West called for the same.

In all the prayers that were inscribed to last, there has been a desire for peace, for the peace of the world.

SHAMBHALA

"LAMA, tell me of Shambhala!"
"But you Westerners know nothing about Shambhala—you wish to know nothing. Probably you ask only out of curiosity; and you pronounce this sacred word in vain."

"Lama, I do not ask about Shambhala aimlessly. Everywhere, people know of this great symbol under different names. Our scientists seek each spark concerning this remarkable realm. Csoma de Koros knew of Shambhala when he made his prolonged visit to the Buddhist monasteries. Grunwedel translated the book of the famous Tashi Lama Pal-den ye-she, about *The Way to Shambhala*. We sense how, under secret symbols, a great truth is concealed. Truly, the ardent scientist desires to know all about Kalachakra."

"Can this be so, when some of your Western people desecrate our temples? They smoke within our holy sanctuaries; they neither understand nor wish to venerate our faith and our teaching. They mock and deride the symbols whose meaning they do not penetrate. Should we visit your temples, our conduct would be completely different, because your great Bodhisatva, Issa, is verily an exalted one. And none of us would defame the teaching of mercy and righteousness."

"Lama, only the very ignorant and stupid would ridicule your teaching. All the teachings of righteousness are as in one sacred place. And each one possessed of his senses will not violate the sacred place. Lama, why do you think that the essential teaching of the Blessed One is unknown to the West? Why do you believe that in the West we do not know of Shambhala?

"Lama, upon my very table you may see the Kalachakra, the Teaching brought by the great Atticha from India. I know that if a high spirit, already prepared, hears a voice proclaiming *Kalagiya*, it is the call to Shambhala. We know which Tashi Lama visited Shambhala. We know the book of the High Priest, T'aishan—*The Red Path to Shambhala*. We even know the Mongolian song about Shambhala. Who knows, perhaps we even know many things. We know that quite recently a young Mongolian Lama issued a new book about Shambhala."

The Lama studies us with his piercing glance. Then he says:

"Great Shambhala is far beyond the ocean. It is the mighty heavenly domain. It has nothing to do with our earth. How and why do you earthly people take interest in it? Only in some places, in the Far North, can you discern the resplendent rays of Shambhala."

"Lama, we know the greatness of Shambhala. We know the reality of this indescribable realm. But we also know about the reality of the earthly Shambhala. We know how some high Lamas went to Shambhala, how along their way they saw the customary physical things. We know the stories of the Buryat Lama, of how he was accompanied through a very narrow secret passage. We know how another visitor saw a caravan of hill-people, with salt from the lakes, on the very borders of Shambhala. Moreover, we ourselves have seen a white frontier post of one of the three outposts of Shambhala. So, do not speak to me about the heaven Shambhala only, but also about the one on earth; because you know as well as I, that on earth Shambhala is connected with the heavenly one. And in this link, the two worlds are unified."

The Lama becomes silent. With eyes half-concealed by the lids, he examines our faces. And in the evening dusk, he commences his tale: "Verily, the time is coming when the Teaching of the Blessed One will once again come from the North to the South. The word of Truth, which started its great path from Bodhgaya, again shall return to the same sites. We must accept it simply, as it is: the fact that the true teaching shall leave Tibet, and shall again appear in the South. Really, great things are coming. You come from the West, yet you are bringing news of Shambhala. We must take it verily so. Probably the ray from the tower of Rigden-jyepo has reached all countries.

"Like a diamond glows the light on the Tower of Shambhala. He is there—Rigden-jyepo, indefatigable, ever vigilant in the cause of mankind. His eyes never close. And in his magic mirror he sees all events, of earth. And the might of his thought penetrates into far-off lands. Distance does not exist for him; he can instantaneously bring assistance to worthy ones. His powerful light can destroy all darkness. His immeasurable riches are ready to aid all needy ones who offer to serve the cause of righteousness. He may even change the karma of human beings. . . ."

"Lama, it seems to me that you speak of Maitreya; is it not so?"

"We must not pronounce this mystery! There is much that may not be revealed. There is much which may not be crystallized into sound. In sound we reveal our thought. In sound we project our thought into space, and the greatest harm may follow. Because everything, divulged before the destined date, results in untold harm. Even the greatest catastrophes may be provoked by such light-minded acts. If Rigden-jyepo and the Blessed Maitreya are one and the same for you—let it be so. I have not so stated!

"Uncountable are the inhabitants of Shambhala. Numerous are the splendid new forces and achievements that are being prepared there for humanity...."

"Lama, ancient teachings tell us that very soon new energies shall be given to humanity. Is this true?"

"Innumerable are the great things predestined and prepared. Through the Holy Scriptures we know of the Teaching of the Blessed One about the inhabitants of the distant stars. From the same source we have heard of the flying steel bird ... about iron serpents which devour space with fire and smoke. Tathagata, the Blessed One, predicted all for the future."

"Lama, if the great warriors are incarnated, will not the activities of Shambhala take place here on our earth?"

"Everywhere—here and in heaven. All benevolent forces shall come together to destroy the darkness. Each one who will help in this great task shall be rewarded a hundredfold, and upon this very earth, in this incarnation. All sinners against Shambhala will perish in this very incarnation because they have exhausted mercy."

"Lama, we certainly know that Pan-chen-rinpoche is greatly esteemed everywhere. In different countries we have heard how highly not only Buddhists but the people of many nations talk about His Holiness. It is even said that in his private apartments, long before his departure, the details of his coming travels were outlined in the frescoes. We know that Pan-chen-rinpoche follows the customs of all the great Lamas. We have been told how during his flight he and his followers escaped many of the greatest dangers.

"We know how at one time his pursuers from Lhasa were already quite upon him, when a heavy snowfall cut off the pursuers' road. Another day, Pan-chen-rinpoche arrived at a lake in the mountains; a difficult problem confronted him. His enemies were close behind; but in order to escape, it would be necessary for him to make a long circuit around the lake. Thereupon, Pan-chen-rinpoche sat in deep meditation for some time. Arousing himself, he gave orders, that despite the danger, the entire caravan would have to spend the night on the shores of the lake. Then the unusual happened. During the night, a heavy frost arose, which covered the lake with ice and snow. Before sunrise, while it was still dark, Tashi Lama gave orders to his people to move on speedily, and he, with his three hundred followers, crossed the lake over the ice by the shortest way, thus escaping danger. When the enemies arrived at the same spot, the sun was already high, and its rays had melted the ice. There remained for them only the roundabout way. Was it not so?"

"Verily, so it was. Pan-chen-rinpoche was helped by Holy Shambhala throughout his travels. He saw many wondrous signs when he crossed the uplands hastening to the North."

"Lama, not far from Ulan-Davan we saw a huge black vulture that flew low, close to our camp. He crossed the direction of something shining and beautiful, which was flying south over our camp, and which glistened in the rays of the sun."

The eyes of the Lama sparkled. Eagerly he asked:

"Did you also feel the perfumes of the temple incenses in the desert?"

"Lama, you are quite right—in the stony desert, several days from any habitation, many of us became simultaneously aware of an exquisite breath of perfume. This happened several times. We never smelt such lovely perfume. It reminded me of a certain incense which a friend of mine once gave me in India—from where he obtained it, I do not know."

"Ah—you are guarded by Shambhala. The huge black vulture is your enemy, who is eager to destroy your work, but the protecting force from Shambhala follows you in this Radiant Form of Matter. This force is always near to you but you cannot always perceive it. Sometimes only, it is manifested for strengthening and directing you. Did you notice the direction in which this sphere moved? You must follow the same direction. You mentioned to me the sacred call—*Kalagiya!* When someone hears this imperative call, he must know that the way to Shambhala is open to him. He must remember the year when he was called, because from that time evermore, he is closely assisted by the Blessed Rigden-jyepo. Only you must know and realize the manner in which people are helped because often people repel the help which is sent."

THE STONE

Champa, half-Tibetan, half-Mongol, from Kokonor, has returned to our camp from the bazaar, and whispers mysteriously:

"They say, that somewhere here is hidden some stone on which is a bronze belt."

"What may this be? And where could one find out, where the stone is?"

"Who knows, perhaps one can find out from the Lamas. Only this is very difficult as they are not communicative about the stone."

We think that the matter concerns some newly discovered Hun burial mounds, or some treasure trove, or finally some legend. Firstly, the interesting point seemed to be not so much the stone, but the belt. A belt has from antiquity been the symbol of rulership. Often we find in history that the robbing or the insult of the belt led to serious consequences.

Thus we discussed around the evening bonfire the strange news about the stone and the bronze belt, and thought that it will probably be difficult to discover any more details. If this concerned a treasure, then it would be still more difficult, as people are always reticent to speak of treasures.

Indeed one can hear often of treasures and legends found in sandy *barkhans.* Sometimes they will be connected with great names of ancient legendary warriors and rulers. Also the name of Chingiz Khan will repeatedly be mentioned since this glorious name is heralded at every opportunity.

Several days pass. New interesting herbs have been found. George is busy with the Buriat Lama, who is a famous medicine man. Unexpectedly a high official arrives from the local Prince. The Prince sends his cordial greetings, and requests that we should not touch and break the stone with the bronze belt. What a mystery—again the same stone! We make inquiries, thinking that means some special ore. We ask: "Where could it be and who has found it?" The reply arouses certain recollections.

"The stone moves about and appears near sacred and famous places. Here, where your camp is, near Naran Obo, the hill is sacred. The Prince knows that you collect useful herbs and flowers. This is very good. But do not disturb the stone, which may appear here and there. You are great people, and the stone may come your way."

This reply proved that the chief significance is not so much in the bronze belt, but in the stone itself. And this stone turns out to be the legendary fabulous precious stone, which visits important regions at preordained dates. Thus the Prince's messenger asked us in quite official tones not to disturb the miraculous stone. And we, of course, ask him to transmit to the Prince that he should not worry. We shall not disturb the stone; we will not break it or otherwise violate it.

One can well imagine how surprised the local Mongols would have been, if we were to tell them all the well-known legends and sagas about the wandering stone—*lapis exilis*—which is glorified throughout centuries from the Pacific coast to the medieval Meistersingers, to the famous Wolfram von Eschenbach. In our case the circumstance was new that not a legend was narrated to us but we were asked not to harm the very stone itself. It means that not a folklore saga but the knowledge of the very stone was living without any doubt up to our days.

Another new detail about the belt on the stone may mean that the stone possesses power. In other variants there was no mentioning of this belt. It is true that one may find in legends indications about signs on the stone, which appear and disappear. It is said that the stone warns his temporary owner of various significant events. On special occasions the stone emits cracking sounds, it may become very heavy, or on the other hand may lose weight considerably. At times the stone radiates light. The stone is usually brought to the new owner quite unexpectedly by some strangers. Numerous are the qualities of the stone. Not without cause are so many sagas and songs dedicated to it. The stone is also mentioned in medieval scientific and historical chronicles. On the Himalayas, in Tibet, and Mongolia, one constantly comes across references to this miracle. In the same connection the name of the mysterious King—Prestor John—is also often cited, and even the Holy Grail is identified with this stone.

It is strange to coordinate the remarkable sagas, which are imbued with deep symbols and signs, with the arrival of the official, asking not to injure nor to take away the stone. Here is an especially sacred place. It is said that near Naran Obo, the miraculous stone has already been seen. It is prohibited to kill any animals in this place. The Tashi Lama himself ascended Naran Obo, and has blessed the place.

"The Tashi Lama gives passes to Shambhala."

Of course, this information is also interpreted in many different ways. But nevertheless up to now some people come to the Tashi Lama with the request for such a permit.

Again old signs coincide with modernity in such unexpected forms.

We have also heard how certain people scolded and stopped the narrators about such signs. Ardent guardians of secrets will whisper, and the bard will at once interrupt his story. And if the listeners still insist, the bard will conclude with some stereotypical joke, which in no way corresponds to the inspired beginning. This means that up to now the ancient rule about the keeping of secrets still exists. And people know how to guard these great mysteries, they know how to divert the conversation to some ordinary routine matters, and they suddenly draw the attention to some insignificant outside event.

And we again remember, how once a Hindu said that he would never reveal a certain secret, and that he would rather admit the assertion that nothing of the kind exists. As in ocean waves one may discern several different currents, so also the depth of human consciousness may treasure many secrets.

Some may scoff at such a steadfastness, at such a guarding of the foundations. But others will revere it, seeing how people conquering their selfishness remain firm and adamant.

"Oh, Stone—thou precious treasure—thou art known to many people." They preserved and kept the knowledge of the stone in the most sacred treasury. If an official arrives and requests not to harm, and not to take away the stone, thereby he does not reveal the secret. He himself never said what stone he had in view. It was but his duty to warn that such a stone sometimes appears in the vicinity. It means that by such a warning he did not reveal the meaning of the stone.

The messenger was happy to have our assurance that we shall not harm the stone. Who knows, perhaps in the intonation of our reply he felt that we know more of the stone than he anticipated? Anyhow, our promise not to harm the stone was received with sincere gratitude.

To know how to guard secrets already means to prove a high quality of the spirit. Who can undertake to draw the dividing line between reality and fantasy? Recently some scientists proved that epical heroes were actually living persons, creators of life, lawgivers, whose deeds, transgressing the boundary of human consciousness, were crowned with wonderful inspiring legends.

Do you know, whether or not that the Stone exists, which is glorified by so many people?

Timur Khada.

HOLY GUARDIANS

THUS said the Mongolian Lama:

"The Holy Keepers also visited our *yurtas*. Nobody knows when They shall appear. It is not known from where They come and whither They go, but They are usually in haste. It is told that They lay foundations for monasteries, where these are necessary. Sometimes the place of their visitation is being marked by *suburgans* or by ordinary *obos*. When the news of Their approach passes through the desert, then people rejoice in all *yurtas*. It is said that there are no illnesses in those places. And all plans and deeds are successful."

We asked: "Perhaps such success is due to mental suggestion? Such beneficial thoughts and ordainments are known."

"We know of this force and we ourselves believe that success is sent. Once the Holy Keeper was asked: 'Is it true that according to His thought many benevolent deeds are done? And how does He suggest them?' It is said that He replied: 'This happens in many ways, but the main thing is that you act as is necessary.' And they hasten in order to give to the people more good thoughts, in order that people everywhere can do the best within the needed time."

We asked: "Are They at once recognized by the people?"

"To say the truth, only a few recognize them. And the others become aware, only after Their departure. And then they again begin to wait. Stupid people!

When something is given, they do not agree; and when it is taken away they again begin to wait for it."

We asked: "And when They come, where do They stay?"

"Sometimes in Their tents, but usually They go away somewhere, and no one knows properly, from beyond what mountains They come and where Their path lies. But wise people expect Them, and expect Them very much, especially for the day of the Blessed One. And when the news of Their arrival comes, joy radiates everywhere. From *yurta* to *yurta*, messengers gallop at full speed. And hardly have the people time to gather, when He has already left. People, of course, say that They use some subterranean passages, but no one knows anything definite about these. When They suddenly appear amid the desert, people wonder how such a long waterless path was accomplished. We ponder whether somewhere there are hidden roads. Even very deep and endless caves were found, and no one knows whither they lead. And in the darkness of these caverns no one was able to find his way."

We asked: "Do you narrate all this about the ancient past, or does it happen now?"

"It was, and is, and shall be. They guard the people. They keep justice. They send new thoughts. And not long ago, and may be even now there may appear a Rider. Either alone, but sometimes two, and no one knows Their ways."

We asked: "And are there any signs of Their coming?"

"No, never. None! Everything great and wonderful comes unexpected. So sudden that human thought cannot anticipate. But the heart perhaps may feel. When the time of Their approach comes, the heart longs and strives and flics to meet Them. Sometimes, the heart flutters as a bird, and perhaps at that moment They pass nearby. How often does a steed neigh, no one knows why; perhaps it sensed Their steeds. Very often dogs appear watchful apparently without reason, but never will a dog bark at Them. Sometimes it happens in caravan, during night-camping. It seems as if someone rides past, and when they listen—there is nothing to be heard. Sometimes a wonderful fragrance, as if from the best flowers, arises over the desert. It is said that this is due to Their approach. Some have seen an unusual white dog, like a Borsoi. Old people say that this was Their dog, and the dog runs alone, but as if with some purpose, and does not respond to calls: no doubt it hastens. Others have seen in the desert white birds—like doves, and believe that these were Their messengers. There are many inexplicable signs in our desert. Sometimes we find most remarkable stones. No doubt someone has placed them there. They are carved, sometimes with unknown inscriptions, sometimes round like eggs." We said: "There, you see many signs in the desert, but for foreigners the desert appears boring and dead." "That is because they do not know the language of the desert. The foreigners cannot judge the wind, nor do they smell the fragrance; and even should they meet Them, they will not recognize Their greatness."

We said: "What are They like? Some people must have seen Them."

"As circumstances require, in order not to attract the people's attention unnecessarily. I was told that in one camp They were taken for traders, in another as shepherds, and yet in another as warriors; everyone judges by himself. But They are not offended at our remarks. One, who recognized Them, tried to find what he should do. And He replied: 'You will do as is necessary, don't worry about it, but always do good deeds, everywhere and in everything.' They always teach to do good."

Again we asked: "But why do They tolerate these dead deserts?" The Lama looked at us very cunningly, and said: "And this will come in time. And the rivers will rise, and forests will grow, and grass will cover everything. Everything comes in time. As it left us because of human sins, so it will come, thanks to the Keepers' thoughts. They will send, when necessary, when we shall be able to recognize and to accept."

We asked: "And has no one any signs or tokens from Them?"

"Perhaps some have. No doubt they have. But only if anyone receives them, he will never say so."

We questioned: "And does anyone know Their names?"

"They can assume different names, but again, if anyone

was lucky to hear Their name, he will never repeat it to anyone else. No one will transgress this law."

Our friend became silent and piercingly followed with his eyes a moving point on the far-off sandy hills. Perhaps he pondered whether his luck had come. In his eyes glimmered the long-waited-for expectation. We felt that he knows, has heard, and seen much more. But much longer must one sit at the bonfire, until the heart opens up. Even if the heart would be ready to reveal, the will knows how far these gates can be opened toward foreigners. To passersby, many mysteries of the desert remain close. The desert can only entrust them to their own—only to him whom it can fully trust, to him who thinks quietly about the past and the future, to him who is content with the little that is incalculable for contemporary luxury.

The desert has assumed that aspect, in which it appears to the passerby, in order not to show its significance and magnificence. The heart of Asia is hidden with all its wealth, with all deeply buried signs, and the sons of Asia know how to guard the ordained, they guard the Teaching of the Blessed One.

Perhaps tomorrow the Lama will tell us about Shambhala.

ERDENI MORI

(Mongolian Epics)

I

IN folklore and sagas we meet with the white steeds of heroes. We know of the white steed of St. George. We know of the white horses of St. Flora and St. Laurus. We have also met with the white fiery Pegasus.

We have seen the white horses of the Lithuanian ancient god Svetovit. And the Germanic Valkyries also were riding on white steeds.

We have heard of the white horse of Isphagan in ancient Iran. We have seen the huge steeds of Arjuna, the guardians of the Temple.

We have heard of the steed of Ghessar Khan, the great hero of ancient Asia, and we have seen the trails of its hooves on the rocks in Tibet. We knew of the steeds from Himavat, with the blessed treasure Chintamani.

Erdeni Mori—the white steed—is the Mongolian carrier of the same treasure of happiness.

On Chinese paintings the white deer carries the same fiery sacred sign on its horns, as if like the deer of St. Hubertus. And the trail of the white horse marks the boundary of the Wall of China. All heroes are on white steeds. And also in Mongolia Tzagan Mori—Erdeni Mori is the white steed, venerated in all legends. The Ruler of Shambhala, Rigden-jyepo, also is seen riding on it, and the steed appears in a wondrous flame. And when the people await the future, then the great Ruler directs the waiting ones toward the predestined.

Verily the white steeds in all folklore belong to the

hero. But sometimes the wise white horse brings alone the great message.

On Scythian bronzes the predominant place is given to the horse. They, of course, carry the traditions. And in fairy tales most prophetic qualities are attributed to the white steed. The hero enters one ear of the horse and comes out wise from the other ear. In sagas the horse warns the warrior of danger. The steed never survives its master. And in burial mounds the bones of the horse are always inseparably with those of the hero.

* * *

Today Mongolia is on everyone's tongue.

Let us listen to some Mongolian prophecies.

Listen to the prophecies of the wise Mongolian seer, Molon Baksha, as written down by his grandson Sangey Zibikov, and translated by the Mongol Shagdorov and Shagdor Dabayev.

"In the year of the cycle of the pig, there will be an earthquake. In the year of the dog there will be confusion amongst those who have power. A great hero will be born in a little hut. And a great Khan will pass by, attracting no one's attention. Near the house troops will pass. People, who have no claim to nobility, will become rulers, and will govern the people. Honest people will withdraw, and will take a place near the threshold; whereas liars will take possession of homes.

There shall come a time when truth will be overpowered by hypocrisy. The spotted serpent will eat its own head, and the red-spotted serpent will devour the flesh of his own body. The horse, eating its body, shall also consume its head. Hence a chief, who embezzled the people's property, shall pay with his head.

And there will come a time when a wooden cart will cost as much as a horse. For the bad horse the road is long, and for a miser a friend is far. As the dead one has no title, so the poor one has no property.

You will fell timber with an axe that has no handle.

An iron serpent will obscure the earthly light—and the whole world is a fiery serpent.

In 1904 there will be a great event.

In the year of the ox there will again be a great occurrence. In the year of the tiger there will be destruction. The year of the hare will be the year of patience and endurance.

On the eastern boundary there will be robbery, because the chiefs will let the wolf upon a herd of sheep enclosed in a yard.

There will come a time that will be called 'neither mine nor yours,' a traveling brass kettle and a leather *yagtan* will be needed.

The fiery serpent will dominate everywhere during the time of migrations.

From the side, where the sun rises, will appear a miraculous white stone with an inscription. If you try to obliterate the inscription with an axe, it will appear again.

Beyond this stone will be the desert, which you will reach. Those who can reach this region will again become human, and the animals will again turn into animals. It will be hard for the senile ones, and for children. Loads will be carried even on oxen, cows, and horses. Images and books you will have to carry yourselves. For the old ones you will have dry meat and fried barley. To drink black tea is nourishing.

And further Molon Baksha foretold that later there will come two to four men who will subdue unrest and will construct a religious, righteous state."

Molon Baksha died at the age of eighty in the year of the ox. His song was:

> Why does the reed wave
> On the right side of the Selenga?
> Why does the reed wave,
> On yonder side of the Kudara?
> And foreseeing sufferings in life
> Why do I already feel sorrow?

When singing this song he used to cry.

* * *

And there is another prophecy:

"The great people of Kidan will not perish. They will meet the people of Shambhala. They will carry most reverently the sacred images and will honor the country's laws.

On the white stone they will read and will call for the great Teacher to reveal the word of truth.

From great bonfires the inscription on the stone will shine. What is coming? Why does the steppe grass move? Who is coming?

Erdeni Mori itself comes. Erdeni Mori itself approaches. And the people will not remain in their previous state.

What shines above the steppe grass? Why do the holy obo (cairns) radiate? Why is the great *suburgan* already alight?

There, where Erdeni Mori has passed, the steppe grass glimmers. There the wolves become silent.

And the falcons hasten their flight."

* * *

From ancient times Erdeni Mori appears, and its treasure radiates. At sunrise and at sunset everything is submerged into silence, this means that somewhere the great white steed, carrying the treasure, is passing. As long as the people know of the ordained treasure, they will remain on the righteous path. Their path, although long and unusual, is inevitable. As inevitable as is the service to perfection. For someone it may be a fairy tale, and for another it is a reality. And someone will become afraid. And others will unfold the pages of the given book.

The book of doves also came from heaven. And the treasure came from above. And not soon was a wise man found to read the book. And many peoples remember these given great gifts. And to all evil ones the light is unbearable. Why are they so horrified? They are afraid of themselves, they have not read the great book, and they have turned away from Light. And having turned away from a small light, how can their eyes stand the brilliant radiance of the Great Light!

Menhe Tengri!

. . . the great blue sky that Chengiz Khan worshipped! Endless are the plains of Mongolia. Boundless are the steppes! Numberless are the mountains, hills, ranges, and ravines, where the glory is hidden!

It seems that the desert is lifeless, but suddenly there appears a camp on the slope. Behold, many *yurtas* rise, and unexpectedly there shines a white monastery or *suburgan.* And a small blue lake glimmers in the distance.

And again the desert becomes lifeless. And again riders in bright kaftans and in yellow *kurmas* and red-topped hats approach with the speed of the wind. The saddles are sil-ver-laid, just as they were in the times of Chengiz Khan. But where are the arrows and bows? Long are their rifles on the back.

And again there is silence. But the dark outline of the caravan proceeds. The steppes are spotted with herds of black yaks. Droves of fine horses are scattered over the desert. Like snow the herds of white sheep glitter in the sun. Antelopes rush along the hillside. A marmot disap-pears in a hole. Camels, wolves, foxes, hares . . .

Where are the birds? Only an eagle circles in the heights. Black ravens appear here and there. A lark sings its beautiful song. A partridge and a quail fly up. And from the lake comes the noise of geese and ducks. A bustard runs along swiftly. Cranes and herons are flying in forma-tion. . . . Many birds!

From where comes thy great silence, beautiful des-ert? Does it come from thy boundlessness? Does it come from the high blue heavenly dome, from the great Tengri, which was always benevolent toward Chengiz?

At night all starry signs shine. The beautiful stellar

runes are awakening. The book of Glory is open. Beyond the hills a ray of light flashed.

Who is there?

Who passed there?

Erdeni Mori!

On the rocks of Shara Muren are the signs of the treasure. Naran Obo guards the miraculous stone. Everywhere Erdeni Mori has passed.

II

The banner of Chengiz Khan was white. In different campaigns he used various symbols—the lion, the steed of happiness, the falcon, or the panther. Fundamentally the color of the Mongols is blue.

The laws of the Great Khan are extant even to this day, and we may recall many that are applicable to our present life. His severe penalties for theft, murder, adultery, and other offenses could be placed upon the pages of our law even in the present times. Similarly with his other official acts, his orders to his officers, and his steps for the progress of his country were broadly introduced by the Great Khan.

In order to prevent pride and vanity among the khans, Chengiz Khan forbade the adoption of pompous titles. Freedom of religion and speech were observed and the love of God acknowledged. Clergy and physicians were freed from public taxes. Capital punishment was prescribed for spies, perjurers, sorcerers, and those who accepted bribes. The marriage laws forbade marriage between the next of kin. And to raise the sense of honor, it was forbidden to employ one's next of kin as servants. To abolish intoxication, Chengiz Khan constantly discountenanced the use of strong beverages, and urged his people to eliminate the use of these entirely.

A regulation is also known to have aimed at the abolishing of excessive superstitions. The ordinances of

Chengiz Khan encouraged hospitality among his nomad population and insured the safety of travelers throughout the vast extent of his empire. Rules were given in regard to camp sites, and divisions of *yurtas* were made into tens, hundreds, and thousands.

Along the caravan routes, military stations with guards were established, and at intervals of a day's journey, posts for horses were set. The army was divided into divisions of tens, hundreds, thousands, and ten thousands. Capital punishment was meted out to all officers who deserted their posts.

Judging by everything that has come down to us, Chengiz Khan was a great leader and organizer.

"The Lord preserve us from the Mongols!" Such were the inscriptions found in destroyed cities of Asia. Danish fishermen did not venture into the open sea for fear of a Mongolian invasion.

This is one of the earliest descriptions of the Mongols, presented to Europe in the thirteenth century, which was created by fear and terror:

"Lest human joys be especially prolonged, and the world's benevolence endure too long without tears [wrote Matthew Peris in the year 1240], reviling creatures of Satan himself, the countless Tartar hordes broke loose and swept out of the boundaries of their encampments surrounded by mountains. Swarming like locust over the earth, they brought terrible devastation to Western Europe, and by fire and sword reduced it to a wasteland. They are inhuman, bestial, more monsters than men. They thirst for blood and gorge themselves with it. They rend and devour dogs and human flesh, and dress in skins with their chests and backs naked except for armor. They are small in stature, stocky, hairy, invincible. With zest they drink the pure blood of their herds. Their horses are stout, strong, and eat branches, and even trees. Due to their short thighs, they have to mount these horses with the aid of three-stepped ladders. . . . They know no laws; they are completely lacking in any idea of comfort, and are more ferocious than lions or bears. . . . they have pity neither for age nor sex nor position. . . . they know no language to converse in besides their own, which no one understands, because up to recent times there was no contact with them, and they themselves never came beyond the boundaries of their country. Thus there is no information available about their customs and personalities, such as is gained through the mutual intercourse of people. They travel with their herds and wives, and the latter are accustomed to fight as well as the men. To the destruction of Christendom, they suddenly appear, and with the speed of lightning ravage and annihilate everything on their way, terrorizing everyone, and arousing terrific hatred everywhere."

This was the reputation of the Mongols when their name first reached Europe, accompanied by the sensational terror that usually preceded their attacks. The very word Tartar aroused terror; they were considered the scourge of God. The old writers called them the "plague of God"—demons sent against men in punishment.

Europe did not regard the Mongols as human beings. It denied them the honor of being enemies or customary adversaries, and considered them some sort of superhuman creatures. In those times Europeans sincerely believed that Mongols had dogs' heads and devoured human flesh. This was the sort of wild terror that gripped Europe before the appearance of the Tartars. The danger, which threatened humanity, was regarded as so extreme that even Danish fishermen did not venture into the open sea for fear of Mongols.

The same picture is apparent at that time within the boundary of the Far East as well as in the Far West—on the shores of the Pacific as well as on shores of the Black Sea. One of the Chinese historians of that period exclaims with dismay that "since the creation of the world, no nation has been as powerful as the present Mongols. They devastate entire countries more easily than we pluck grass. Why do the heavens permit it?"

Another writer, describing the consequences of Mongolian supremacy, significantly remarks that "in Asia and Western Europe a dog can hardly bark without the permission of the Mongols."

After overwhelming all Asia, and reaching the threshold of Europe, the Mongolian invasion seemed such an ominous threat that the rulers of Europe began frantically to take council with each other as to ways of meeting the threatening danger. It was decided to undertake united resistance against this human deluge, as no single country could cope with it alone. No proof is more evident of the fear that these Mongol hordes inspired, even within the limits of the greatest European countries of that period, than the call of Frederick II, Holy Roman Emperor, to the entire Christian world to repel the invasion of the dreaded Mongols. Just imagine an appeal addressed to "Germany, ardent in battles; France, nursing at her bosom a fearless army; militant Spain; England, powerful in men and ships; Crete; Sicily; wild Hibernia; and cold Norway," asking them to organize international crusades against the nomad conquerors who came to Europe from far-off Mongolia.

Once during the conquest of Persia by the Mongols, a few Mongols met some Persians, and not having any arms with them, told the Persians to keep sitting by the roadside until they go to fetch their swords to behead them. And the Persians calmly obeyed. Thus history tells us.

Excerpts from the manifesto of Frederick II eloquently describe the "Mongol Terror" that surrounded Europe in 1240:

"These people [wrote the Emperor] have emerged from the far ends of the world, where they have long been concealed in an atmosphere of terrific climatic extremities, and have suddenly and brutally swept upon the Northern countries, swarming like locusts. No one knows whence this fierce race has gained its title of Tartar, but one thing is certain, it is apparently God's will that this race has been preserved from prehistoric days as a weapon to scourge people for their transgressions, and mayhap even for the fall of Christendom. This brutal savage people has not the least conception of humane principles. They have a leader whom they revere, and whose command they blindly obey, calling him the earthly god. They are small in stature, stocky, strong with great resistance, and have unbreakable faith. At the least sign from their leader they throw themselves with reckless valor against the most incredible perils. They have broad faces, slanting eyes, and emit the most terrifying shrieks and outcries, which indicate vividly the savagery of their hearts. They know no other raiment except the skins of oxen, asses, and horses, and up to now their armor is only crudely and badly soldered iron plates. But now—and we cannot mention this without a shudder—they begin to improve their armor by looting that of the Christians. Soon the Lord's wrath will descend on all of us, and these barbarians will begin to kill us, to our shame, with our own weapons. The Tartars already are learning to dress richly and elaborately, and at present they eat the most savory food. They ride beautiful horses, and are inimitable archers. It is said that their horses, when they have no other fodder, eat foliage, bark, and roots of trees, and yet preserve their courage, strength, and agility."

Thus Europe estimated the Mongol conquerors.

In later times these estimates become more exact and more detailed. For instance, Timur, instead of the former evaluation of a destroyer, received from the French savant, Grousset, a completely different estimate. Grousset says that Timur "who combines the subtle strivings of Iran-Hindu culture with the austere mold of an ascetic, appears as one of the most colorful figures of the Indo-Iranic world." Thus the great son of Chengiz Khan in the clan of Barlass is presented in a new light by the reflective scientist Grousset. Similarly, many rulers of the world, who were hastily condemned, as quickly revealed themselves in a completely different light. Is this not the case in Russian History with Ivan the Terrible and Peter the Great?

In recalling the description of Grousset and the notes of Plano Karpini about the interest in arts and sciences of Mongolia, we may consider that the Mongolian apotheosis reached the zenith in Akbar the Great. Of course, there have been prejudiced judgments of him as a bloodthirsty tyrant, but there has finally emerged a brilliant picture of the resplendent unifier and cultured ruler of a great country. And to this luminous image of Akbar, already apparent, new studies can only add new valuable signs. And the wisdom of the people, which is just at its base, will add the aureole of a saint to the image of the Great Emperor. Thus through the centuries the people can revere a consistently great service. In regard to the characteristics of Mongols, I also recall other notes by contemporaneous travelers. There are many valuable and benevolent tokens. One should likewise remember the sacred Mongolian books, with their covenants about the Bodhisattvas, and their admonitions to compassion, self-sacrifice, and help to one's neighbor. Let us also recall the Nestorian times. In short, let us not in any way disparage that which was so real a factor in the life of this strong and courageous people.

How many beautiful hours we recall from our own travels in Mongolia. I remember the hearty greeting of welcome of the Mongol Rin-chin. How much we valued also the fiery exclamation of the grey-headed Buriat, "Light conquers darkness!" I remember how valiantly the Mongols acted in our encounter with bandits. I remember the building of the *suburgan,* and the gracious offering of their treasures. If we go by the marks of benevolence, we will find many of them. No matter how often a nation finds rebirth, its foundations still prevail. The same may be observed with many other peoples. Circumstances may change, bringing happiness or ill-fortune, but the soul of the people remains. And one may trace this folk-soul by its ancient songs, its sayings, and its parables. In these indestructible folk mementos, one can find the worthiest characteristics.

In the laws of the Mongolian Khans, in the heroic epic of these people, is reflected a nature that is firm, courageous, often ascetic, patiently enduring the vicissitudes of their time.

And perceiving these covenants of the past, which have not been lost in the currents of the present day, should we not help this people who desire peaceful progress?

There was a time when the circumstances of life, and the yearnings of their heart enticed the Mongols into far-off places, because man often thinks that the beyond is more alluring—"splendid are the drums beyond the mountains." But contemporary thought has directed the Mongols toward the treasures of their own lands. To appreciate our own possessions, to learn to evaluate that which is defined by destiny, is a great accomplishment. It so happens that the Mongols as such, having concerned themselves with remote places, did not as yet exhaust their own inner treasures. Not to use means not to waste. Therefore, it is but just to direct attention to Mongolia with benevolence and friendship.

No one will make the error of exclaiming again, "Lord preserve us from the Mongols." On the contrary, thoughtful persons will send hearty wishes for the peaceful regeneration of their people.

Rigden Djepo himself, in resplendent armor, is galloping on. The Mongols do not forget the visions of the Great Lama in 1927. So it is also said in the prophecies:

"On the slope toward the sunrise, a white stone will be revealed with an inscription.... and though you hew out this inscription, it will never disappear but will forever emerge again."

Greetings to our Mongolian friends. Greetings to Mongolia!

*   *   *

Tzong-Kha-Pa in his Teaching "Lam-Rim-Chen-Po" ordains:

"As the shadows of birds flying in the sky move together, so also good and evil deeds follow the living beings.

Do not neglect even the smallest sin, thinking that it may be harmless. The accumulation of drops of water by and by fills even a large vessel.

Habits for good and evil deeds constantly dominate over man. Deeds, even over a hundred world-periods will not disappear but will accumulate; and when the time is ripe, their consequences will arise for the reincarnated.

How happy are the travelers who have taken care to carry along sufficient food, so also living beings who have done good deeds ascend to a blissful life."

*   *   *

The Lama proclaims:

"Let life be firm as adamant, victorious as the banner of the Teacher, mighty as an eagle, and may it last for eternity."

Callingly resounds the conch shell over the vastness of Mongolia!

[59]

GIFTS OF THE EAST

THERE is before us an ancient Mongol coin. On it are reproduced the sun, the moon, and the seven stars of the Great Bear or the Seven Elders. This is a broad dream of the heavens. A dream of miracles and wonders of the Great Blue Sky of Chengiz Khan.

Verily a broad concept.

Is it not striking that the Mongols bathed their horses in the Adriatic? The Mongols were in Paris, Lyons, and Valencia. The Mongols supplied helmets to the army of Philip the Beautiful. Alançon comes from the Alans. The Alans are esteemed in the Mongolian camps.

All this is boundless, as is also the whole advance of the East to the West, under the sign of the Crusades and following the trails of great travelers. The West often forgets how many heritages of the East it has accepted during many ages in the time of Marco Polo, Plano Karpini, Rubruquvist, Lonjumo, d'Anselico, and other daring spirits.

"The Mongol invasions have left such a hatred behind them that their artistic elements are always neglected. It is forgotten that the mysterious cradle of Asia has produced these quaint people and has enwrapped them in the gorgeous veils of China, Tibet, and Hindustan. Russia has not only suffered from the Tartar swords, but has also heard through their jingling the wonder tales known to the clever Greeks and the intelligent Arabians, who wandered along the Great Road from the Normans to the East.

The Mongol manuscripts and the annals of the foreign envoys of these days tell us of an unaccountable mixture of cruelty and refinement with the great nomads. The best artists and masters were to be found at the headquarters of the Tartar Khans."

Thus I emphasized in my lecture "Joy of Art."

In 1202, the Italian, Leonardo da Pisa, writes the mathematical treatise *Liber abacci* already with Arabic figures. He also uses for the first time the Arabic cipher—zero, voidness—vacuum. Arabic figures! But the Arabs themselves in full justice call them Indian figures. Often we come across the Indian cradle. The gifts of the East are unlimited. And even now the Khozars, this old tribe, lives in Afghanistan.

Algebra, Alidad, Zenith, Nadir, Azimuth, and finally Aldebaran, Algol, Altair—they all come from the Arabs, from the East.

From the same source there come many conceptions in medicine and the natural science. Alcohol, alembic, alkal, amalgam, and many others—are from the East. In Spain we see an Arabian university at Kordova, and the same in the south of Italy at Salerno. The physician of the Sultan of Egypt cures Louis IX. The words sirop, julep, elixir, camphor, and many others were already recorded in the medicine of the East.

Even in agriculture the East gave useful advices to the West. Maize is from Asia, the sugarcane, rice, indigo, saffron, tea, and a whole series of fruit trees and vegetables have their home in the East. Many pilgrims carried in their traveling bags various seeds, and saturated with them their home country. The apricot was called the pear of Damask. The eschalot is from Askalon. Artichokes, spinach, estragon—are all from the Arabs. The wines of Cyprus, Ghaza, Askalon, the raisins of Greece and Palestine are all the gifts of the East. Arabian horses, karabahs, karashars, donkeys, mules, and finally the hunting leopards, so beautifully depicted on the canvasses of Gozzolo—all this is from the vastnesses of Asia. It is stated that even the windmills are from Asia.

The industry of the East has since long tempted

Europe—the sugar of Antiochia and Tripoli; the cotton from Beyreuth, Aleppo, Akra; the silk from Tyre, Tortosa, Tiveriada; the muslin cloth from Mossul, Muar; the taft and saffron from the Arabs; the carpets from Iran; the Eastern compositions of color; the leather from Kordova, the celebrated Spanish-Mauritian faiences.

In the terminology of seafaring—bussol, admiral, arsenal, musson, feluka, corvet, shalanda, tartana—all from the East.

On the battlefields the Eastern armies were mighty enemies. More than once, the West, during encounters with the East, learned new military strategies, discipline, watchfulness, and alertness. Powerful orders of knights were inaugurated after coming in contact with the East. Western warriors imitated from the East excellent armors. Swords of Damask up to now have the reputation of the highest quality. Torches, small shields, came from the East. Saracinian (armor) *bakhteret*, the Eastern helmets (*misurka*), and a quantity of manifold armor and saddlery has its origin in the East. Let us not forget that the word *ulan*, which is applied in many armies, is a purely Mongolian word. In the Russian, Polish, and Lithuanian vocabulary there are many Mongolian and other Eastern words that have become deeply enrooted: *essual* (an officer's rank), *kuyack* (a helmet), *meren* (a horse), *tamga* (a seal), *yam* (a postal station), *yarlyck* (a label), *yar* (a steep river bank), *karaul* (a watchman), *dokha* (a fur coat), *chumbur* (bridle), *argamack* (a steed), and many other similar and widely applied words.

In the East the crusaders, in order to be distinguished during battle, began to depict on their shields the first symbolic signs, which remained afterward as coats of arms. Many heraldic animals have their origin in the East: the unicorn, elephant, lion, griffin, dragon. On our shield the stars are Eastern. The very coloring of the shield, even in terminology, brings to mind Iran and other countries of the East.

Innumerable scents, perfumes, pomades, and all sorts of cosmetics came from the East. Many terms in the households, and of furniture came from the same source—divan, baldachin, alcove, sunduck, carafe, jar—all are from there, as also the name of many precious stones. Even the word *galeta* reminds us of Galata.

Often the Eastern nations were pictured by prejudiced chroniclers as intolerant, cruel, even treacherous and immoral. Yet at the same time we have irrefutable historical data about their tolerance, humaneness, honor, and charity. We admire the valor and daring of Chengiz Khan, and of many warriors of the East. The Saracinians were called by some historians ignorant barbarians, yet at the same time in their universities and from their cultures in science, in art, one could see how they excelled the conceited Westerners of those days. Contact with Eastern nations was one of the main impulses of the Middle Ages. It called forth in several domains of life a kind of awakening. This was a precursor of the Renaissance.

The first impressions of a foreigner crossing Mongolia will be unfavorable as regards the military strength of this country, but in reality the military force of Mongolia is not so small as a casual observer may think. Every Mongol is an excellent rider and marksman. The whole population loves hunting as a sport. The Mongols shoot from their saddle and, from childhood, are accustomed to archery and lassoing from galloping horses.

The bow and arrow, even quite recently, were the main weapons of the Mongols. Archery competitions are up to now the main entertainment during the Annual Festival. A sure eye and a steady hand are required to mark the target when turning back from a horse at full gallop. In this way the Mongols also have become masters of the rifle, with which they acquaint themselves with surprising ease. Almost no shot in a battle misses its aim.

The Mongols love their country more than many other people. They have many advantages in the defense of their country. They quickly judge distances, are used to the air of the heights; they are clever in maneuvering across their hilly country.

The Mongols can endure great hardships without food and water, and can stand the terrific local hurricanes.

Besides an active resistance, the Mongols also have great patience and persistence. The Mongol population living in *yurtas* can leave their whole settlement overnight. The cattle will be driven away, the well will be destroyed, and the intruder will find himself in an empty desert without food and water, left to the mercy of the harshness of nature.

The Mongols can stand a great deal, and the heroic deeds described in annals since the time of Chengiz Khan are not fairy tales.

The same may be stated of many peoples in the East. And the West in the past has acquired many gifts from the East. Religion, philosophy, and many other most precious treasures of spirit and culture in full justice should be ascribed to the East, to Asia. Why this is so is not for us to judge. The historian can but base himself on reality. And no one can diminish the great value of the gifts of the East.

I was glad to receive the book of Dr. Hara Davan about Chengiz Khan. The author belongs to the East, and therefore his enlightened judgment is the more convincing. He knows of what he speaks. He understands the deep culture at the foundation of many great movements, which may be incomprehensible to outsiders. Also the recently deceased Vadimirtzeff correctly evaluated the treasures of Asia.

Gratitude is the quality of Arhats. Following with great ordainment, let us be grateful for all great gifts, in all their multifacetedness and significance.

Let us remember all the great gifts of India. Let us remember how unexpectedly appreciation was often expressed there, where in medieval distances one might have expected insufficient knowledge. Dante in his *Paradise* inspiringly mentions the Orient, the Ganges, and the Blessed One!

> *"Di questa costa, là dov'ella frange Piu sua rattezza, nacque al mondo un sole, come fa questo talvolta di Gange.*
> *"Però chi dèsso loco fa parole non dica Ascesi, chè direbbe corto, ma Oriente, se proprio dir vuole."*

Dante. *Paradiso.*

THE SWORD OF GHESSAR KHAN

WATER is served around in a tin cup. This little cup still exists; it has traversed all of Tibet, China, and Mongolia. And here is a *yagtan* that was made some time ago in Kashmir. The old thing outlived the whole of Asia, endured all methods of transportation. It should be well taken care of; it knows so much, and here is the Banner of the former expedition—*Maitreya.* Since then we have met under various aspects of this growing conception. Far away is the Tibetan painter who painted this Banner. Lama Malonov who decorated the Banner with Chinese silks is no more. And the Banner witnessed much. It won the wild goloks over to our side. It astonished and softened the Tibetan Governor; it smote the forehead of the Amban of Khotan. And during the construction of the *suburgan* at Sharagolchi, it glowed with its vivid colors. Now it is in the Himalayan Institute, which is a fruit of the Expedition.

May it guard over all the curative herbs of the Himalayas in which are inherent so many of the best potentials!

Every object that crossed Asia with us has become unusually dear and unforgettable. The very difficulties of the path have been transmuted into unusual joys because they are surrounded by a spaciousness that has absorbed so much of the wondrous past.

The little bells of the caravan mules are again ringing. Again, steep ascents of the mountain path. Again, we encounter travelers, each carrying his own secret of life. Again tales about local spiritual treasures, about memorable places. Again the heroic sword of Ghessar Khan is lit in the rock. And again caves and peaks of the sacred pilgrimages are before us. The eternal travelers pass us with their packs upon their back. Not faith alone, but an unconquerable attraction to this strange life entices them along the difficult mountain paths.

We are going to Lahaul. It is again a continuation of the expedition. One feels just as before, save that then there was no mail, no information of the world reached us for many months. But here we are still on the rim of the last mail runners, and the world's turmoil can knock at our door weekly. Beyond the Rotang Pass, the dry Tibetan air blows up the same curative and inspiring air that healed all those in quest of spiritual ascent. At night in the clear sky covered with its countless stars, with the Milky Way and with its newborn and dying luminaries, glowed strange flashes of light. These are not simple heat lightning, but the remarkable Himalayan radiance of which literature has spoken more than once.

After having crossed Tibet and Ladak, one can appreciate Lahaul. The snowy peaks, colorful shrubs, fragrant juniper, and brightly tinted wild roses are not inferior to those of the most fertile plains of Tibet. Many of the sanctuaries, stupas, caves of hermits are not poorer than in Ladak. On the rocks are the same ritual figures of archers pursuing with their arrows the sharp-horned mountain rams. The ancient ibex was the symbol of light. The same burial rites in sepulchers lined with stones and in stone burial vaults. Above Keylang rises the majestic mountain of "spiritual tranquility" with its sacred three-peaked summit, similar to Narbu-rinpoche.

How many medical books and writings are kept there by the Lamas! The famous local Lama doctor is already working for us with a coolie boy, and like Panteleimon the Healer, he fills his baskets, slung over his back, with herbs and roots. It is good that George,* who knows the Tibetan language so well, is with us. It is good that Lama

---

*   Dr. George Roerich, son of Prof. Nicholas Roerich and a well-known authority on the Tibetan languages.

Mingyur, who knows so much of Tibetan literature, is with us. The first few days, some books were brought to us, which as yet had never been translated. Among them are also medical writings and a poetic description of the local sanctuaries. The environs are filled with famous names: here are the caves of Milarepa, who hearkened at dawn to the voices of the Devas; here lived also *Padma Sambhava.* All the great apostles of the teachings were in need of the irreplaceable radiation of the Himalayas. Not far from here is the waterfall, Palden Lhamos upon the rocks; Nature itself has designed the figure of the austere goddess riding on her favorite mules. "See how the mule has raised its head and its right leg. Look how distinctly the head of the goddess is seen." We see, we see! And we hear the continuous song of the mountain stream. We pass caves and the rocks of the *Nagis.* These are inhabited by some remarkable snakes. We are amazed at the ancient palaces of the Takhur of Gundla. We are amazed to see how some of the gabled roofs and balconies remind us again of Norway. It is instructive to observe the flat roofs, which are an unmistakable heritage of ancient Asia, and these sharp and unexpected gables that remind one of the North.

We do not forget the reception arranged for us at Keylang, the capital of Lahaul. Decorated with garlands of flowers, preceded by trumpets and drums, we entered Keylang.

As we approached Keylang, an unexpected and touching spectacle awaited us. On the roofs stood Lamas in high purple tiaras, with gigantic trumpets. From the flat roofs the yellow and red petals of wild roses were showered at us. The crowd thronged in festive attires. The school children, standing in rows, shouted greetings to us at a sign from the Wazir. And on the arches and houses were colorful signs with touching inscriptions. Approaching our summer headquarters of the Himalayan Research Institute with an ever-growing procession, we were again met with trumpets by Lamas; and the daughter of our neighbor, Anu in a high turquoise headdress, presented us with the sacred milk of a yak. Thus Keylang, lost amid the snow peaks, wanted to express its cordiality.

We were overwhelmed not only by new discoveries, but we succeeded in seeing the rare Lamaistic mystery, "The Breaking of the Stone." A group of nomadic Lamas from Spiti presented in our yard this unusual mystery, never written about. George gives a complete translation of it in the journal of the Institute.[*]

It began when the Lamas dragged a huge stone, which was more than a yard and a half long, from our hill. Two people could hardly carry it. An extempore altar was set up, and a long row of ritual dancers, with chants and prayers, depicted the destruction of the evil forces.

There was also an exhibition of the piercing of their cheeks with needles. There was a remarkable dance with swords, which included jumping on the blades of the swords. One must admit that this procedure truly demanded great skill, otherwise the two swords pressing the stomach could very easily have pierced the intestines. Amid these dramatic episodes, as is to be expected, a semi-humorous interlude was also introduced. The ruler of a wild country appeared disguised as a shepherd; he was greeted with the laughter of the spectators, aroused by a dialogue about the secret treasures of this ruler. But toward the end of the mystery, all humorous interpolations ceased, and one noticed a more concentrated inner preparation. These conjurations and preparations ended as follows: One of the Lamas lay down on the ground, and two others with great effort lifted the huge stone prepared for him, and placed it on his stomach. At the same time, the old Lama, who had pierced his cheeks and thrust himself upon the swords, lifted the round stone, which was the size of about two human heads high above his head, and threw it with all his force on the stone, which was lying on the stomach

---

[*]   See the article titled *"The Ceremony of Breaking the Stone," "Pho-Bar Kdo-Goog,"* by G. Roerich, in the Journal of the Urusvathi Himalayan Research Institute, Vol. II, 25–51.

of the Lama. He repeated this same action with similar force. Upon the second blow, to the amazement of all present, the long stone split loudly into two parts liberating the Lama who was lying on the ground. Thus, the heavy material world was conquered. The evil forces were conquered, and the mystery play ended with a joyous choir, and the dancing of the Lamas to the accompaniment of a kind of Tibetan-painted balalaika. Of course, the forms of this unusual mystery with its victory over the low material world are heavy, but no less heavy are the actual material forms of common life. Let us also not forget that upon the broken stone was an image of a man, drawn with charcoal and chalk, whose physical substance the Lamas pierced with the magic daggers, *phurpa*, in a previous ritual dance.

A Lama from Kolong comes to us. George and Lama Mingyur are writing down the local chants. We are going to look at the ancient images on the stones. Once more we are convinced that the Chortens, attached to the old images of hunters and mountain sheep, are the latest additions. As before, we think that these sharp-horned sacred sheep—the symbols of light—and their searchers, the tireless archers, are symbols of far more remote cults. Here again, we are touching upon the still inexplicable solar cults, which recall the remote concepts of Druidism.

Again we pay visits to the monasteries. There are interesting books about hermits. From the flat roofs we admire again the vast glaciers, snow peaks, and deep ravines with thundering torrents. Here is the mountain of spiritual tranquility; here is Peak Mand; here are also the enticing roads to Ladak and sacred Kailas.

Here are the dances of the Lamas. Those who are unfamiliar with them call them "devil dances."

"Ignore this foolish name. The dances of the Lamas have a deep symbolic meaning."

"And what about the horns?"

"The protectors of the animal kingdom and the rulers of the elements have this symbol, but have nothing in common with the devils. Soon you shall mistake the rays of Moses also for horns. Oh, what ignorance!"

After a long ritual full of age-old gestures, the dance ended with the mystery in honor of the black-headed Lama, who defeated the impure king, Landarma, the cruel persecutor of the faith.

Karga, an ancient plot of land. The remnants of an ancient fortress. Chortens, Mendangs, covered with stones with the inscriptions of prayers. People say that there are also ancient graves here, but we do not excavate, in order to avoid any controversies with the archaeological department. Our attention is mainly attracted to the numerous carvings on the rocks. Again sheep and archers. Very ancient ones. Lama Mingyur beckons to us with pride to see a stone upon which is an image of a sword. This is why the painting *The Sword of Ghessar Khan* was conceived. Where did we see these characteristic forms of the sword-dagger? We saw them in Minusinsk, we saw them in Caucasia, we saw them on many Sematic and Celtic antiquities. This sword, which is so distinctly carved on this ancient, brownish-purple surface of the stone, polished by the ages, points to the very same theory of the transmigrations of peoples. Is this a sign of a battle? Is this a sign of a courageous crossing?

Here is also the legend about the warriors of Ghessar Khan, who came from afar and settled here. They also brought the first apricot pit. Of course, those are not the Mongols, who reached Lahaul in the seventeenth century. The folk memory preserves something far more ancient and significant.

And opposite, beyond the river, high on the rock, rises the most ancient monastery of this region, Gonde-La, founded by Padma Sambhava himself. The antiquity of the seventh century. Old, calling places.

Here is old Pinzog, a singer-narrator of the saga of Ghessar Khan. He sits on the floor in my studio, and tells, mixing his story with chants, the poem dedicated to the great hero of Ladak, Tibet, and China. Does not this chanting originate from the sixth century, and are not from the same time the meaningful gestures of the bard? Who could suspect in the worn-out appearance of Pinzog, such rhythmic refinement of gesture and the ennobled variations of improvisations of his song. Everything is stressed—how the hero is preparing to start against the enemy, how before his march he received wise counsel from his aunt, how he prepares his arms....

Pinzog depicts how the hero inspects his armor, tries his bow, and spots the enemy on the hillside. "And do you know here, that in Kham are castles of Ghessar Khan, where instead of beams lie innumerable swords of the warriors of Ghessar Khan?" "Not only in Kham but also in Tzang, the warriors of Ghessar have built such monuments of glory," inserts our listening Lama. We know this, know it well, because when in Tibet, people offered us swords; they always whispered that these were from the palace of Ghessar Khan. In one afternoon the bard cannot finish his story of all the glorious conquests of Ghessar. He must also tell of Bruguma, the wise wife of the hero. He cannot omit his chiefs and warriors either, nor all the victories of the invincible defender of truth. What doesn't one hear in the mountains of the Himalayas! The newspapers just reported of a man swimming on the Jumuna river holding on to the tail of a tiger. Even such a story is not a fairy tale.

The Hindu Doctor writes to us that cancer, this increasing scourge of humanity, is absolutely unknown on the Himalayan heights.

The Tibetan Lama Doctor brings Tibetan medicines; among them are also remedies for cancer. We also recollected the official statement of a successful cancer cure, by the deceased Buryat Doctor, Badmeav. Lama Mingyur informs us of the edible roots, which are found in the woods of Sikkim; he promises to obtain them for us. From our friend, the Colonel, we received news that the workmen of Captain B. were terrified during the whole night by a giant who appeared, frightening them to such an extent that they abandoned the work and ran away. To this the Lama added that in Sikkim also, cases are known of similar apparitions of giants, messengers of Dharma Pala, who are sent with forewarning, or to divert wrathful actions. Thus life is multi-varied.

Here is the house of the Thakur from Kolong; the old building is in the style of the Tibetan fortified courtyards. The host and hostess meet us at the entrance. The servants arc adorned with silver and Chinese brocade. The trumpets of the Lamas thunder. First of all, we are invited to the solemn service in the house chapel. There are many family relics, many excellent *tankas*. Here we find Shambhala and Rigden Jyepo and Milarepa, and many other heroes of achievement. The service proceeds in a Bhutanese fashion. After this, we are shown not only the jewels but also the books and woodblocks for printing. This is not a simple household: the Thakur is ruler of the region, and the family has many acquisitions. It, of course, ends with Tibetan tea and *tsampa*. Here also begin negotiations for the construction of a house on the Thakur's ground. Because it is his patrimony, the Thakur cannot sell the ground, but he is able to lease it for forty years, and if one wishes he can also give it for longer. And he does not even wish any money. He says: "Honor to us if great people come from great places to our small place."

And again the conversation concerns the images on the rocks, the undecipherable inscriptions, stone graves, and secret sacred books. Besides the places in Kulu Valley one place is mentioned near Trilokanath where, according to tradition, books were hidden during the persecutions of the fierce Landarma. On the mountains there are also ruins of some ancient dwellings. They say that when the warriors of Ghessar Khan came, the old Lahaulis left for the summits. The Tchud fled underground from the white king on Altai, and the citizens of Lahaul departed to the summits. From an historical and archaeological point of view this region has been investigated very little.

The painting *Menhirs in the Himalayas*, reminds of

menhir-like stones erected since most ancient times and up to now on mountain passes. The custom has no doubt a connection with the ancient menhirs of Tibet, discovered by our expedition in 1928, which were like the menhirs of Karnack.

The painting *Three Glaves** shows an ancient design on a stone near Keylang, the capital of Lahaul (Lahaul in mutilated pronunciation means "Southern Tibet"). On the background is to be seen the famous mountains of these parts of the Himalayas, called Mt. "M." This place is located on the ancient road from India to Kailas and Tibet, and is known as the dwelling place of many Rishis, of whom Vyasa was the compiler of the Mahabharata, Rishi Vasishta was the discoverer of healing springs, and Kapila, who according to the traditions, possessed the so-called "eye of death." Of Tibetan spiritual leaders in this locality lived Milarepa, Padma Sambhava, and Gutsang-pa. The place, where the stone is situated, is about 11,000 feet high. The local images on rocks and stones are well worth studying. Everywhere are scattered images of crosses of Nestorian and Manichaean origin.

Ladak, Dardistan, Baltistan, Lahaul, the Trans-Himalayas, part of Persia, Southern Siberia (Irtysh, Minusinsk) are rich in rock images that are very much alike in the technical sense, which involuntarily remind one of the rocks of Bohuslän, and the images of the East Goths and other great migrators.

The images of Ladak, Lahaul, and all Himalayan uplands can be divided into two main types. The Buddhist type, which reaches our time in the form of images of the Svastika (in Buddhism, so also the inverted Bon-po), the Lion, the steeds of Ghessar Khan, religious inscriptions, Chortens, and other objects of cults.

The other type of images comes from more ancient

---

*   The paintings *Three Glaves* and *Menhirs in the Himalayas* were presented by Prof. N. Roerich to the Archaeological Institute of America, of which Prof. Roerich is vice-president.

times, with the pre-Buddhist Bon-po and similar cults of fire, and is still more significant in its character, and in its curious similarity to Druidism, which is so interesting in connection with the study of the great migrations of peoples.

The main subject of these images (partly reproduced in the works of Dr. Francke-Tibetische Hochzeitslieder, Folkwang Verlag, Gmbh, Darmstadt, 1923) is the mountain ibex, which is the symbol of fire. Among these images one can distinguish by their technique a whole series of ancient strata (similar to the Swedish *halristningar*), up to the newest, which proves the inner existence of some kind of cult.

Besides the ibex, one can see in various combinations, the images of the sun, of hands, ritual dances of figures, and other signs of oldest folklore. This type of images, with most ancient traditions, deserves a most careful study especially in comparison with similar antiquities in other countries.

To the previous images we have succeeded adding two more significant ones, which previously had not been mentioned. In the locality of Karga and near Keylang itself (Lahaul), we have found images of swords, to which I have dedicated one of my paintings, which I present to your esteemed Institute. The meaning of these images is enigmatic, but it is especially interesting that their form fully corresponds to the form of the bronze swords and daggers of the Minusinsk Siberian type, which are so typical for the earliest great migrators. Let us not make any hasty presuppositions or worse, conclusions, but let us enter this instructive detail as one more indicative milestone.

Let us not forget that an old Catholic missionary, Odorico da Pordenone, who visited Tibet in the fourteenth century, mentioned that the place "Lhasa" was called "Gotha." The ruins of ancient temples in Kashmir strikingly remind of the general character of Alan constructions, which culminated in the "Roman style," which led to the early Gothic style. And Louis de la Vallée Poussin's records of foreigners, Irila and Sita, having built temples in Kashmir. And Sten Konov points out that Irila belonged to the tribe of Gatas, which, according to his conclusions, means Goths. All such signs are most useful for the theme of the great migrations of people.

A telegram from Leh. The Institute's expedition arrived safely.

The caravan has encountered neither sickness nor losses. The collections are excellent. We thought so; we thought that Ladak would not disappoint our collector. Instructive experiments are again ahead.

And who would not be kindled by the wonders of the Himalayas?

Whence, then, comes this unusual lure of the Asiatic paths? The mountains do not stand as barricading giants but as enticing milestones. From behind the peaks, glows the radiation of the Himalayan snowy kingdom. The local people, those who have heard of something reverential, point out this radiation. For it radiates from beyond, from the very tower of the great Rigden-jyepo, who labors untiringly for the welfare of humanity.

Here is also a rare image of the great Ghessar Khan himself. Around the warrior are collected all signs of his incarnations and everything significant that should not be forgotten in this glorious epic. On the steps to the throne stand Tibetan boots. These are the same seven-league boots mentioned in the saga of Ghessar Khan. But they stand close to the throne, and this means that the great warrior of the new era is already preparing for the new heroic deed. Soon he will enter.

GODS OF KULUTA

AND so it was. And there came an astrologer who told what was to come. And there visited us our esteemed neighbor—the goddess *Tripura Smidari,* and touched her chosen one, and he trembled and became pale, and said: "Not everything is as yet completed, not everything is over. Great events are ahead, and everything will be victorious." And the same was confirmed by the goddess's sister, *Batanthi.* And the severe god, *Jamlu,* on his part, affirmed the same future. And the protector of the house, the white-clad *Narsing,* through his Brahmin, heralded the same happy news. And in testimony of the truth, the Brahmin held on the palms of his hands glowing charcoal, which did not burn him.

Sometimes it would seem that all the countries of Asia have already been described. We have admired the curious tribe of the Todas. We have been amazed at the sorcerers of the Malabar Coast. We have heard of the Nagas of Assam, and of the extraordinary customs of the Veddas of Ceylon. The Veddas and Paharis of Northern India are always pointed out as most unique tribes.

Although many articles have already been published about the Northern Punjab, where an incomprehensible conglomerate of ancient hill tribes is massed together, yet the remote hill men have been touched so little by civilization, that the inquisitive observer constantly finds interesting new material.

The mixture of ancient Rajputs, Singhs with Nepalese and Mongolian hill men, has produced quite an individual type, which also produced a religion—a combination of Hinduism and Buddhism.

The sacred Kulu Valley lies hidden on the border of Lahaul and Tibet, forming the most northern part of the Punjab. Whether this was *Aryavarsha* or *Aryavarta* is difficult to say. But the most significant names and events have gathered in this beneficial valley. It is called the Silver Valley. Whether in winter, when the snowy cover sparkles, or in spring, when all the fruit trees are covered with snowy white blossoms, the valley equally well merits this name.

In this ancient place they have their three hundred and sixty gods. Among them also is *Gotama Rishi,* dedicated to Buddhism, which is known to have been here for ages. There are also Akbar the Great, whose statue is in the *Malana* Temple, and all teachers and heroes, who by sword or spirit won great battles.

Deoban, their sacred forest, is entangled with century-old trees. Nothing may be destroyed in the silence of the protective grove. Even leopards, bears, and jackals are quite safe in this abode of the gods. People say that some of these protected trees are over a thousand years old, and some even two thousand. Who has counted their ages? Who knows their beginning? And their end is not near, so powerful are the unembraceable trunks and roots.

Equally ancient are the deodar trees round the *Mahadevi* temple in Manali. Heavy boulders, stones resembling huge mountains, are scattered all over the mountain slopes of the Himalayas. Near the temple are seeming altars built of stone. Here the gods are said to meet during the spring festivals. In the darkness inside the temple rises a rock, washed by a prehistoric stream. Was it here that *Manu* compiled the first commandments for the good of mankind?

On the mountain slope above every village can be seen a comb of ancient, giant deodar pine trees. These are all places sacred to the three hundred and sixty gods of the glorious Kulu Valley, or as the ancient people called it, *Kuluta.* These places were marked by the Indian pundits, by old Tibetans, and by the famous Chinese traveler of the seventeenth century, Hsuan-tsang.

In the Kulu Valley, even up till now disputes are settled by the prophet priest. In the sanctuaries of temples are untold sanctities, which the human eye is not allowed to see. The guardian of a temple enters the sanctuary only rarely, and always blindfolded, and carries out one of the sacred objects to an initiate, for a brief moment.

The people of the mountain nest, Malana, speak an incomprehensible language, and nobody has as yet clearly defined this dialect. They live their own lives, and only rarely do their elected representatives descend into the valley to visit the temples of the god *Jamlu.* In high black cone caps, with long earpieces, and in homespun white garments, these mountain hermits tread the snowy narrow paths.

During the New Year of India, the entire Kulu Valley celebrates the festival. We were told that the goddess *Tripura Sundari* had expressed the wish to visit us. The triumphal procession of the goddess, her sister *Bhutanta,* and the god Nag arrived. In front of our house stood a long row of multicolored banners. Further away was a multitude of drums, pipes, and bent brass horns. Farther on, in finely ornamented costumes, dancing all the way, with bent sabers, came the priests, *gurs, kadars,* and local festival dancers. On the broad terrace the procession halted. Every one of the three palanquins of the gods was covered with silver and golden masks. The music roared, songs were enchanted, and they began a wild warlike sword dance. Like the Caucasian hill men or the swordbearers of Kurdistan, the sons of the ancient militant valley madly but gracefully whirled around in dance.

Then an old Brahmin priest appeared. He took two sabers from the young dancers. . . . As if a miracle had happened, the bent old priest suddenly became full of life, and like a warrior leaped about in a wild sacred dance. The curved sabers flashed. With the back of the saber blade, the old man inflicted on himself imaginary symbolical wounds. It seemed as if he would gash his throat. Then with an unexpected movement the bare steel was run between the open mouth. . . . Was this an old man or a youth masked in a gray beard?

All this was unusual. But the most unusual was to come. The dancers calmed down. The musicians stepped aside. The palanquins of the goddesses were borne upon the shoulders of the men; but the men, who carried them, did not touch the poles with their hands. On the contrary, the palanquins seemed to push them about, and, as if drunk, they staggered around, led by an unknown power. They began turning around with the palanquins on their shoulders. Suddenly the palanquin seemed to rush at a chosen person, propping itself up with the end of the poles against his chest. He shuddered, became pale, and his entire body shook. . . . In a transformed voice he shouted out prophecies. But the goddess also desired to speak through another. Again the palanquin moved around in a circle. And again someone was chosen and endowed. It was a pale youth with long black curls. Again, the blunt look of the eyes, the chattering teeth, the trembling body, and the commanding proclamation of prophecies. The New Year had been honored. The procession lined up again and returned by the steep hilly path to the temple, where drums were to thunder till long after midnight and where the dancers would again whirl round in sacred war dances.

It is good when the gods of Kulu are gracious.

What do the inhabitants of Kulu Valley like most? Dancing and flowers. We visited another sword dance. Skillfully, the sword blades whizzed through the air, and around in a semicircle danced a row of colorfully dressed men, arm in arm, singing drawling songs, accompanied by drumbeats and large kettledrums. On rich stretchers under an ornamented canopy sat Krishna with a blue face and in gold-brocaded garments. Next to him sat Radha, and in front was a small Kali, her face black, like a Nubian, with a long, red, outstretched tongue attached to it. The children, who represented the gods, sat up very seriously with an understanding of their nomination. And round stood the crowd, a mixture of many nations: Paharis, Tibetans, Hindus, Ladakis, and many other types of hill people with strange faces. All this seemed to carry me back to the American Southwest pueblos, where during the festivals, we saw similar rows of people with their arms interwoven, who represented rain clouds, the harvests, and hunting—everything that harasses and delights the people, who live in contact with nature.

During our travels, we heard much of every manner of god. We saw how the Chinese punish their gods, drown them in the river, cut off their hands and feet, and deprive them of their dignity. The Samoyeds either anoint their gods with fat or flog them. In short, all sorts of things may happen even to gods. But that, in our times, a legal contract should be made with a god. . . . such as is done in Kulu still seems a novelty. In the Bible we read of covenants made with gods, but, of course, this was without government revenue papers. But here in Kulu Valley, the gods are very close to life, and they base all of their decisions according to the up-to-date laws of the country. Here I have before me a contract between myself and the god *Jamlu,* concerning the water supply. Such written contracts with gods I have never before seen. Everything becomes modern, and even gods sign contracts on revenue paper.

But not only do contracts with gods occur in Kulu, before me is a deed of sale of an ancient fortress, and there is a special clause that the previous owner retains his right to a quarter part of a golden cock, buried on these grounds. The tale of the *Coq d' Or* . . .

The *gur,* priest of the gods, is the most revered person in all Kulu. He is all clad in white, in a homespun woolen mantle, with a small cap on his black and grey hair. His nose is aquiline, and he has sparkling deep-set eyes. His legs are also covered with white.

The *gur* is seated on a rug, and having completed the

burning of his incense, he gives every one of us a flower as a sign of the grace of the gods.

The gods are very satisfied, he informs us. We did not offend them. On the contrary, we have even collected their images near our house, bringing them from an old ruined temple. There is the statue of *Juga-Chohan* on horseback; there is also the goddess *Kali*, the *Rishi Kartik, Swami Nansigang, Parbati,* and several images of *Narsing,* the protector of this place.

"Tell us, *gur,* have you seen *Narsimha?*" we ask him. "We heard that many people have seen the protector of these regions."

Before the *gur* had time to answer, a Hindu school teacher who was present, replied:

"Certainly many of us have seen *Narsimha.* The old Rajah, who became the protector of this Valley, wanders at night time near his former castle and along the mountain paths. All your servants here have seen how on a moonlight night, a tall majestic figure with a long staff has descended the mountain and disappeared under their very eyes. . . . I have myself seen *Narsimha* twice. Once in this very house. The protector entered into my room at night and, touching me, wanted to tell me something. But it was so sudden that I became frightened, and the vision disappeared. Another night I returned by the mountain road from the castle homeward. And I met the protector himself, who said: "Why walk so late when everybody sleeps?" You can ask Capt. B., and the wife of the planter L. They both know of apparitions of *Narsimha.*"

And the old *gur,* chewing his thin lips, said:

"I have seen *Narsimha.* And also the goddess. She came to me as a small child, and blessed me for my initiation as *gur.* I was very young at the time. At the gates of the temple I imposed a fast on myself and sleeplessness for seventy-two hours. And in the morning after these hours had passed, an unknown little girl came to me. She was about seven years old, dressed in superb robes, as if for a festival, although it was an ordinary day. And she said to me: "Your task is fulfilled. Go and act as you decided!"

The *gur* has told us much about the great local Rishis: the gods in the valley live in prosperity. They have plenty of property and land. Without their sanction nobody is allowed to fell a tree. The gods visit one another as guests. Many people have seen the gods traveling. Sometimes they fly; sometimes they walk with great leaps propping themselves on sticks. Of course, besides that, several times every year they have triumphal processions with drumbeats and trumpets as accompaniment. In the storehouses of the temples are hidden rich garments, pearls, gold, and silver masks—all attributes of the gods.

The wife of the planter told us that, indeed, staying once overnight at the Naggar castle, she was awakened by a noise in the neighboring room; and on the threshold, a white figure appeared of medium height; but she became terribly frightened, and the figure disappeared, making such a loud noise that two English ladies, sleeping next door, on the other side, became very much frightened. And with the same noise, the figure moved along other parts of the castle. The same person also saw another interesting thing. On the maidan of Sultanpur, she saw a dog running, pursued by a white transparent figure.

A Brahmin, in a very large yellow turban, told us how the local gods help the inhabitants of the Kulu Valley.

"Some misfortune happened in the house of a man, and in terror he fled up into the mountains, seeking the help of the gods. Three days he spent on the rocks. Someone invisible brought him food, and a voice said, 'You may return home.' And the man returned and found everything in order. Another man went into the mountains of Manikaran and secluded himself in meditation. An unknown Yogi appeared before him and surrounded him with radiant light. From that day on all the inhabitants of the valley followed that man, paying him homage and trust. This was about fifty years ago. If you want to try to see a Rishi, go up into the mountains, to one of the mountain lakes. And in fasting and prayer, stay there, and perhaps one of the protectors will appear before you."

Thus the people of Kulu regard their deities with familiarity. In this ancient place, as in Naggar, and in Manali, are gathered all the great names. The lawgiver, Manu himself, gave his name to Manali. The great Arjuna, in a miraculous way, laid a passage from Arjunagufa to Manikaran, where he went to the hot springs. After the great war, described in the Mahabharata, the Pandavas came to Naggar, and high above the Thava temple, they built their castle, the remnants of which are still being shown. Here also in the Kulu Valley lived Vyasa, the compiler of the Mahabharata. Here is Vyasakund, the sacred place of fulfillment of all wishes. In Bajaura, near the river Beas, stands a temple connected with the name of Ghessar Khan. Coming from the side of Ladak, the great hero here overtook his enemies and defeated them. On the same river Beas, called in history Hypathos, near Mandi, Alexander the Great once stopped. A hill is shown there connected with the conqueror's name. On the top of the hill are some ruins.

Here also in the neighborhood lies the famous lake Ravalsar, the place where the great teacher, Padma Sambhava stayed. Thousands of pilgrims visit this remarkable place, coming from beyond the mountain ridges of Tibet, Sikkim, Ladak, and Lahaul, where Buddhism prospers. From Kulu came the propagator of Buddhism, Santa Rakshita. It has been ascertained that Kulu and Mandi are the sacred lands Zahor, which so often are mentioned in ancient records. Here, after the persecution of the impious king, Landarma, were hidden the most ancient books. Even the place of these hidden treasures is indicated approximately.

In Naggar is shown the cave of the famous spiritual teacher, Pahari Baba, who converted the cruel Raja into leading a pious life. It is a lovely, quiet place, hidden among dense deodars and pine trees. A small brook gurgles, and birds call to one another. A Brahmin guards the sacred cave, which has now been adorned by a temple. The chief deity of this temple is an image of—as the Brahmin calls Him—Taranata. He brings the image out of the temple, and one cannot fail to recognize in it Tathagata, the Gautama Buddha—the Teacher. In this way the Hinduism of the hill Paharis has become blended with its predecessor—Buddhism. In other temples one can also see Shiva, Kali, and Vishnu, images of Buddha, Maitreya, and Avalokiteshwar. And all these memorial images are reflected in the gathering of the three hundred and sixty Rishis, the protectors and holders of this blessed place.

One cannot omit to mention that under the name of Trilokanath—Lord of the Three Worlds—in upper Kulu, as also in Chamba State and Lahaul, Avalokiteshvara is worshipped. This is confirmed by the typical aspects of the images.

On the border of Lahaul, which is also an ancient former Tibetan principality, on the rocks, are inscribed images of a man and a woman as high as nine feet high. It is said that this was the height of the ancient inhabitants. It is curious that in Bamiam, in Afghanistan, where there are also huge images on the rocks, these are also connected with a legend of the height of ancient giants.

The earthquakes in Kangra have destroyed many of the temples, but the memory of the people preserves the names of heroes and teachers. Here also are erected monuments of a different character, reminding one of things that might well be forgotten. In Mandi and in Kulu, you can see big stone, stelae-like, ancient menhirs, with some timeworn images. In close groups stand these granite blocks, hiding some secret. What is this secret? What memory do they recall? These memorials refer to all the generations of local rajas, and show the number of their wives, who were burned alive together with the body of their deceased sovereign.

These stones speak of the past. But to the north of Kulu rise the white peaks of the main Himalayan range. Beyond them lies the road to Lahaul and Ladak, and the main white giant is called Guru-Giri Dhar—the Path of the Spiritual Teacher. This conception unites all Rishis into a great whole, leading the way to the Heights.

In this Silver Valley the Great Shepherd called to life all living beings by the silvery sounds of his flute. He calls toward joy. And the apple trees, pear trees, cherry trees, and plum trees respond in their enthusiasm of blossoming. The willow tree opens its fluffy blossoms, apricot trees turn lilac, the vigilant nut tree unfolds in rich yellow, and as a healing nectar flows the aromatic sap of the deodars.

Under the apple tree, covered with rose-colored blossom, the eternal Krishna, on his silver flute, plays his divine songs of regeneration.

ANCIENT MEDICINES

DR. Bernard Read does highly beneficial work. From yellowish, forgotten, and often ridiculed records of ancient Chinese pharmacopoeia, he rediscovers for the scientific world many considerations, which attract the attention of contemporary knowledge. For us, the works of this scientist are especially valuable. We have often stressed the necessity of studying ancient pharmacopoeias, and various popular home medicines, amid which one can no doubt find results of experiments of many ages.

Because of such affirmations we have often been scoffed at. Certain scientists of today fear that they may be considered out of date, and may thus lose a leaf from their laurel of modernism. I was recently accused that my considerations may support old-fashioned scientists instead of refuting together with modernists everything that was accomplished before. And I had to explain that we never asserted that everything contained in ancient pharmacopoeias is fully good and useful. We only affirmed that ancient pharmacopoeias should be studied, as one more source useful for certain conclusions of excellent scientists of today.

Of Dr. Bernard Read's researches we have heard long ago. Our friend, the Hon. Charles Crane, had some years ago recommended this excellent scientist for cooperation with our institutions, and this took place. And now we follow with increasing interest how even the newspapers dedicate entire columns to the researches of Dr. Read. It sounds paradoxical: the most modern achievements based upon the most ancient sources! And yet it cannot be expressed otherwise, because Dr. Read, through the knowledge of ancient sources, confirms the most modern discoveries of contemporary science. For a historian these strictly scientific deductions are most instructive, since through them it is affirmed once more how carefully one should approach the past of human life, in which so many observations had already been manifested. In such cases we have to deal not only with civilization but with culture in its entire originality.

It may seem to many that the healing use made of donkey skin, sheep's eyes, deer's horn, dog's brain, odd herbs, etc., all interwoven as they are in folklore, is just so much empty Chinese superstition, and that it is unfortunate that such great faith is placed in such absurd remedies.

However, an extensive survey now being undertaken by Dr. Bernard Read, Head of the Division of Physiological Science, and his associates at the Henry Lester Institute of Medical Research may greatly diminish popular skepticism.

It is the attitude of the Lester Institute that before today's medical science of the Western world can be imposed on the Chinese people, due regard must be given to the empirical observations, which form the basis of the old Chinese medical practice.

Reason has suggested that when certain therapeutic practices have been in constant use for a great many centuries not only in China but in India, and with no apparent relationship to the still more ancient civilizations, as revealed in old manuscripts, it becomes evident that some real benefit is derived.

The work of Dr. Read with his associates and staff is to put such empirical practices upon a rational basis by employing the highly technical skill of modern workers and a more fundamental knowledge of the principles involved to evaluate them by new standards, which emphasize in proper balances, deficiencies and faulty assimilation, and thereby to find fresh avenues for research, which may yield results of value in modern medicine.

Dr. Read has been working in this field for thirty years in China and has been rewarded by his success in chaulmoogra oil and ephedrine—first produced in his laboratories in Peking—among his other important contributions to medical science. Now working under the excellent facilities of the Lester Institute in Shanghai, where he came two years ago to head the divisions of physiological science, more valuable data on the Chinese Materia Medica are being contributed to modern medicine. There is now in progress an investigation into the chemical composition and vitamin contents of a tremendous variety of local Chinese drugs and foods.

The phenomenally widespread use in China of boiled-down donkey skin, called *Ah-Chiao*, as a blood regenerator and internal styptic, and a general nutritive for weak people, especially those suffering from tuberculosis, has led to an investigation into its particular character both chemical and physiological. Dr. T. G. Ni finds that it contains a large amount of glycine, cystine, lysine, argenine, and hystidine. Administered orally it improves the calcium and nitrogen absorption, and raises the calcium level of the blood. This Ah-Chiao used intravenously was found to be effective in restoring a depressed circulation after hemorrhage and shock. Further work is proceeding on its beneficial effects in muscular atrophy. In Hangchow last year, there was a quarter of a million dollars' trade of donkey skin in one store alone.

It has been shown by dietary surveys that large numbers of people live on deficient diets such as may lead to latent or subacute scurvy. In old medical practice, such symptoms as weakness of the knees and general lassitude were treated with numerous remedies that for their action may depend upon the presence of vitamin C. Hence, 120 Chinese foods and drugs purchased in Shanghai markets, as they appeared for sale in ripe condition, and also collected in the country close to Shanghai, have been subjected to a chemical study with a view to ascertaining the vitamin C content. The results are given in value of Pumels report written by Yuoh-Fong-Ghi and Dr. Read.

Among the citrus fruits, pomelo was found to have the highest vitamin C content, being superior to grapefruit and all of the various types of oranges. Many sorts of leaves that are eaten regularly and used medicinally, such as dandelion, mulberry, nasturtium, poplar, shepherd's purse, and amaranth, yielded interesting data. Green amaranth, little known by foreigners, grows in great profusion in the country, and has been found to have a very high vitamin C content and to be superior to spinach in its content of iron and calcium. The high vitamin content of willow and poplar leaves and shepherd's purse suggests good reason for their use in ancient medicine.

Dr. Read states that ancient medicine in China needs considerable clarification before forward or backward-looking people are able to estimate its true worth. As a historical record, it is of worth to the anthropologist, the naturalist, and the physiologist. Dissected from outside influences, it has a vast amount of honest observation of Chinese fauna and flora, their habitat, preparation, and uses as foods and remedies in treatment of disease, suggesting important paths of research.

In China's great classic, the Pen T'sao Kang Mu', common foodstuffs include such extremely toxic seeds as the bastard anise and poisonous terodent fish, and drugs include oranges, gelatin, and licorice. Thus, for practical purposes, no distinction need be made between foods and drugs. The voluminous old Chinese medical literature embraces the whole field of Chinese natural history, a remarkable record of observations for thousands of years.

Dr. Read feels that, apart from its applied value, Chinese medicine needs a more intelligent and sympathetic understanding on the part of modern medicine. It is universally believed in. There is need in Asia for a widespread application of scientific methods to enable people to evaluate ancient medicine at its true worth, and to heighten appreciation of modern ideas in medicine in all of its relationships.

"It is of interest to note [states Dr. Bernard Read in his report on "The Newer Pharmacology and Ancient Medicine"] that the modern medicine of the British Pharmacopoeia only included nine substances of animal origin, and of those, nearly all were quite innocuous things like lard and wax. While modern science is turning to liver, stomach, vitamin A from the eye, adrenalin, etc., it is remarkable to find the use of so many animal tissues in ancient medicine."

In this report Dr. Read presents a table showing twenty-six parts of six domestic animals used in old Chinese medicine. These animals include the cow, horse, pig, chicken, sheep, and dog.

When bitten by a mad dog, the brain of the same animal is applied to the wound. This suggests a connection with modern Pasteur treatment and is worthy of investigation.

The velvet horn of the Skia deer and other species is taken as a drug in powder form and is very highly regarded by the Chinese. Recent studies by Russian scientists show that the male sex hormone is present.

The iris and the lens of the sheep's eyes were given for dimness of vision and conjunctivitis. The eyes of the hawk, parrot, and mackerel were administered for blindness. Recently Wald has isolated vitamin A from the iris of sheep, pigs, cattle, and frogs.

In old Chinese medicine pig's liver was recommended for blindness, beriberi, constipation, etc., and has fairly recently been found to be rich in vitamin A, B, C, D, and E. A great many instances of this sort are cited. Shepherd's purse is given as an excellent example of a medicinal herb cast aside for its apparent lack of potent principles, which has been shown to be moderately rich in three of the vitamins, and well justifies the old Chinese use of it for a number of maladies.

Native remedies claiming to have a power to increase human fertility are often associated with magical ideas, but

Dr. Read believes that in view of the increasing volume of recent scientific work in this field, there is hope that information may be forthcoming whereby these claims can be properly evaluated.

Some people suffer from a deficiency of iodine. Many centuries ago in China, seaweeds were used in the treatment of goiter. It is now believed that these old remedies were often quite efficacious.

Dr. Read says that further extensive reference might be made to a host of other remedies, but that enough has been cited to show that science may progress by looking backward as well as forward; that probably the most suggestive path of progress may be gained by studying the records of old empirical medicine; that the scientists need, more than any other, to keep an open mind regarding the claims of ancient medicine, so that with the aid of modern knowledge and modern technique, an unprejudiced study may be made of the customs of our forefathers, who were engaged in the same life and death struggle against disease.

In China there have been preserved, for something between thirty and fifty centuries, remarkably accurate records of human experience in the field of medicine. These records are not accumulations of divine intuitions but empirical findings which up to the present have only been sifted with the very coarse sieve of last century science.

Thus without destroying anything, without unjust scoffing, one may find new useful possibilities, accessible to all. Dr. Read's experience of many years but confirms that when scientists go along the path of honest goodwill, they discover much of that which would remain concealed to the evil-doubting eye. Honest investigation and self-conceited skepticism are two entirely opposite things, and the way of suspicious disbelief is obscure and crooked.

In all ancient records one can find remedies that merit thorough investigation. The particles of Truth remain everywhere indisputable. Sometimes the formulae of ancient wisdom remain enigmatic for the superficial student—but yet truth remains truth when these hieroglyphs are studied without prejudice.

The path of negation is always branded as the path of ignorance. The latest discoveries but confirm the continuity of human thought through all ages. The obscure formulae often were due to the peculiarity of the language or to a deliberate desire to retain, but in certain hands, the precious knowledge. Such caution should not be condemned, for "one should not throw pearls before swine." This ordainment has been repeated in many different ways. "There is no prophet in his own country"—this sad truth also was given for the benefit of future humanity not without deep reason.

There will come a time when ignorant, self-conceited negation, in all walks of life, will be replaced by a radiant unprejudiced research. One should especially rejoice at every benevolent study—in it is contained true goodwill.

Guru Charaka,* the great Ayurvedist, still wanders along the blossoming Himalayan uplands. Wisdom knows in its straight-knowledge how many innumerable precious remedies were given to humanity.

There is no old or new age, there is no antiquity, nor modernism for the ever life-giving Panacea.

---

* Prof. N. Roerich's painting *Guru Charaka* is in the Roerich Hall in Benares (Bharat Kala Bhawan).

GREETINGS TO THE GREAT ARTIST!

DR. ABANINDRANATH TAGORE

DURING the present days of Armageddon, not many joys are spared for troubled mankind. Amid the Eternal values, Art has a predominant place. Verily we blessed all, who in spite of difficulties gather and create in the name of Beauty. They know that in this creative work is being born the majestic Renaissance of their Motherland.

It is our superb duty to reveal true heroes of the nation. The coming generation should know precisely to whom it is indebted for its upliftment and why it has been privileged to have for its uses all attainments and creations.

The life of an artist is not an easy one. But because of this very eternal struggle, this life is a beautiful one. For eighteen years I have been connected with India, and long before I had already felt the virility and essential strength of its growing self-expression. And now, observing the glorious development of Indian Art, so manifold, I see how true was my first impression.

As a powerful Beacon stands Dr. Abanindranath Tagore, as a guru of an entire School of Art. He blessed the best living artists of India. By his own untiring example, he opened the gates for a resplendent future.

The emotion packed in his paintings, in their imaginative genuine rhythm, is full of poetic symbolism. His paintings seem to say of their master: "We are the singing of his hand and heart."

My fraternal greetings to Dr. Abanindranath Tagore.

THE BUILDER

CAN the sower know for certain what his sowing will produce? Will hail fall, will there be enough horses to take out the given harvest? The sower can only surmise; it is not given to him to know. Vigor and tenacity are given him in drawing each new furrow of the field. The sower knows the dates of sowing and makes haste not to let them pass, even in a single premise.

The builders of wonderful temples and strongholds have not known if it would be given to them to complete them. Yet for all that, they laid the foundations in steadfast confidence, and kept on erecting, as long as there were forces and possibilities. Sometimes only in the course of centuries was the structure crowned, but those who began new foundations were not distressed by this and did not grow cold in their constructive zeal.

Construction is prayer of the heart. Sowing is a necessity of the spirit. If one has doubts and grieves beforehand at all the dangers that may happen to the future harvest, then, of course, this will be not life but the worst dissoluteness. If the spirit be crushed by the unlikelihood of completing the structure, then, of course, this will be a retreat into savagery.

A writer inspires readers unknown to him. A singer composes his tunes for listeners unknown to him. A creator sends his attainings to the need and joy of the world. Does the bird sing for itself or for the world? It cannot help singing each morning. Not fearing a marauder, the bird builds its nest on the ordained date.

The builder has to construct. He cannot live without buildings. Construction is his song, his prayer, his most pleasant task. The builder lays the foundation of strongholds and temples and storehouses, not enfeebling himself with the thought of who will complete the roof of the building and when. The builder does not let pass the dates of beginning, knowing about the growth of the seed.

Does the builder stop because of uncertainty about resources for the roof? The seed grows, and with it grows everything surrounding. The ship does not know all the whirlwinds breaking out along its path, yet nonetheless it spreads the needed sails in good time. If we examine the history of all buildings, we are actually amazed at how possibilities came to life while walls and towers went up.

And creator and steersman and builder are not acquainted with fear. The foundations are not made strong in fear and tremblings. The seed is small, yet already it has within itself the whole store of growth and flowering and fragrance. The seed will produce also the succeeding seeds. The sower is not afraid to sow, the builder does not fear to construct, if only the heart knows the undeferrable need of harvest and building.

For any beginning a small seed is needed. It is also possible to teach in a very small house. It is possible to create in a cramped corner. It is possible to stand guard in the plainest armor. In each striving for construction will be a search and thirst for perfection. In these quests is the basis of life. Its steadfastness is composed by irresistible striving for attainment. Indeed these attainments are both goal-fitted and commensurate.

The so-called Babylonian towers will not be lasting whose sole *raison d'être* is to surpass each other. The true builder strives for perfection, but the thought is alien to him of merely outdoing something. The true builder first of all co-measures in order that his building stay within the needful proportions, and by its harmony only enhance the consonances of the epoch. The builder understands that such evolution is eternal spiral motion in its infiniteness and unceasingness.

Any incommensurate ugliness will be repulsive to the builder. A feeling of harmony, of commensurateness is manifested as a distinctive quality of the true builder. It is impossible to teach a man these inborn constructional proportions and provisions. If these qualities are present but dormant, they may be awakened. The sleep of the qualities is broken by the most unexpected means, sometimes unsurmised and unspoken. Wise conversations, quests of broader horizons, the art of thinking, all may awaken in secret the innate constructional needs. By all admissible means, it is needful to uncover these secrets, the treasures of which can produce a true usefulness for humanity.

Likewise, it is also necessary to develop in oneself the consciousness of how a sturdy tree always grows up from a small seed. So many times people have tried to plant in the ground large adult trees, and almost never have these incommensurate plantings produced lasting results. But in order to realize the goalfitness of planting from the seed, one has to understand in spirit and to grow to love all the miracle-working power of the seed.

The observation and investigation of seeds give rise to most unusual meditations. Even while it knows beyond question what giants grow out of the tiniest seeds, the human mind is always hesitant about this miracle. How is this possible, that within the tiniest envelope there have already been conserved all the forms of the future structure, all its curative and nutritive properties? The builder must think upon these seeds, from which so strongly and goalfittingly grow the whole succeeding tree in many ages.

It is possible for the builder to delay his constructive thoughts until all the means of fulfillment shall be mechanically collected together. It needs to be remembered that the resources grow together with the process of construction. If the means be exhausted before the structure is finished, this only means that somewhere new stores have already come into being, already been composed, and it is necessary to look for them.

The work of the builder must be joyous work. In his heart he knows his building to be completed. The fuller and deeper the builder realizes this summation, the more joyful will his path be. In his very being the builder cannot be an egoist, for surely he does not build for himself! The builder first of all understands the meaning of formational movement, and therefore in his thinking, he cannot be immobile.

Each immobility is already death; it is the forerunner of dissolution and downfall. And just as precisely is each construction the forerunner of life. Therefore at each decision of the builder, there starts up an outpouring of new energy. What appeared unbearable yesterday becomes easy when the necessity of the new building is affirmed in the spirit. Verily in each new structure is manifested the beautiful.

Builders are of all kinds. They touch all earthly limits. Let this creative diversity be preserved; for in the very greatest creativeness, there is primarily an incalculable multiformity. Wherever there is even the embryo of constructiveness there will no deserts come to life. Aside from all the physical deserts, there remain most terrible the deserts of the spirit. But each builder will already be an enlightened reviver of these most menacing deserts.

Long live beautiful construction!

SRI RAMAKRISHNA

WE are in the desert of Mongolia. It was hot and dusty yesterday. From far away thunder was approaching. Some of our friends became tired from climbing up the stony hills of Shiret Obo. While already returning to the camp, we noticed in the distance a huge elm tree, *Karagatch*, lonely, towering amid the surrounding endless desert. The size of the tree, its somewhat familiar outlines, attracted us into its shadow. Botanical considerations lead to believe that in the wide shade of the giant, there may be some interesting herbs for us. Soon all coworkers gathered around the two mighty stems of the Karagatch. The deep shadow of the tree covered over fifty feet across. The powerful tree stems were covered with fantastic burr growths. In the rich foliage, birds were singing, and the beautiful branches were stretched out in all directions as if wishing to give shelter to all pilgrims.

On the sands, around the roots, innumerable trails made by animals were visible. Next to the broad imprints of a wolf were small hooves of the *dzeren*, the local antelope. A horse had also passed here, and next to it was the heavy footstep of a bull. All sorts of birds had been here. Apparently the entire local population visited the welcoming shelter of the giant. The elm Karagatch especially reminded us of the huge banyan trees of India. Such trees were the meeting place of blessed gatherings. Many travelers found there both bodily and spiritual rest. Sacred narratives were chanted under the inviting branches of the banyan tree. And thus the lonely, giant Karagatch in the Mongolian desert vividly turned our memory to the shadow of the banyan. The mighty branches of the karagatch reminded us also of other great achievements of India. What a joy to think of India!

Thoughts turned to the radiant giant of India—Sri Ramakrishna. Around this glorious name there are so many respectful definitions. *Sri Bhagavan Paramahansa*—all the best offerings through which the people wish to express their esteem and reverence. The consciousness of a nation knows how to bestow names of honor. And after all, above all most venerable titles, there remains over the whole world the one great name—Ramakrishna. The personal name has already changed into a great all-nations, universal concept. Who has not heard the Blessed Name! The conception of goodness and benevolence truly befits him. Except for petrified hearts, who would oppose the Good?

We recollect how in various countries has grown the understanding of the radiant Teaching of Ramakrishna. Beyond shameful words of hatred, beyond evil mutual destruction—the word of Bliss, which is close to every human heart, spreads widely like the mighty branches of the sacred banyan tree. On the paths of human searching, these calls of goodwill were shining like beacons. We ourselves witnessed, and have often heard how books of Ramakrishna's Teaching were as if unexpectedly found by sincere seekers. We ourselves came across the book in a most unusual way.

Hundreds of thousands, even as many as a million pilgrims gather on the memorable day in the name of the Blessed *Bhagavan*. They gather, being called by an inner impulse of the heart, in goodwill, and they become rejuvenated by blissful remembrances and strivings. Is this not a most remarkable expression of the voice of the people! This is the nation's judgment, the reverence of the people, which cannot be compelled nor forcefully commanded. As wonderful lights, they spread from one to another forming an inexhaustible flame; hence, such national reverence is not dimmed but radiates throughout the times of contemporary world commotions.

Too many crises grip the people at present. It could happen that the spirit of the people could become confused and distracted from the spiritual fundamentals. The wail about the shattering of the foundations is so often heard nowadays. But are not the millions of pilgrims, who assembled by their own free will, the best living proof that above the confusions of today, there lives in the hearts an inexhaustible spirituality and striving toward the Good? We are optimists and conquer all obstacles through goodwill.

Behold, on an unbearably hot day, not being frightened of distances, pilgrims are hastening in order to venerate the memory of Ramakrishna. Is this not a remarkable event? For it is not an official duty that brings together all the multifarious travelers. A pure heart and a sincere striving imperatively lead them to the places consecrated by the name of Ramakrishna. Such a spiritual gathering is the most precious evidence in our days. It is wonderful that amidst the heavy labor, amid doubts, amid depression, people yet can be lit by the flame of gratitude and veneration. Their hearts call them together. They are gathering not for destruction, nor for quarrels, nor for insults, but in order to unite their thoughts upon the Good.

Great power is contained in a united benevolent thought. Humanity should value such sublime manifestations, which are the cause of all these unifying and constructive thoughts. Creative is the thought of Good! The good never destroys; it untiringly elevates and builds. By commands of good are affirmed those eternal foundations, which have been ordained to humanity on all the best tablets. The call of the Blessed *Bhagavan* for creative Good will forever remain the great spiritual heritage of humanity.

Light is especially precious during the hours of darkness. May the Light be eternally preserved! In his parables about the Good, Ramakrishna never belittled anyone. And not only in the Teaching, in parables, but in his own deeds, he never tolerated bemoaning. Let us remember his reverent attitude toward all religions. Such broad understanding will move even a stony heart. In his broad outlook, the Blessed *Bhagavan*, of course, possessed a real straight-knowledge. His power of healing he in turn gave out freely. He never hid anything useful. He exhausted his strength in innumerable blessed givings. And even his illness, of course, was due to such a constant, self-sacrificing outpouring of his spiritual energy for the healing of others. And in these generous gifts, Ramakrishna manifested his greatness.

In all parts of the world, the name of Ramakrishna is venerated. Also is revered Swami Vivekananda, who symbolizes true discipleship. The names of Ramakrishna, Vivekananda, and the glorious host of their followers remain on the most remarkable pages of the history of the spiritual culture of India. The astounding depth of thought, which is characteristic for India, the beautiful manifestation of *Guru* and *Chela*—remind the whole world of basic ideals. Ages pass, whole civilizations change, but the *Guru* and the *Chela* remain in the same wise relationship, which since antiquity was established in India. Many millenniums ago the words of wisdom were already recorded in India. And how many more millenniums were they reserved even before, in verbal transmission. And in this sacred mouth to ear transmission, they were kept perhaps even safer than on written records. The ability to keep up the correct meaning depends on a developed, wise consciousness, and in this is contained the application of precious stones of the past for the radiant future.

Not only the everlasting value of the Teaching of Good affirmed by Ramakrishna, but precisely the necessity of these words especially for our times is unquestionable. When spirituality, as such, is being so often refuted through wrongly interpreted formulae, then the radiant constructive affirmation as a beacon becomes especially precious. One has but to know the colossal number of editions of the Ramakrishna Mission. One has but to remember the large number of cities in which these Missions have their branches. These figures require no exaggeration. There is no unnatural nervousness, and no premeditatedness in these quiet thought-creating gatherings. Everything is deeply realized not in tumult and rush but grows in highest co-measurement.

The thoughts about the Good, which Ramakrishna so generously taught, should awaken the best sides of human hearts. Ramakrishna always preached against deniers and destroyers. He was in all respects a builder for the Good, and his admirers should unfold, on the examples of his Teaching, the best hidden treasures of their hearts. Such beneficial creativeness is very active. And it naturally is also transmuted into the best achievements on all paths of life. Gathering on the memorable day of Ramakrishna's anniversary, the pilgrims do not fear the dust of the road; they are not frightened by the fatiguing heat, but they are filled with a striving toward the Good, toward the great service to humanity. Service to Humanity—great is this ordainment of Ramakrishna!

Reverence to the Teacher!

I recall a small Hindu who found his Teacher. We asked him: "Is it possible that the sun would glow to you if you would see it without the Teacher?"

The boy smiled. "The sun would remain as the sun. But in the presence of the Teacher, twelve suns would shine to me!"

The sun of the wisdom of India shall shine because upon the shores of a river there sits a boy who knows the Teacher.

TAGORE AND TOLSTOY

"**B**Y ALL means visit Tolstoy," thundered the gray-bearded Stassov, Director of the Slavonic Department of the St. Petersburg Public Library. This happened during my visit to him, after graduating from the Academy of Fine Arts in 1897.

"I do not care much for academic diplomas and distinctions. But let the great writer of Russia recognize you as artist. That will be a real distinction. And no one will appreciate your *Messenger** better than Tolstoy. He will at once understand with a message your envoy is speeding. Don't delay, in two days I am going with Rimsky-Korsakoff** to Moscow. Come along with us. Elias (the sculptor Hinsburg) will also join us. Come along, come along!"

Thus we are together in the railway compartment. Stassoff, a septenarian, took the upper berth, grumbling that otherwise he cannot sleep. His long white beard was hanging down. A heated dispute starts with Rimsky-Korsakoff about his new opera. To a realist like Stassoff, the entire epic of "Grad Kitej" does not appeal.

"Just wait, you have to discuss this matter with Tolstoy. He says that he does not understand music, but he weeps when he hears it," says Stassoff jokingly to Korsakoff.

At that time there was much talk about Tolstoy's *What Is Art* and *My Belief.* All sorts of fables about Tolstoy and his life were whispered, as is usual around great men.

---

* *Messenger* is the name of Roerich's first painting, now in the Tretyakoff Gallery in Moscow.

** Rimsky-Korsakoff, famous Russian composer of national operas.

Gossipers had a wide field for their imagination. They could not grasp how Count Tolstoy could plough the field or make shoes. Absurd anecdotes about Tolstoy's so-called godlessness were in circulation. These slanderers concealed the fact that a godless person could never have written the beautiful parable about the three hermits.

I regret that I do not have at hand the actual text of this narrative, but everyone who wishes to cognize the great personality of Tolstoy should know at least a short summary of it.

On an island there lived three old hermits. They were so simple that the only prayer they used was: "We are three—You are three—have mercy upon us!" And great miracles were manifested during this simple prayer. The local bishop came to hear about these hermits and this inadmissible prayer, and decided to visit and teach them the canonical prayers. He arrived on the island, told the hermits that their prayer was undignified, and taught them many of the customary ones. Then the bishop left on a boat. And he saw that across the sea, following the boat, was a radiant light. As this light approached, he discerned the three hermits, who were holding their hands and running upon the waves hastening to catch the boat. When they had approached, they asked the bishop: "We have forgotten the prayers you taught us, and have hastened to ask you to repeat them." When the bishop saw this miracle, he said to the hermits: "Continue to live with your old prayer."

Could any godless person give such a remarkable image of hermits, who attained illumination in their simple prayer? Indeed to Tolstoy, the great seeker, everything basic and truthful was near to the heart.

Everyone also remembers also his *Fruits of Enlightenment,* which is full of sarcasm about ignorantly interpreted spiritistic séances. Certain people wished to see in this the negative attitude of Tolstoy toward the entire metaphysical domain. But the great thinker only scourged ignorance.

In his epic *War and Peace, Anna Karenina,* and many other

essays and parables, there was manifested a wide comprehension of psychology in its highest sense. In the heat of argument Tolstoy may indeed have asserted that a simple folk dance for him is equal to the highest symphony. But when one had an opportunity to witness how deeply Tolstoy was moved, especially by symphonies, one understands perfectly well that in his paradoxes was contained something by far finer and broader than the public may have wished to see in its own interpretation. Tolstoy, the great teacher, before his very end, started out to the Optina Pustyn,* and did not this spiritual act signify a remarkable apotheosis of his wonderful life!

The morning following our arrival in Moscow, we went to Tolstoy's home in Homovniki. Each of us brought something: Rimsky-Korsakoff, his latest compositions; Hinsburg, a bronze statue of Tolstoy; Stassoff, some new books; and I, a photograph of my *Messenger*.

Those who know the quiet side streets of ancient Moscow, the old residences divided from the street by a ward, and the special atmosphere of those historical dwellings—they will understand the whole unforgettable impression of those surroundings. There was the fragrance of apples in the air, mixed with the aroma of libraries and old furniture. Everything was simple and yet refined. We were welcomed by Countess Sophia Andreevna, the wife of the great thinker. Stassoff took command of the conversation, and Tolstoy himself only joined later. He appeared in his typical *tolstovka*,** quite in white, and there remained forever the first impression of his radiantly white appearance.

Only in great men can this simplicity be combined with majestic convincingness. I know that his definition of "majestic" would not please Tolstoy, and he would

---

* *Optima Pustyn* is a well-known hermitage in Russia.

** *Tolstovka* is a kind of workman's overshirt, which Tolstoy liked and usually wore.

probably have interrupted it with some harsh remark. But he was never against simplicity.

Only such a gigantic philosophical and literary talent and unusually expanded consciousness can create that grandeur, which was expressed in the entire figure, gestures, and sayings of Tolstoy. It was said that his face was a simple one. This is not so; he had a strong, typically Russian face. Old, wise peasants and so-called old believers, who sometimes live far away from cities, have such faces. Indeed, the expression of such faces may be severe. But in them there is no mean irritation; on the contrary, there is expressed a mighty thought. India also knows such faces.

Tolstoy admired the work of Hinsburg, making some abrupt remarks to the point. Then my turn came, and Stassoff had been quite right supposing that the *Messenger* would not only be approved but would even call forth some remarkable comments. On my painting, a messenger is seen hastening in a boat to some ancient Slavonic settlement, carrying the important news that some tribes had attacked their neighbors. Tolstoy said: "Did you ever cross a swift river in a boat? You must aim higher than the desired destination, or you will be carried downstream. So also in the domain of morality, one should always steer much higher—life anyhow will carry one down! Let your Messenger aim very high—then he will attain!" Very often in life this advice of Tolstoy was remembered by me. Then Tolstoy dwelt on folk art, on certain paintings from peasant life as if wishing to direct my attention toward the people. "Know how to suffer with them" was also one of Tolstoy's ordainments. Then we talked about music. Again there flashed some paradoxes, but behind them there was such a love for art, such a searching for Truth, and such a care for the people's education that all those disputes merged into a beautiful symphony of service to humanity. And from morning till evening there resounded an unforgettable *Tolstoviana.*

On the following morning, starting on our return

journey, Stassoff said to me: "Now you have been bestowed with the true distinction of an artist!"

Amazing is the whole life of Tolstoy as a great writer and greater teacher of light. Every event of his life increased the deep veneration of the people to him. And when his excommunication from the Church took place, the undivided sympathy of the masses was with him.

Besides the many published works of Tolstoy, there circulated everywhere in Russian society many banned essays and letters. The causes and effects of Tolstoy's excommunication were discussed in whispers, there were rumors about his private meetings with the Emperor. Also certain prophecies of Tolstoy were discussed; later these remarkable predictions were widely announced through the press. In these the prophetic writer already foresaw the great war, and many other stirring events.

All news about Tolstoy's sayings was attentively received; as if above official authorities, Tolstoy's mighty thoughts dominated. Besides his thundering statements about non-resistance to evil, about pan-human love, about true education for all, there were also such touching descriptions, as for instance, on the death of a tree. India would especially value these simple, truthful words, which contained a deep thought about life omnipresent. Through one of his feminine heroes Natasha, Tolstoy exclaims: "Yes, I was thinking that we are hastening, and think we are hastening home. But God only knows whereto we are going in this darkness. And perhaps we shall arrive, and will find ourselves not in *Otradnoye* (estate) but in a fairy-tale kingdom. And then I thought. . . ."

The sacred thought of a beautiful realm lived in Tolstoy's heart, when he followed the plough like the true ancient hero of the Russian Epos Mikula Selianinovitch; or when like Boehme, he made shoes; or when like the great Carpenter, he stood at the bench, seeking contact with all phases of labor. Untiringly this sower cast in his precious seeds, and they took firm root in the consciousness of the Russian people. Innumerable are in Russia the homes in the name of Tolstoy: Tolstoy museums, Tolstoy libraries, and reading rooms. And can one imagine a more glorious end for Tolstoy than his departure to the Optina Pustyn and passing away at a small railway station? A significant end for a great traveler! This passing was beyond all imagination, and Russia at the first moment could not even believe it. I remember how Elena Ivanovna[*] brought this news to me, repeating sorrowfully: "It is unbelievable, it is unbelievable. As if something basic, some part of Russia itself, has left us. As if an epoch is closed. . . ."

And now, as I write these lines there suddenly appears a radiant rainbow across all the purple and snowy ridges of the Himalayas, from the very earth to the very sky. A blessed sign from Heaven to Earth.

Again Elena Ivanovna brought news, but of a quite different kind. She often, through her great intuition, found in bookshops something new, needed, and inspiring. Thus she brought Tagore's *Gitanjali* in a translation by Baltrusaitis. These beautiful, sonorous poems radiated like a rainbow; and in the Russian translation of Baltrusaitis, they sounded as a clarion call. Until that time, Rabindranath Tagore was not known in Russia in his entire scope; it was known that Tagore's name was acclaimed all over the world, but we Russians had no occasion to cognize the depth of the heart of this great poet.

Gitanjali came like a revelation. The poems were read at gatherings and at private "at homes." Only true talent could create such a precious mutual understanding. The quality of convincingness is mysterious. The foundation of Beauty is ineffable, and every pure human heart rejoices at the reunion with Light. This realization of Beauty, this universal response of the soul was brought by Tagore. What may he be like? Where and how does this giant of thought and beautiful images dwell? The inborn love for the wisdom of the East finds its application in the touching, calling, persuasive chords of the poet. Now everyone

---

[*]   *Elena Ivanovna* is Madame Helena Roerich.

at once became imbued with love for Tagore. It was evident how even the most contradictory people, the most irreconcilable psychologists were united by the call of the poet. As if under the beautiful dome of a temple or in the consonances of a majestic symphony, the inspiring song victoriously united all human hearts. Just as Tagore himself proclaims in his uplifting *What Is Art:*

"In Art the person in us is sending its answer to the Supreme Person, who reveals himself to us in a world of endless beauty across the lightless world of facts."

Everyone knows that Tagore does not belong to the earthly world of petty facts, but to the world of Truth and Beauty. And the persistent desire arose: "How and where to meet?" Will not fate bring about a meeting here, on this plane, with him who so powerfully called toward Beauty the Conqueror? Strangely, Providence transforms imperative dreams into reality. Indeed unforeseen are the paths. Life itself weaves the beautiful web as no human imagination can visualize it. Life is the best fairy tale.

We dreamed of meeting Tagore, and there he himself appears in my studio on Queen's Gate Terrace in London in 1920. Tagore had heard of my Russian paintings and wanted to meet me. And just at that time I was painting a Hindu series *Dreams of the East.* I remember the amazement of the poet at such a coincidence. We recall how beautifully he entered, and how his spiritual appearance impressed us. Verily, the first impression is the true one.

At the Luncheon of the World Fellowship of Faiths in 1934 in New York, Dr. Kedarnath Das Gupta recalled our first meeting with Tagore in the following words: "This occasion had its beginning about fourteen years ago in London. At that time, one day I was at the home of Rabindranath Tagore, who said to me, 'Today I am going to give you a very great treat.' I followed him, and he took me to South Kensington to an apartment filled with superb canvases and paintings, and there were Nicholas Roerich and Mme. Roerich. As Mme. Roerich showed us the paintings I thought of our beautiful ideal of the East:

prakriti and *purusha,* man revealed through the woman. That visit has never been out of my mind."

Just as unforgettable for us remains this visit of Tagore, with his inspiring talks on art; his letter about paintings also remains as a cherished memento. Then we met in America, where the poet lectured so convincingly about the immutable laws of beauty and about mutual human understanding. In the rush of the leviathan city, the words of Tagore sometimes sounded as paradoxical as the fairy-tale realm of Tolstoy. The greater was the attainment of Tagore, who untiringly traveled all over the world, with the imperative call about Beauty. The poet said in China: "Civilization expects the great culmination of the expression of its soul in Beauty." One may quote at length, from the books of Tagore, his prayers and ordainments for a better life, which are so easily carried out in the beautiful domain of the poet's heart.

Are these calls far from life? Are they but the dreams of a poet? By no means! This whole truth, in its entire essence is preordained and realizable in earthly life. Ignoramuses will assert in vain that the worlds of Tagore and Tolstoy are utopian. This is thrice wrong! Is it a utopia that one should live beautifully? Is it a utopia that one should not kill and not destroy? Is it a utopia that one should learn to imbue one's surroundings with knowledge? These are not utopians but reality itself, as real as the fact that one should help wherever possible. If the light of Beauty would not penetrate at least through dimmed sparks into the earthly plane, life itself would be unbearable. What deep gratitude humanity should render to those giants of thought, who self-sacrificingly taught the eternal foundations of life! Without these laws of the Beautiful, life would turn into such bestiality and ugliness that every living breath would be choked.

Horrible is the curse of ugliness. Terrible is the persecution that throughout history tried to destroy true seeking and cognizance. When an ignoramus orders that everyone should think according to his code, this is tantamount to the demand of nonsense and imbecility, for it is destruction. Majestic are the gifts of Tolstoy and Tagore to humanity. They are not selfish misers but most generous donors; they give and give endlessly. Tagore's heart strives to spread real education. Santiniketan—this stronghold of enlightenment—is forever linked with a host of great names. So many artists and cultural leaders of India and many foreign coworkers participate in the ideals of Santiniketan.

The ploughland of Culture is not easy. People sometimes believe that the accomplishment of colossal historical events was always crowned with laurels. History sometimes records entire periods of difficulty in but a few stingy words. Yet how many thorns were met on the way, and how much priceless energy was expended in order to lay the steps of human achievement despite all obstacles, enmity, and ignorance. The more joyful is it to witness how esteemed are the harvests of Tagore's sowing. In Tagore we see a wonderful synthesis of the thinker, the poet, the bard, the artist, and the teacher of life. From the depths of ages we heard that such coordination of happy manifestations is possible. But when it takes place before our very eyes, here on our *terra dolorosa,* against all attacks of chaos, then such attainments verily open for us new vistas. The human hearts become filled with gratitude when witnessing such glorious deeds. The giants of thoughts are not in need of such gratitude. But it is necessary for space, as building material for a more radiant future.

One cannot name any sphere of Culture to which Tagore is indifferent. With everything educational, creative and constructive, Tagore will not only sympathize but he will find forceful helping suggestion. It is but natural that Rabindranath Tagore responded cordially to the pact for the protection of the world's cultural treasures. Whose soul could vibrate with greater ardor for the safeguarding of the fruits of creativeness than Tagore's? But he knows the difficulty of the present moment. He feels what malice and hatred hover above the world at present. Not from newspapers but through his wise heart, he comprehends what danger to peaceful labor threatens during the present Armageddon. Tagore does not conceal these dangers. As always he speaks daringly of questions of peace and education. One can imagine how ignorance is hissing somewhere at his call for peace.

The last letter I received from him recently sorrowfully defines the present world situation: "My dear Friend, the problem of peace is today the most serious concern with humanity, and our efforts seem so insignificant and futile before the onrush of a new barbarism that is sweeping over the West with an accelerating momentum. The ugly manifestations of naked militarism on all sides forebode an evil future, and I almost lose faith in civilization itself. And yet we cannot give up our efforts, for that would only hasten the end."

The heart of the great poet is filled with grief at the current confusion. The thinker knows that every worker of Culture should valiantly defend his post and self-sacrificingly stand up for the treasures of the world. And in this self-sacrifice is also manifested the sign of Tolstoy's service to humanity. As Tolstoy was never a politician, so also Tagore stands adamant as the mighty teacher of life.

One cannot name anyone, who with such convincingness, combines modernism with the ordainments of ancient wisdom. Such a synthesis to the majority of people seems even irreconcilable. Even the esteemed philosophers often state their forbidding "or"—"or," as if life is not of one source and as if the cosmical laws are not immutable. Even the most ancient ordainment proclaimed through the *Rig Veda:* "Truth is one—men call it by various names." I often had occasion to hear how even educated people said that it is old-fashioned to quote Confucius or the Vedas. They suspected a certain lack of progress when someone studied ancient wisdom. Only now is science, in the person of some advanced research workers, beginning to reaffirm the value of knowledge that has reached us from the depths of antiquity. In Tagore such wisdom

is inborn, and his deep understanding of modem literature and science gives that equilibrium, that golden path,
which to the majority seemed a utopia. But this attainment is right in front of us, one has but to admit it in full
attentiveness and goodwill.

On the seventieth anniversary of Tagore's birthday, we
wrote: "*Vijaya, Tagore!*" Difficult is such a victory, but the
more precious it is to admire the radiant hero in the service of humanity.

To the superficial outside observer, Tolstoy and Tagore
may seem different. Some people who like to revel in con-
tradictions will no doubt also try to apply their wit in this
case in order to separate. But if we shall analyze both the
thinkers benevolently, and without prejudice, we shall but
regret that there exist no portraits of Tolstoy and Tagore
taken together—in a hearty talk, in deep wisdom, and in
the desire to bring good to humanity. On the occasion of
Tagore's seventieth birthday, we rejoiced to see Tagore's
portrait in the Latvian newspaper *Segodnia*. The renowned
poet of Latvia, Rudzitis, has beautifully characterized the
great Tagore in a monograph, and now from Praha Prof.
V. Bulgakoff sends me a beautiful postcard of Tolstoy and
himself, taken in 1910 in Yasnaya Poliana. And again
the great images of Tagore and Tolstoy rise before me in
their great service to humanity. Together on one picture,
I would like to see these two giants of thought.

Deep homage to Tagore and Tolstoy!

GURU—THE TEACHER

O^{NCE} in Karelia I sat on the shores of Lake Ladoga with a farm lad. A middle-aged man passed us by, and my small companion stood up, and with great reverence took off his cap. I asked him afterward: "Who was this man?" And with special seriousness, the boy answered: "He is a teacher." I again asked: "Is he *your* teacher?" "No," answered the boy, "he is the teacher from the neighboring school." "Then you know him personally?" I persisted. "No," he answered with astonishment. . . . "Then why did you greet him with such reverence?" Still more seriously, my little companion answered: "Because he is a teacher."

Almost a similar incident happened to me on the banks of the Rhine near Cologne. Again with joyous amazement, I saw how some young man greeted a school teacher. I recall the most uplifting memories of my teacher, Professor Kuinjy, the famous Russian artist. His life story could fill the most inspiring pages of a biography for the young generation. He was a simple shepherd boy in the Crimea. Only by incessant, ardent effort toward art was he able to conquer all obstacles, and finally become not only a highly esteemed artist and a man of great means but also a real Guru for his pupils in the high Hindu conception.

Three times he tried to enter the Imperial Academy of Fine Arts, and three times he was refused. The third time, twenty-nine competitors were admitted, and not one of them left his name in the history of art. Only one did, but Kuinjy was refused. The Council of the Academy was not of the Gurus and certainly was short-sighted. But the young man was persistent; and instead of uselessly trying, he painted a landscape and presented it to the Academy for Exhibition. And he received two honors without passing the examination. From early morning he worked. But at noon he climbed up to the terraced roof of his house in Petrograd, where, with the shot marking each midday, thousands of birds completely surrounded him. And he fed them, speaking to them and studying them as a loving father. Sometimes, very rarely he invited us, his disciples to this famous roof. And we heard remarkable stories about the personalities of the birds, about their individual habits, and the ways to approach them. At this moment, this short, stockily built man with his leonine head, became as gentle as Saint Francis. Once I saw him very downcast during the entire day. One of his beloved butterflies had broken its wing, and he had invented some very skillful means to mend it; but his invention was too heavy, and in this noble effort he was unsuccessful.

But with pupils and artists, he knew how to be firm. Very often he repeated: "If you are an artist, even in prison you shall become one." Once a man came to his studio with some very fine sketches and studies. Kuinjy praised them. But the man said: "Well, I am unfortunate because I cannot afford to continue painting." "Why?" asked Kuinjy compassionately, and the man said that he had a family to support, and he had a position from ten to six. Then Kuinjy asked him piercingly: "And from four to ten in the morning, what do you do?" "When?" asked the man. Kuinjy explained: "Certainly in the morning." "In the morning I sleep," answered the man. Kuinjy then raised his voice, and said: "Well, you shall outsleep your entire life. Don't you know that from four to nine is the best creative time? And it is not necessary to work on your art more than five hours daily." Then Kuinjy added: "When I worked as a retoucher in a photography studio, I also had my position from ten to six. But from four to nine, I had quite enough time to become an artist."

Sometimes, when the pupil dreamed about some

special conditions for his work, Kuinjy laughed: "If you are so delicate that you have to be put in a glass case, then you had better perish as soon as possible, because our life does not need such an exotic plant." But when he saw that his disciple conquered circumstances, and went victoriously through the ocean of earth storms, his eyes sparkled, and in full voice, he shouted: "Neither sun nor frost can destroy you. This is the way. If you have something to say, you will be able to manifest your message in spite of all the conditions in the world."

I recall how once he came to my studio on the sixth floor, which at that time was without an elevator, and severely criticized my painting. Thus, he left practically nothing of my original conception, and in much uproar he went away. But in less than half an hour, I heard again his heavy steps, and he knocked on the door. Again he climbed the long steps in his heavy fur coat, and panting said: "Well I hope you shall not take everything I said seriously. Everyone can have his point of view. I felt badly when I realized that perhaps you took our discussion all too seriously. Everything can be approached in different ways, and really truth is infinite."

And sometimes, in the greatest secrecy, he entrusted one of his disciples to bring some money anonymously from him to some of the poorest students. And he entrusted this only if he was completely confident that this secret would not be revealed. In the Academy it happened once that a revolt against the vice-president, Count Tolstoy, arose, and as no one could calm the anger of the students, the situation became very serious. Then finally at the general meeting came Kuinjy, and everyone became silent. Then he said: "Well, I am no judge. I do not know if your cause be just or not, but I personally ask you to begin your work because you have come here to become artists." The meeting ended at once, and everyone returned to the classrooms, because Kuinjy himself had asked. Such was the authority of the Guru.

From where his conception of real Guruship, in the

refined eastern understanding arose, I do not know. Certainly in him it was a sincere self-expression, without any superficial intention. This was his style; and in the sincerity of this style, he conquered not only as an artist but also as a powerful vital type, who gave to his disciples the same broad, inflexible power to reach their goal.

Long afterward in India, I saw such figures of Gurus, and I have seen the faithful disciples who, without any servile obeisance but rather with great enthusiasm of spirit, venerated their Gurus with that full sensitiveness of thought, which is so characteristic of India.

I have heard a lovely story about a small Hindu who found his Teacher. He was asked: "Is it possible that the sun would grow dark to you if you would see it without the Teacher?"

The boy smiled: "The sun would remain as the sun. But in the presence of the Teacher, twelve suns would shine to me." India's sun of wisdom shall shine because on the shores of a river there sits a boy who knows the Teacher.

In the same teachings of India it is said: "Blessed are you, India!—because you alone have guarded the concept of Teacher and disciple. The Guru can dispel the attack of sleep. The Guru can raise up the drooping spirit. Woe to him who has dared to lay claim falsely to someone as his Teacher, and who lightly pronounces the word Teacher while honoring himself. Verily, flowers that spirit who understands the path of ascent; and he fails who has drooped in duplicity of thought."

One may ask a Hindu boy if he wishes to possess a Guru. No word is needed in reply because the boy's eyes will express desire, striving, and devotion. The fire of Aryavarta will glow in his eyes. The stream of Rig Veda will glow on the slopes of the mountains.

"Who can describe in words the entire possession of the Teacher? Either there is the realization of it, as a serpent of knowledge, or lacking this, there is darkness, sleep, obsession. There is no need to terrify, but one should tell all who have approached Yoga: Your support is the Teacher.

Your shield is devotion to the Teacher. Your destruction is indifference and duplicity."

"He who smiles alike on friends and foes of the Teacher is unworthy. He who does not betray the Teacher, even by reticence when speech is needed, may enter the step of the threshold."

Thus speaks Agni Yoga, which foresees the splendid future of humanity if humanity will master its possessions.

Not only in India but in the whole East, we have the same conception of the Teacher. Certainly in many Eastern countries now, the storm of the coming civilization roars. You can imagine how many misunderstood conceptions may harm this supreme feeling of the hierarchy of knowledge. So many symbols and beautiful signs are swept away through such superficial mechanization of life. And still, even in the most remote places, you can distinguish this instinctive understanding of Guruship. How can one express in the customary words the dignity, the noble understanding, of accepting the chalice of knowledge?

The sense of conviction is the most hidden quality of high creation in art. The most skillful criticism cannot explain why we believe and cherish many of the Italian and Netherlands primitives, or why so much in modernism cannot be explained. This quality of inner rhythm, of inner contracts of color and line, the hidden law of dynamic proportions cannot be fully expressed by the conventional rhetoric; and still they exist, and they govern our creations. Certainly there exist some inexpressible conceptions. I remember how in one philosophical society the most important contemporary poet-philosopher, Block, ceased to attend the meetings. And when he was asked the reason, he shrugged his shoulders, and said, "Because they speak of the unspeakable." And still everything unspeakable and unconvincing in common conversation becomes clear and convincing under the benevolent touch of the master.

Every art creation is a dynamo, charged with infinite uplifting energy, a real generator of enthusiasm. Certainly this is comparative. Some of the creations are charged with this primary energy for one hour and some for eternity—this is relativity. But the most uplifting moment is when the Teacher and the disciples, sometimes even in a half-silent way, are touching this fountain of the Beautiful. Everyone knows how often, without a word, one rhythmic gesture covers the abyss of misunderstanding. And is it not the misunderstanding that we have to conquer? Verily, where can there be evil, especially in the vast field of Beauty? Certainly there can be ignorance and ugliness born of ignorance; there can be the offspring of ignorance—misunderstanding. In our day of so much confusion and corruption, when the spirit is bound with heavy chains of conventionality, how we need to watch each beginning of misunderstanding, and how we must extinguish these ugly parasites which grow so rapidly and pervert the most beautiful garden into a jungle of refuse.

And who can heal this disease of ugliness? Only the Teacher. In what aspect can he act? As a Guru. Is it so difficult and so inapplicable for our days?

I am happy to speak to Teachers. All of you know better than anyone else the inner meaning of the sacred conception of Guru and Teacher. If we all know it, one may ask then, why speak of it? But we also know the strength of prayer; we know the meaning of incantation, we know the charms of chants; then let us know, "What is the meaning of Guru?" "What is the meaning of a teacher of life?" And still, in the best moments of our life, we shall repeat this high conception; because in repeating it, we are cementing the space with the best stones of the future.

Evolution, the young generation, future heroes of a country, future martyrs of wisdom and beauty, we know our responsibility to you! With every affirmation of the Beautiful and of the Highest, we are creating the quality of the future life. Is it possible to create this future life and some happiness for the coming generations, without joy and enthusiasm? And from where does this flame of enthusiasm, of incessant creative ecstasy come? Certainly it comes from the flowers of the field of beauty. If we shall take from life all expressions of beauty, we shall change the entire history of humanity.

The teachers of art—are they not the teachers of synthesis? In old teachings, art and beauty are explained as the highest conceptions. You recall the story from the Upanishads, when during the search for Brahma, Brahma was found in the smile of beautiful Uma. Lakshmi, the Goddess of Happiness, is the most beautiful Goddess. Ugliness really has nothing to do with happiness. In our service to art and beauty, is it not the most gratifying and uplifting feeling to know that we serve the real synthesis of the coming evolution? And in spreading the seeds of beauty we are creating the beautiful life. Where and how can we amalgamate all the strange formations of the conglomerate of contemporary life? Verily, verily, only the veil of beauty can cover and magically transform the grimace of misunderstanding into the enlightened bliss of real knowledge. Not only for teachers but also for pupils, life is so complicated. How to find the balance between a healthy body and the ugliness of exaggerated sports? How to compromise the highest grace of the dance with the dullness and conventionality of some of the extreme modern dances? How to pacify the noble striving for music with some of the disturbing jazz of today?

How to connect the highest spiritual factor with the lowest state of matter? Are these antitheses quite unapproachable, or can a true unifying basis be found, not alone in dreams and thought but here also on earth? Modern thought demands facts. The most calculating positivism wants to draw heaven to earth. Let us recall what one of the most positive contemporary philosophers, Prof. Nicholas Lossky, in his remarkable studies, *Matter and Life*, says: "After all that has been stated, it is not difficult to give a conception of the most characteristic traits of the teachings of matter in the system of organic world perception. If matter originates in the highest existence—existence that is also capable of creating forms of reality other than matter—then the laws of material nature are conditioned to a far greater extent than physicists admit. Naturally, one doubts that the formula of each law should permit a wide range of conditions, most of which are even still uncrystallized; the law is not always an exact one; in other words, it is usually too broad.

"For instance, to expect that under all conditions, water will boil at one hundred degrees is to take the complexity of nature too little into account; in addition to the necessary temperature, a normal atmospheric pressure is needed, as is chemical purity of the water, etc. The physicist recognizes these incalculable additional conditions; but as he deals with matter alone, he has become accustomed to think of all these conditions as being purely physical.

"Therefore in establishing the most common laws, such, for instance, as the law of the indestructibility of matter when the question concerns the general nature of matter, the physicist presumes that there is no need to include the additional details into the formula of the law. Even further to the mind of such a physicist who tends toward materialism, any limitation of this law seems inconceivable. And truly, so long as we remain in the domain of material processes, the annihilation of matter through physical means, pressure, or impetus seems inadmissible and even inconceivable.

"But let us presume that matter is not the only form of existence in nature, and further, let us presume that matter is something evolving subject to the action of the highest principles of the elements, then the place of matter in nature becomes far less durable than the mind of a materialist considers.

"Thus it is not difficult to also conceive conditions when the annihilation of a particle of matter is also possible."

Thus we see that even in the conception of the most positive scientist is clearly expressed the relativity of matter. In this relativity is an open window for the highest conceptions. Let them approach our earth. Let them saturate the coming evolution, not only as an external transfiguration but also as the evolution of the innermost being. The facts are needed, but the understanding of these facts should be without hypocrisy and superstition. In the field of teaching, it is a special joy to expel not only ignorance but that ugly offshoot of ignorance superstition; and the freedom of discipline enters where ugly superstition is destroyed. The self-denying study of the facts opens to us the highest degree of matter. The cosmic ray is no longer a fairy tale but has entered the laboratory of the scientist, and the scientific mind knows how many more rays and forms of energy can enter our life, and can be applied for the upliftment of every breath. The benevolent transfiguration of life is on the threshold; even more, it knocked on our portals because so many things may be disturbed at once without delay. How many social problems can be solved without hostility, and with only one condition—that they be solved in a beautiful way! Well, we can evoke the energies from space; and we can enlighten our life with powerful rays, but these rays shall be beautiful—as beautiful as is the conception of evolution.

Our responsibility before the Beautiful is great! If we feel it, we can demand the same responsibility to this highest principle from our pupils. If we know that this is a necessity, as during an ocean storm, we can require of our companions the same attention to the keenest demand of the moment.

We are introducing, by all means, art into all manifestations of life. We are striving to show the quality of creative labor, but this quality can be recognized only when we know what is the ecstasy before the beautiful; and this ecstasy is not that of a transfixed image, but this is motion, this is all-vibrating Nirvana, not only the falsely conceived Nirvana of immobility but the Nirvana of the noblest and most intensive activity. In all ancient teachings, we have heard about the nobility of action. How can they be noble if they are not beautiful? You are the teachers of art; you are the emissaries of beauty; you know your responsibility to the coming generation, and in this is manifested your joy and your invincible power. Your actions are noble actions.

And to you, my young unseen friends, we are sending our call. We know how difficult it is for you to begin the struggle for light and achievement. But the obstacles are only new possibilities to create beneficent energy. Without battle, there is no victory. And how can you avoid the venomous arrows of a dark enemy? By approaching your enemy so closely that we shall lack space even to send an arrow. And after all, nothing enlightened may be achieved without travail. So, blessed be labor. And blessed be you, young friends, who are walking in victory! The Gurus of the past and future are with you.

Gurus, to you my invocation and my reverence!

RAJ-RAJESWARI

O Raj-Rajeswari!

O Mother of the Peace!

FROM the most ancient days, women have worn a wreath upon their heads. With their wreath, they are said to have pronounced the most sacred incantations. Is it not the wreath of Unity? And this blessed Unity, is it not the highest responsibility and beautiful mission of Womanhood? From women one may hear that we must seek disarmament not in warships and guns but in our spirits. And from where can the young generation hear its first caress of Unification? Only from the Mother. To both East and West, the image of the Great Mother—womanhood—is the bridge of ultimate Unification.

Raj-Rajeswari—All-Powerful Mother. To you, the Hindu of yesterday and today sings his songs. To you, the women bring their golden flowers, and at your feet, they lay the fruits for benediction, carrying them back to their hearths. And glorifying your image, they immerse it in waters lest an impure breath should touch the beauty of the world. To you, Mother, is dedicated the site on the Great White Mountain, which has never been surmounted. When the hour of the extreme need strikes, there you will stand; you will lift up your hand for the salvation of the world. And encircled by all whirlwinds and all light, you will stand like a pillar of space, summoning all the forces of the far-off worlds.

Throughout the entire East and in the entire West, there lives the image of the Mother of the World, and deeply significant salutations are dedicated to this High Being.

The Great Features of the Face are often covered; and under the folds of this veil, glowing with the squares of perfection, may one not see the One Great Unifying Aspect, common to Them All!

"Peace be to the World!"

Verily, when wrath obscures the judgment of the mind, only the heart finds saving solutions. And where is the heart which can replace the woman's? And where is the courage of a heart-fire, which can be compared with the courage of a woman at the brink of the insoluble? What hand can replace the calming touch of the conviction of a woman's heart? And what eye, having endured the pain of suffering, will respond so self-sacrificingly in the name of Bliss?

You, daughters of the Great Mother of the World, your hands weave the Banner of Peace unfurled in the name of the most Beautiful!

Devastated are the ancient temples. The columns are cleft. And shells have pierced the stone walls.

At Goa the Portuguese ships landed long ago. Upon the high prows of the caravels, the images of the Madonna glittered with gold, and in Her Great Name, cannon balls were fired into the ancient sanctuaries, by the Portuguese, for *La Virgin de Los Conquistadores*!

In Sevilla in the Alcazar, there is an old painting by Alexandro Fernandes that bears this very title. In the upper part of the painting in the radiance of the celestial light of clouds, stands the Holy Virgin with a benign smile, and under her broad mantle is sheltered a host of conquerors. Below there is a turbulent sea, covered by galleons, ready to sail to new, far-off soils. Perhaps these are the very ships that will destroy the sanctuary of Elephanta! And with a benign smile the compassionate Virgin regards the conquerors, as if She Herself will rise with them to destroy the alien acquisitions. This is no longer the threatening warning of Elijah, the prophet, nor the Archangel Michael, the constant warrior. But She Herself, the Peaceful, is raised in the folk consciousness for battle, as if it befitted the Mother of the World to concern Herself with the deeds of human slaughter.

My friend is indignant. He says: "Look! This painting is certainly frank! In it is apparent the entire psychology of Europe. Look at the conceit! They make ready to lay siege to foreign treasure troves, and to the Mother of God they ascribe protection for their deeds! Now compare how different is the mood of the East, where the benevolent Kwan Yin covers the children with her garment, defending them from danger and violence."

Another friend present defends the psychology of Europe and also refers to certain paintings as true documents of the psychology of each era. He recalls how in the paintings of Zurbarán or Holbein, the Holy Virgin covers all who come to her with her veil. Referring to the images of the East he recalls fearful horned idams, adorned with frightful attributes. He recalls the dance of Durga upon human bodies and upon necklaces made from skulls.

But the exponent of the East does not concede. He points out that in these images there is nothing of a personal element, and that the seemingly frightful attributes are the symbols of the unbridled elements, and only by knowing their power may man understand that he can conquer them. The lover of the East pointed out how the elements of terror have been used everywhere, and that flames no less terrifying, nor horns less demoniac, were represented in the Hells of the frescoes of Orcana in Florence. All the horrors of the brush of Bosch or the austere Grunwald rival the elemental images of the East.

The devotees of the East cited the so-called Tourfan Madonna as being, in his opinion, an evolution of the Goddess Marichi, who after being a cruel devouress of children gradually evolved into their solicitous guardian, becoming the spiritual comrade of Kuvera, god of fortune and wealth. Recalling these benevolent evolutions and high aspirations, one may mention a custom still existing in the East. Lamas ascend a high mountain and, for the salvation of unknown travelers, scatter small images of horses, which are carried far off by the winds. In this action lies a sense of benevolence and renunciation.

To this, the answer made to the lover of the East was that Procopius the Righteous, in self-renunciation, averted the stone-cloud from his native city, and on the high bank of the Dvina, he always prayed for the unknown travelers. And it was also pointed out that in the West many saints like Procopius renounced their high worldly position for the good of the world. There are in the West many "kefalo-fori Saints, with their heads in their hands, as a symbol of complete renunciation."

In these deeds, and in these *oraisons* "for the unknown, for the unsung, for the unstoried" lies the same great principle of anonymity and the realization of the transitoriness of incarnation, which also is so attractive in the East.

The lover of the East stressed the fact that this principle of anonymity, or renunciation of one's temporary title, and this inspection of benevolent disinterested giving has been carried to a much broader and higher level in the East. In this regard he reminded us that the art works of the East were almost never signed, because the gift of the heart never needs its accompanying note. In response, however, his opponent recalled that all Byzantine, old Italian and old Netherlands primitives, and Russian icons and other primitives were also unsigned, and that the beginning of personal signatures appeared much later.

The talk turned to the symbols of omnipotence and omniscience, and it was again evident that the identical symbols have passed through the most varied manifestations. The conversation continued, because life afforded inexhaustible examples. In answer to each indication from the East, an example from the West was brought forward. One recalled the white ceramic horses, which, up to the present time, stand in circles in the fields of Southern India, and upon which, it is related, women in their astral bodies take their flights. In answer to this was placed forward the images of Valkyries, and even the contemporary projection of astral bodies. It was then recalled touchingly how the women of India each day adorn the thresholds of their homes with some different design, the design of well-being and happiness; but at the same time it was remembered that the women of the West embroider their many designs for the salvation of those dear to their hearts.

One recalled the great Krishna, benevolent shepherd, and involuntarily compared him with the ancient image of the Slav, Lei, a shepherd resembling in every way his Hindu prototype. One recalled the songs in honor of Krishna and the Gopis, and compared them with the songs of Lei, and the choral dancers of the Slavs. One recalled the Hindu woman on the Ganges and her torches of salvation for her family. And they were compared to the wreath cast on the river during the celebration of the Trinity—a custom dear to all Aryan Slavs.

Remembering the conjurations and evocations of the sorcerers of the Malabar coast, one could not overlook the very same rites of the Siberian Shamans, the Finnish witches, the clairvoyants of Scotland, and the red-skinned sorcerers.

Neither the separation of oceans nor continents had affected the essence of the folk conception of the forces of nature. One recalled the necromancy of Tibet and compared it with the black mass of France and the Satanists of Crete. . . .

By countering the facts, the exponents of East and West found themselves speaking about identical things. The seeming diversities became only various degrees of human consciousness! These two conversationalists looked at each other with astonishment—where was the East and where the West? Which one was so accustomed to contrast?

The third silent person present smiled, "And where is the boundary of East and West altogether? And is it not strange that Egypt, Algeria, and Tunis, which are south of Europe in the general conception, are really considered as the Orient? And the Balkans and Greece, lying East of them, are regarded as West?"

I remembered then how walking on the San Francisco shore, with a professor of literature, we asked each other: "Where are we really—in the extreme West or the extreme East?" If China and Japan, in relation to the Near East, Asia Minor, are considered as the Far East, then, continuing the same line of argument, would not America, with her Incas and Red skins, be considered as the Farthest East? What then can one do with Europe, which would then appear to be surrounded by "Easts" from both sides?

We recalled that during the time of the Russian Revolution, the Finns considered Siberia their own, giving as their reasons the tribal similarities. We recalled that Alaska almost touches Siberia, and the fact that the Red Indians, compared with many other indigenous peoples, appear strikingly to have an Asiatic face.

In this way it happened that for a moment all superstition and prejudices were laid aside by all adversaries; the exponent of the East spoke about the "Hundred-armed, One" of the orthodox churches, and the exponent of the West exalted and admired the images of the many-armed, all-benevolent Kwan Yin. The exponent of the East spoke with reverence about the gold-embroidered garment of the Indians and felt the deep penetration of the paintings of Fra Angelico; and the lover of the West gave reverence to the symbols of the many-eyed, omniscient Dukhar. They remembered the All-Compassionate. They remembered the multitudinous aspects of the All-Bestowing and All-Merciful. They remembered how correctly the psychology of the people had conceived the iconography of symbols, and what enormous knowledge lay hidden at present under the dead lines. There, where preconceptions disappear and prejudice is forgotten, appears a smile!

And as if freed of a great burden, they spoke of the Mother of the World. With affection they recalled the Italian cardinal who was in the habit of advising worshippers: "Do not overburden Christ the Savior with your request, for He is very busy. Better address your prayers to the Holy Mother. She will pass your prayers on to whoever is necessary."

They remembered how a Catholic priest, a Hindu, an Egyptian, and a Russian once set out to investigate the origin of the sign of the Cross, and how each searched for a meaning to suit his own purpose but all arrived at the same unifying meaning.

They remembered attempts that flashed through literature, intended to identify the words "Christ" and "Krishna," and again they remembered Joseph and Buddha. And since, at that moment, the benevolent hand of the Mother of the World turned away all prejudices, the conversation ran in peaceful tones.

And instead of sharp contradiction, advocates of East and West turned to a creative reconstruction of images.

One of the speakers recalled the story of a pupil of Ramakrishna, who cited the great reverence given to the wife of Ramakrishna, who according to Hindu custom, was called Mother. Another likened the meaning of the word "Mother" to the conception of "Materia matrix."

The images of the Mother of the World, of the Madonna, the Mother Kali, the Benevolent Dukhar, Ishtar, Kwan-Yin, Miriam, the White Tara, Raj-Rajeswari, Niuka—all these great images, all these Great Self-Sacrificing Entities, flowered together in the conversation as a benevolent Unity. And each of these in his own tongue but comprehensible to all pronounced that there should be not division but construction. All pronounced that the day of the Mother of the World had come, when Supreme Energies would approach our Earth; but because of wrath and destruction, these Energies, instead of the predestined creation, might result in disastrous catastrophes.

In the smile of Unity, all became simple. The aureole of the Madonna, so odious to the prejudiced, became a scientific physical radiation—the aura, long since known to humanity.

The symbols of today, so poorly interpreted by rationalists from being regarded as supernatural, suddenly became accessible to the research worker for investigation. And in this miracle of simplicity and understanding, there became distinct the breath of the evolution of Truth.

One of the speakers said: "Here we now speak of purely physical experiments, but did we not begin with the Mother of the World?"

Then the other took from a drawer of his writing desk a slip of paper and read it: "A Hindu of today, graduated from many universities, thus addresses the Great Mother, Raj-Rajeswari Herself:

"If I am right, then Mother, Thou art all—
The ring, the way, the dark, the light, the void,
And hunger, sorrow, poverty, and pain—
From dawn to dusk, from night to morn, and life and
      death—if death there be—
All things art Thou.
If thou art they, then hunger, poverty, and wealth are
      only transitory shapes of Thine.
I do not suffer nor enjoy
For Thou art All, and I am surely Thou.
If Thou art He, to mortals manifest,
Then pass me through Thy Light to Him—The Truth.
The only Truth—to us so dimly known in Thee.
Then lash this mortal body as Thou wilt,
Or embed in golden comfort rich and soft—
I'll feel it not, for with Thy Light I'll know
      The Truth."
And the third one added: "At the same time, on the
      other end of the world, people sing:
"Let us glorify Thee, Mother of Light!"

And the old libraries of China and the ancient Central Asiatic centers guard, since most ancient days, many hymns to the same Mother of the World. Her temple is found in Kish, one of the most ancient cities so far excavated.

And when we were all joyfully united on the adoration of the Mother of the World, one of my friends asked me

what I would read to them on this occasion from my book
Flame in Chalice. I read them my poem "Light":

LIGHT

How shall we behold Thine Image?
The all-penetrating Image.
Deeper than feeling and reason,
The intangible, the silent,
The unseen. I summon
The heart, wisdom and labor.
Who has apprehended that which has
No form, no sound, no taste,
Which has no end and no beginning?
And the darkness when all shall cease?
The thirst of the desert and the salt of the Ocean?

I shall await Thy Glory.
Before Thine Image
The sun does not shine. The moon does not
Shine. Nor the stars nor the flame
Nor the lightning.
The rainbow does not shine.
The Light of the North does not glimmer.
There shines Thy Image.
Everything gleams through Thy Light.
In the darkness are shining
Particles of Thy Glory.
And in my closed eyes
Dawns Thy wondrous
       Light Of the Eternal.

II

THE BEAUTIFUL VICTORY

THE BEAUTIFUL VICTORY

Himalayas

IN India I was once asked what is the difference between East and West, and I answered: "The best roses of East and West have the same fragrance." So, while we are speaking about opposition and differences, essentially we have the great "One," because really all law is One; and under this law, everything is One. We have only to serve this One; and if we are unable to do so, we may say *mea culpa*, for we are guilty of having failed to follow the law.

Very often we are trying to discover how to build the next life—how to build the next evolution. Well, that is our duty. And all will very soon wish to build up our own lives, and certainly you will wish to build up a happy life. What is the best medium to reach this happiness? Only through the Beautiful. We are divided in so many experiences, and yet everything is this same feeling of the Beautiful. You note that I am underlying the Beautiful, not Beauty, because I am speaking not only about art, or about some expression of art, music, drama, song, but I am speaking about the *sense* of the Beautiful, and it is our duty to introduce into our lives this general sense of this great conception.

Perhaps someone could ask me: "Well, it is very good to have such a dream—to make life somehow beautiful. We often think that this Beautiful is only for those who are rich. And he who must work, how can he dream about the Beautiful?"

In various countries, we have seen many collectors and real workers in art, and some of them have been very poor. They have been of the working class, and still this sense of the Beautiful was so strong in them that, even with their modest means, they found the possibility to approach the Beautiful.

The chief thing is to have this inner sense of the Beautiful. Because not everyone has the medium in art, but practically everyone has *thought*, and very often our creation in the *realm of thought* is far greater than reflections in some medium of art. I am underlining this because very often people come to me saying over and over the same story: "I have no prospects in life. How can I dream about something beautiful when I have no time to study?" But in a few moments you can see that this man is really gifted—that he has wonderful conceptions and thoughts, and really can project his thoughts and his conceptions into space.

Every thought is recorded in space. So the chief thing is to create in thought—to be real cooperators in this beautiful creation of the whole universe. Because in this way of creation, we will reflect the best creative powers, and then we will really be cooperators and coworkers toward the Supreme.

How can we introduce this spirit here? To do this in a vital way, we have to realize the power of thought. We speak often about willpower, but very seldom do we employ this power. We speak about telepathy, and we think that it is something very difficult and supernatural, phenomenal; but there are no phenomena, and there is no occultism.

To children, even the telephone is a most occult thing. But when you know how energy is employed, you know that there is nothing extraordinary involved.

We should introduce these possibilities into our lives.

In Asia, they speak about Agni Yoga, the Teaching of

Fire. Is it something supernatural? No. They are explaining how to use this element of Fire—the flame of Space— this all-embracing element. And you will be told that very soon the Era of Flame is approaching our land. You will hear it in a quite scientific way, and then you will remember that Professor Millikan discovered the cosmic ray and is about to discover the keenest application of that ray.

In Asia, for ages and ages, they have spoken about this same beautiful energy. In the Vedas, vital precepts arc given.

In the time of the Buddha, they knew about the iron birds that would serve humanity. They knew from the most ancient times about iron serpents, also for the sake of humanity. So, you see how, for ages, real knowledge was being given out but in another language, or with other symbols, for if you will regard our prejudices in full honesty, we can have a multitude of very useful facts.

But the problem is how to approach facts honestly. "We have to take science as science, without any prejudice or superstition." At the same time not infrequently, the scientists themselves fail to regard facts in the pure light of honesty. We should take these facts through ourselves— through our own understanding—and sometimes we will find ourselves more superstitious than some of the people in the desert. When we have such scientists as Einstein, as Millikan, as Raman, we feel that our coming evolution is in good hands.

Is it not a great joy to see how an eminent scientist speaks in so broad a way? In him there is no superstition. And he is experiencing this same state of the Beautiful. Every scientist in the moment of discovery is the same as the artist because he is in the same creative spirit of the Beautiful. Sometime you can ask a discoverer how his discovery was made—what happened in the moment of discovery. And if the man is honest, he will tell you that something happened at that moment. It was not an accident. At that moment, he touched the Supreme—the highest Cross of Eternity.

Some big businessmen are also artists, and it is very easy to speak to and to receive understanding from a big man because his consciousness is already expanded. And if you are speaking to him about something difficult, still his experience is so big that he can understand everything; and from his understanding emanates his tolerance. Please remember this quality—tolerance. You will need it. So many things have been broken through ignorance.

Intolerance is ignorance.

Sometimes we think we are tired. But we are not tired. We are only using the same nervous center too long. If we are tired, it does not mean that we need relaxation—that we need to sleep. We should only change our work—change the center; and in this change of different nervous centers, you will become rested.

Remember, the chief poison is the poison of irritation and anger, and this is a most powerful poison. For, with every irritation, we physically create in our nervous system some poisonous emanation.

Our best scientists and physicians already know that something physical is created through irritation. In Asia, they will tell you about this crystal of anger. How can we be happy if we know that through our anger, we are creating poisons? The only remedy is not to be irritated—not to be angry. When you remember forever that anger is something hideous, then it is not so difficult not to be irritated. If you know that someone is coming to irritate you, you must encounter him with a smile. And when you know that, you are already strong.

I should not like to feel that some of you today think that I am speaking of something abstract, or occult, or something mystical. What is "mystical?"

Something from mist. But we have nothing to do with mists or clouds—only with facts and lights. And with facts we can enlighten our life.

We are speaking about the Beautiful; because when you will realize this scientific energy, the greatest power that is in each of you—then you will release this energy, and energy will grow.

Very often people ask how to release this energy. This energy is our property. One time a young group asked how to release this energy. I asked them: "Each of you, please tell me something unusual about your life." They all became silent. There was nothing unusual to tell! "Our lives are routine." "I am working in a bank." "I am working in a factory." But it is not strange that Boehme, one of the great philosophers, was a shoemaker? And one was a carpenter! Certainly this routine of life is our *pranayama*. That is a new word meaning the use of the energy, the processes of learning how to use the energy. You can achieve through this—but I can tell you that your routine work is the *pranayama*.

When we keep the quality of our work, we begin to be successful. He is the highest artisan, who can attain the quality of art in work. We can even wash the floors spiritually. For then someone will at once remark: "This man is doing this work in such a beautiful way that he is not in his place. Sometimes higher should be given to him." And when we refine the quality of our work, another thing happens—we have the joy of work.

The greatest misfortune is that people often work in expectation of a rest for a holiday; but when we know the joy of work, then we need no conventional holidays. We can celebrate our holiday in labor, with the clearest conception and with the best thought. And we shall not be tired because we shall be enthusiastic, we shall keep our enthusiasm. We shall not sleep too much because we shall not need to sleep much. When we are sleepy, when we are not thinking, then we are not vigilant, and everything bad happens. But if we are producing any work for the quality of the work, in this creative enthusiasm, we are strong and impersonal; this feeling of the impersonal is the greatest aspect of the Beautiful.

Impersonality is the greatest aspect of the Beautiful. Then we can understand that "I" is isolated, and that "We" is strong. Through the "We" is the real beginning of organization, and the real cooperation.

In India we have a beautiful conception of Guruship, the Teacher—it is not a feeling of slavery—on the contrary, it is a great feeling of cooperation. In this way; a chain of cooperators can be created. You know your Master, and someone considers you as a Master; in this way there is a precious chain to the Supreme.

When we know the one Road of Ascent, then many things are easy for us.

CREDO

LYSIPPUS was a blacksmith's apprentice before he ever became a sculptor. The heart of a great artist has never been withered by anguish of a reflective spirit or distress of a hungry body. There is no drought that can destroy the seed of creativeness once it is ready to sprout. Amid the most burdensome labors the folksong sounds a call to renewed creativeness. It is implanted in the quality of each task. Art, knowledge, labor—these are sons of that same creativeness that guides and uplifts.

From the most ancient times, the aims of art have been characterized by the most diverse words. However multiform these definitions may be, everywhere their essence is perceived to be one and the same. First of all from art is demanded persuasiveness. It is said that to be convincing, one must see through beauty. And so it is. To view with the eye of beauty, this means one must comprehend the very best in composition. What sort of composition is this? Much has been said about conventional premeditated arrangement, about a tendency to pretentious subjectiveness. Many times people have tried to express their just indignation at something that in their opinion weighed down the lofty concept of creativeness and rendered it incapable of soaring flight.

Such in reality is conventional composition. In the last analysis artificial composition will always provoke boredom and weariness. But there is also another composition that is natural and yet indefinable in words. The artist may see so clearly and constructively, so to speak, that you do not miss a word of his song. It is precisely as in nature, when the most varied elements are combined in complete harmony. When one examines a cluster of crystals, it is forever amazing how, even when unexpected forms are encountered, they always make up a harmonious, conclusive whole. Thus it is in all artistic creativeness. Its productions have crystallized so naturally that any argument about composition simply falls to the ground. In such a crystal of creativeness is expressed that convincingness that can be definitely felt, but words will be powerless to define it or to give any recipe for it.

When a picture has been naturally built up, you can add or subtract nothing. You cannot shift its parts, and this, not for the reason that you must not violate "symmetry," but that you must not deprive the picture of its vital balance. You have the desire to live with such a picture because you will find in it a constant source of joy. Each object that sheds joy around it represents a veritable treasure. You are indifferent to what school or trend it belongs as an *objet d'art*; it will be a persuasive guide of the Beautiful and will bestow upon you many hours in which you will feel a love for life. You will be grateful to him who has helped you meet life with a smile, and you will take good care of this hieroglyph of Beauty. And you will become better, not at the dry command of morality but from the creative radiation of the heart. In you will awaken the Creator, which is latent in the depths of the consciousness.

In its best disclosures, science proves to be art. Such striking scientific syntheses are forever imprinted upon the human brain as something overwhelmingly conclusive. Then science ceases to be a conventional synchronization of facts and advances triumphantly into the domain of new cognition, leading humanity along with it.

Creativeness, whether it be in symbols or in art, or in any of the realms ruled by the Muses of the classical world, will be attractive, that is to say, convincing. Science is already entering such immense fields as thought. Now it is coming to light that thought acts according to some sort

of laws not set down in human words yet already perceptible in series of experiments being carried on at present.
The mind of the thinker will be a creative one.

It has always been required of art that it be creative.
This demand is no more than just. After all, art cannot be
other than creative. Be it a most intricate picture, landscape, or portrait, once this work emerges from the hands
of the true artist, it will be creative. In the complexity
of present-day concepts, it may be that the very idea of
creativeness has fallen to pieces. Sometimes people begin
to assume that creativeness must be expressed in forms
having nothing in common with reality. Some may still
remember the joke originating at a French exhibition,
where a picture turned out to have been painted by a donkey's tail. In their quests of creativeness, instead of liberation (for creativeness must always be free) people begin to
seek some new limitation and conventional recipes. In this
is forgotten the most fundamental condition of creativeness; first of all, it does not tolerate anything convention-
ally imposed and self-restrictive.

For example, let us cite Gauguin. Can one possibly call
his pictures conventional or tendential? Precisely in the
freedom of creativeness, Gauguin strode over all the limiting frames of his subject as well as any sort of restrictive
technical rules. He always remains a creative artist, that is
to say, a true and convincing master craftsman. The power
of persuasiveness of this artist is not in any recipes or rules
devised by reason. He has created just as a bird sings,
which cannot but sing because its song is the expression
of its essential nature. His persuasiveness lies in the fact
that he has been capable of viewing each of his pictures as
a part of creative nature.

This inner vision of a picture, to the extent that it is
requisite and convincing, will always be far outside the
methods of technical rules. Creators of all times and
peoples have created their productions not only by intuitively seeing them in their best form of expression but by
extending their creativeness to the very material in which

they worked. The sculptor having inspected the block of marble creates from it the best possible. The master woodcarver employs each quality of his piece of wood in working it into the forms appearing to his creative eye. The painter intuitively selects colorful material for each of his expressions. The artist would probably be unable to explain afterward why precisely he employed oils or tempera or watercolor or pastel. And so it must be. Why does an orator raise and lower his intonation? Why does the musician discover those ineffably enchanting harmonies, which even he cannot always repeat?

Intuition is being much discussed at present. Volumes are being written about intuitive philosophy. The solution of problems is being sought not only in calculations but also in intuitive synthesis. One artist has said: "Do thus, in order that people may believe you." Another, discussing a certain realist, asked: "Does he have to depict all the wayside filth just because it exists in reality?" Yet at the same time let us not condemn realism. Of course, it is only in striving for the actuality that in turn produces that convincingness, for the sake of which one must see with the eye of beauty.

Recently much has been said about the synthesis of art. In all the arts, synthesis is nothing but a condensation of all good possibilities. Once Brulov[*] said, in jest, that art is extraordinarily easy: "One has but to take the right color and apply it in the right place." In essence the master and great technician spoke truly. Precisely one must do what is needful in applying the color, and something whispers what this "needful" is. The master knows when it would be impossible to do otherwise, yet when you ask him by what canons and rules he has done exactly so and not otherwise, no artist can explain to you what laws he followed in doing as he did.

Comparing the works of art of different times and peoples, we see that frequently the most apparently diverse

---

[*] A famous Russian artist of the mid-nineteenth century.

productions go together excellently in a common grouping. One can easily picture to oneself how certain primitives; Persian miniatures; *objets d'art* of Africa, China, and Japan; Gauguin and Van Gogh can all appear in one collection, and even hang on one wall. Not the material or technique but something else enables these entirely different examples to live together in harmony. They are all truly products of creativeness. Moreover, all kinds of art and sculpture, painting, mosaics, ceramics—in a word, absolutely all things in which have been expressed the creative outburst of a master—will be friends and not mutually exclusive antagonists.

Each of us has often listened to contradictory pronouncements. One says that he understands only the old school. Another vehemently raises the objection that all must be in movement and, therefore, he finds joy only in the modernists even though their works may be harsh and strident. Some esteem only oil painting, while others admire the delicate watercolor. Some affirm that they like only "finished pictures," while others assert that they treasure sketches most highly, as the first inspired impulses of the creator. Some can be enraptured only by monumental works, while others feel warm affection for miniatures. Some limit their taste to the grandiose; others find repose of the spirit in small artistic *bibelots*. Do all such limitations denote limitedness of soul on the part of the art lover, or rather, may it not be that these amateurs have simply dammed up their possibilities?

Very often one's preferences and one's collection depend upon some accidental initial impulse. Perhaps some time a man has heard that a picture is painted with oils, and this expression took root in his brain. Perhaps in the family circle a child has been impressed by a word spoken about watercolors, or he may have been given a set of them and from this chance beginning has followed his interest in precisely this medium. In all manifestations of life and particularly in the matter of artistic impulses, one often has occasion to encounter initial fortuity. Indeed, these "accidents" often prove to be for matters of chance. A man has begun to respond precisely to one thing rather than another and, in this, may have been expressed his dormant accumulations. Spring has come, and buds open out naturally, which have long been asleep through the winter cold. New creativeness has begun!

What a beautiful word—"creativeness"! In various languages it rings out appealingly and convincingly. In its own way it speaks about something latently possible, about something triumphant and conclusive. So mighty and beautiful is the word "creativeness" that all conventional obstacles are forgotten in the face of it. People rejoice at this word as a symbol of advancement. The command of creativeness covers over all whisperings of the limited mind about rules, about materials, about all that is so often answered with the suppressive word "impossible." To creativeness, all is possible. It leads humanity along with itself. Creativeness is the banner of youth. Creativeness is progress. Creativeness is mastery of new possibilities. Creativeness is peaceful conquest over stagnation and formlessness. In creativeness has already been implanted movement. Creativeness is the expression of the fundamental laws of the universe. In other words, in creativeness is expressed Beauty.

It has been said that Beauty will save the world. People have smiled at this formula with sympathy or with derogation, but no one can refute it. There are certain axioms that may cause wonder but which one cannot overthrow. Humanity dreams about freedom; it inscribes this great hieroglyph upon the facades of buildings. At the same time, mankind exerts every effort to restrict and reduce this concept. Great freedom of thought is manifested in true creativeness. That will be true that is beautiful and convincing. In the secret places of the heart, for which man himself is responsible, has been implanted trustworthy judgment as to what true conviction is, what creativeness is, what Beauty is.

As Velasquez said: "Not a picture but truth itself."

Let us recall two excellent passages from Anatole France's *Garden of Epicurus.*

"Whatever wins its vogue only by some trick of novelty and whim of aesthetic taste ages quickly. Fashions change in Art as in everything else. There are catch-words that come up, and pretend to be new, just like the gowns from the great dressmakers in the Rue de la Paix; like them, they only last a season. At Rome in the decadent periods of art, the statues of the Empresses showed the hair dressed in the latest mode. Soon these coiffures looked ridiculous, so they had to be changed, and the figures were given marble wigs. It were only fitting that a style as rococo as these figures should be re-periwigged every year. The fact is, in these days when we live so fast, literary schools last but a few years, sometimes but a few months. I know young writers whose style is already two or three generations out of date, and seems quite archaic. This is doubtless the result of the amazing progress of industry and machinery, which sweeps modern communities along. In the days of MM. de Goncourt and railways we could still spend a fairly long time upon a certain form of artistic writing. But since the telephone, literature, which depends upon contemporary manners, renews its formulas with an altogether disconcerting rapidity. So we will merely agree with M. Ludovic Halévy that the simple form is the only one adapted to travel peacefully, not down the centuries, that would be assuming too much but at least down the years.

"The only difficulty is to define what the simple form is, and one must admit this difficulty to be a great one.

"Nature, at any rate as we can know her, and in milieux adapted to life, offers us nothing simple, and art cannot aspire to greater simplicity than nature. Yet we understand well enough what we mean when we say that such and such a style is simple, and such and such another is not.

"I will say this much then, that if there is no simple style, there are styles which appear simple, and it is just these which carry youth and longevity with them. It remains but to inquire whence they get this fortunate appearance. Doubtless we shall conclude that they owe it, not to their being less rich than others in diverse elements, but rather because they form a whole in which all the parts are so well blended that they cannot be distinguished separately. A good style, in fact, is like yonder beam of light which shines in at my window as I write, and which owes its pure brilliancy to the intimate combination of the seven colors of which it is composed. A simple style is like white light. It is complex but does not seem so. This is only a simile after all, and we know what such parallels are worth when it is not a poet who draws them. But what I wished to make plain is this; in language the true simplicity, which is good and desirable, is only apparent, and it results solely from fine co-ordination and sovereign economy of the several parts of the whole."

"If you would taste true art, and experience a profound impression before a picture, examine the frescoes of Ghirlandajo in Santa Maria Novella at Florence, depicting the *Birth of the Virgin*. The old master shows us the room of delivery. Anna, upraised on the bed, is neither young nor beautiful, but one sees immediately that she is a good housewife. She has ranged at the head of the bed a jar of sweetmeats and two pomegranates. A serving-maid, standing between the bed and the wall, offers her an ewer on a platter. The babe has just been washed, and the copper basin still stands in the middle of the floor. Now the infant Mary is taking the breast; her wet-nurse for the nonce is a young and beautiful lady of the city, a mother herself, who has offered her bosom to the end that this child and her own, having imbibed life at the same fount, may keep the savor of it in common, and by force of their blood love each other as brother and sister. Near her stands another young woman, or rather a young girl, like her in features, perhaps her sister, richly dressed, wearing the hair drawn away from her brow, and plaited at the temples like Aemilia Pia; she stretches out her two arms toward the infant with a charming gesture, betraying the awakening of the maternal instinct. Two noble ladies, clad in the Florentine fashion, are coming in to offer their felicitations. They are attended by a serving-maid bearing on her head a basket of water-melons and grapes. This figure is of a large simple beauty; draped in flowing garments confined by a girdle, the ends of which float in the wind, she seems to intervene in this pious domestic scene like a dream of pagan antiquity. Well, in this warm room, in these gentle womanly faces, I see expressed all the life of Florence, and the fine flower of the early Renaissance. This goldsmith's son, this master of the Primitives, has revealed in his painting, which has the clearness and brilliancy of a summer dawn, all the secret of that courtly epoch in which he had the good fortune to live, and which possessed so great a charm of its own that his contemporaries themselves were wont to exclaim: 'The gods are good indeed! Oh, thrice-blessed age!'

"It is the artist's part to love life, and to show us that it is beautiful. Without him, we might well doubt the fact!"

Leonardo ordained:

"He who despises the art of painting, thus despises a philosophic and refined conception of the universe, because the art of painting is the daughter, or rather grandchild of Nature. Everything that exists was born from Nature and has borne, in its turn, the science of painting. This is why I say that painting is the grandchild of Nature and relative of God. He who blasphemes the art of painting, blasphemes Nature.

"The painter must be all-embracing. O artist, may thy multiformity be as infinite as the manifestations of Nature. Continuing what God has commenced, strive to multiply not the deeds of human hands but the eternal creations of God. Never imitate anyone. And every creation of thine, be a new manifestation of Nature!"

History records the manifold remarkable achievements of Leonardo da Vinci in all domains of life. He left amazing mathematical writings; he investigated the nature of flying; he conducted medical researches and was a distinguished anatomist. He invented musical instruments, studied the chemistry of paint; he loved the wonders of natural history. He adorned cities with magnificent buildings, palaces, schools, libraries; he built large military barracks, constructed one of the best ports in the Adriatic, and planned and built great waterways; he founded mighty forts, constructed war machinery, sketched military plans. . . . Great was his versatility.

But after all these remarkable achievements, he remained in the memory of the world as an artist—as the great artist. Is this not a true victory of Art?

ARMOR OF LIGHT

I REMEMBER how Puvis de Chavannes always found a sincere, benevolent word for the most different creations. But I cannot forget how another famous artist used to go around all exhibitions but with the foam of bitter criticism that he defamed. I noticed that he spent about three-quarters of an hour on abuse and only a quarter of an hour on rejoicing. Taking leave of the artist, I said, "I know how to make you stay longer—with things that are detestable to you!" And the abuse of this artist was most refined, but his praise very poor and dry. Of course, in his creativeness Puvis de Chavannes was far higher. Did not the benevolent criticism of Puvis originate because of his greater creative ability?

Why disparage and act maliciously where a general enthusiasm and a general joy of creativeness have been ordained?

Since time immemorial innumerable are the commandments about the beautiful. Whole kingdoms, whole civilizations were built by this great ordainment. To beautify, to ennoble, to uplift life means to reside in the good. All understanding and all forgiveness and love and self-denial are generated in the attainment of creativeness.

And should not all young hearts strive for creativeness? And so they do; and plenty of ashes of vulgarity are required to choke this sacred flame! How often can one open new gates to the beautiful by the single call, "Create, create"! How much decrepitude is expressed in the fossilized program: First, I shall learn to draw; then, I shall go over to colors; and after this, I shall try to start composition. Innumerable are the cases when the flame of the heart was extinguished before the pupil reached the forbidden gates of creativeness! But how much joy, daring, and vigilance is developed in the consciousness of those who from their childhood dared to create! How enticingly attractive can children's composition be before their eyes and hearts become hardened by the all-deadening conditions of standard!

Where are the conditions of creativeness? In the genius, in the imperative tremor of the heart, which calls forth constructiveness. The earthly conditions are of no importance for the creator who has been called. Neither time, nor place, nor material can limit this impulse of creativeness. "Even if imprisoned, an artist will become an artist," was one of the sayings of my teacher, Kuinji. But he also used to say, "If you have to be kept under a glass cover, then the sooner you disappear the better! Life has no need for such touch-me-nots." He understood well the significance of the battle of life, the battle of light and darkness. A small clerk came to the teacher; the latter praised his work, but the clerk complained: "Family and office stand in the way of my work."

"How many hours do you spend in the office?" asked the artist.

"From ten to five."

"And what are you doing from four to ten?"

"What do you mean, from four to ten?"

"Yes, from four in the morning?"

"But I sleep."

"Well, then you will spend your whole life sleeping. When I worked as a retoucher with a photographer, our work was from ten to six; but the whole morning from four to nine, I had at my own disposal. And to become an artist, even four hours per day are sufficient."

Thus said the venerable master Kuinji, who, beginning as a shepherd boy, through labor and unfolding of his talent reached an honorable place in the art of Russia. Not harshness but knowledge of the laws of life suggested to him his replies, full of realization of his responsibility, full of consciousness of labor and creativeness.

The main thing is to avoid everything abstract. It does not exist in the actuality just as emptiness does not exist. Every recollection of Kuinji, of his teachership, both in the art of painting and in the art of life, always brings to memory unforgettable details. How necessary are these milestones of experience when they bear witness of tested valor and of actual constructiveness!

I remember, how after my graduation at the Imperial Academy of Arts, the Imperial Society for the Encouragement of the Arts invited me to become assistant editor of their periodical. My colleagues were indignant at such a combination of activities, and prophesied the end of my art. But Kuinji firmly advised me to accept the appointment, saying: "A busy person succeeds in everything. An open eye perceives everything. But for a blind man to paint is anyhow impossible." I remember how Kuinji once criticized my painting *The March*. But half an hour later he returned short of breath, having run up to the studio, and said smilingly, "You must not be grieved. The ways of art are innumerable. The main thing is that the song comes right from the heart."

Another teacher of mine, Puvis de Chavannes, who was full of well-wishing and inexhaustible creativeness, always called with profound wisdom for the labor, self-expression, and joy of the heart. Love for humanity and the joy of creativeness were not dead in him, but one will remember that his first steps were not encouraged. For eleven years his paintings were not accepted by the Salon. This was a hard testing-stone for the greatness of the heart!

My third teacher, Cormon, always encouraged me to individual, independent work, saying: "We become artists when we remain alone by ourselves.'

Blessed are the teachers when they lead with a benevolent, experienced hand toward wide horizons. It is a great happiness when one can remember one's teachers with the full tremor of a loving heart.

The teachership of old India, the deep conception of Guru—teacher—is especially touching and inspiring. Yes, it is inspiring to see how a free, conscious veneration for the teacher existed until today. Verily, it forms one of the basic beauties of India. No doubt the same conception existed also among the old masters of Italy, and the Netherlands, and among Russian icon painters. But in these countries it is already a beauty of the past; whereas in India, it is living and will not die out, I hope.

Every spiritual impoverishment is shameful. From the subtler worlds the great masters are watching sorrowfully, grieving over the folly of impeded possibilities. In the articles *"Spiritual Values," "Revaluation,"* and *"Flame—the Transmuter,"* we spoke sufficiently about everything that should not be lost at the crossroads. I cannot forget the deep saying of my deceased friend, the poet Alexander Block, about the ineffable. Block ceased to frequent the Religious Philosophical Society because, as he expressed himself, "They speak there of the unspeakable." Precisely, there is a limit to words; but there is no limit to feelings, to the capacity of the heart. Everywhere is the beautiful. All pilgrims of the good, all sincere searchers landed at this coast. People may quarrel ever so much and may even become like beasts, but still they will unitedly be silenced at the sound of a mighty symphony and will desist from all quarrels in a museum or under the dome of the Notre-Dame in Paris.

The same love of the heart is evoked when we read in all ordainments the lightnings of beauty.

The Persian apocrypha about Christ is most touching: "When Christ was walking along with his disciples, they came across the carcass of a dead dog, lying near the roadside. The disciples turned away in disgust from the decaying corpse. But the teacher found beauty in this instance and pointed out the beautiful white teeth of the dog."

At the hour of passing, Buddha the Lord remembered: "How beautiful is Rajagriha and the cliff of the vulture!

Beautiful are the valleys and the mountains. Vaishali! What a beauty!"

Every Bodhisattva, besides all his other abilities, has to also be perfect in art.

The Rabbi Gamaliel says: "The study of the law is a noble work if connected with some art. This occupation, which is accompanied by art, leads away from sin. But every occupation that is not accompanied by art leads nowhere." And the Rabbi Jehuda adds, "He who does not teach his son art, makes of him a highway robber." Spinoza, who reached considerable perfection in art, answered indeed to this ordainment of harmonization and ennoblement of the spirit.

Of course, the high ordainments of India also affirm the same basic significance of creative art. "In ancient India, art, religion, science were synonymous with Vidya, viz., culture." "*Satyam, Shivam, Sundaram* are the eternally triune manifestation of godhood in man—immutable, blissful, and beautiful."

Let us remember the Museion—the home of the Muses—of Pythagoras, Plato, and all those great ones who understood the cornerstones of the foundations of life, and

Plotinus—speaking on the beautiful!

From the depths of hard experiences of life, Dostoevsky exclaims, "Beauty will save the world!" Ruskin, who glorifies the stones of the past, reiterates the same. A well-known head of the church looking at paintings, exclaimed, "A prayer of earth to Heaven!"

The old friend of all creative searchers, Leonardo da Vinci, says:

"He who despises the art of painting, thus despises a philosophic and refined conception of the universe, because the art of painting is the daughter, or rather grandchild of Nature. Everything that exists was born from Nature and has borne, in its turn, the science of painting. This is why I say that painting is the grandchild of Nature and relative of God. He who blasphemes the art of painting, blasphemes Nature.

"The painter must be all-embracing. O artist, may thy multiformity be as infinite as the manifestations of Nature. Continuing what God has commenced, strive to multiply not the deeds of human hands but the eternal creations of God. Never imitate anyone. And every creation of thine, be a new manifestation of Nature!"

The "stubborn sternness" of Leonardo da Vinci—was it not strengthened by the clear joy for the far-off worlds, by the firm prayer of the heart for Infinity?

How many of the best personalities affirmed the prayer of the heart, the prayer for beauty, for the beauty of creativeness, for victories of Light! From all lands in all ages, many affirm the significance of creativeness as the leading principle of life. Ancient monuments retain glorious images of Egypt, India, Assyria, Maya, and China; and are not the treasures of Greece, Italy, France, Belgium, and Germany living witnesses of the significance of highest creativeness?

How wonderful that, even now, amid all spiritual and material crises, we can affirm the kingdom of the beautiful! And we can do this, not as abstract idealists but armed with the experience of life and strengthened by all historical examples and spiritual ordainments.

Remembering the significance of creativeness, humanity must also remember the language of the heart. Are not the parables of Solomon, the Psalms, the Bhagavad Gita, and all fiery commandments of the hermits of Sinai written in this language? How precious it is to realize that all ordainments lead not to division, this limitation, and not to savagery but to the ascent, the strengthening, and purification of the spirit!

Dr. Brinton reminded me that when leaving America in 1930, I told him, "Beware of the barbarians." Since then many barbarians have broken into the domain of culture. Under the sign of financial depression many irremediable crimes have been committed within the wall of the spirit. The list of dark oppressors, like tablets of shame, has indelibly been recorded on charts of education and enlightenment. Uncultured retrogrades hastened to destroy and uproot much in the field of education, science, and art! Shame, shame! Chicago has no funds to pay the municipal teachers. A church in New York has been sold in auction. In Kansas City, the capitol has been sold in the same way. And how many museums and schools have been closed! And how many hardworking men of science and art have been thrown overboard! Yet the horse races were visited by fifty thousand people! Shame, shame! The stones of ancient monuments can cry out against all the apostates of culture, the source of everything blissful and precious. Do not the scorners of culture trample their own well-being? Even the blind ones see more than these gloomy servants of darkness.

"Beware of the barbarians!"

Still, we cannot be reconciled with an unstable value. We can unite only on the steps of culture, in the name of everything, creative, beautiful. Still it will always be considered a good and noble deed to support everything creative and educational. Ascending these steps, we ourselves become enlightened.

Assembling around the sign of culture, let us remember how we addressed womanhood: "When there are difficulties in the home, we turn to the woman. When accounts and calculations are no longer of aid, when enmity and mutual destruction reach their limits, we turn to the woman. When evil forces overcome one, the woman is invoked. When the statistical mind becomes helpless, then one remembers the woman's heart."

And thus now, times are difficult for the universal abode of culture. And again we hope that the heart of the woman will understand the grief for hampered creativeness, for culture. She will understand the grief for spiritual treasures and will come to aid in realms of the beautiful.

Youth should not be educated upon the wails of despair. When we wrote about the preordained beautiful gardens, we did not lure into illusory domains. On the contrary, we called to the strongholds, affirmed by life. Especially in the days of distress we must affirm the prayer of the heart to the beautiful. We must remember that the beautiful is within the reach of everyone.

To rise from a shepherd boy to venerated masterhood, like Kuinji, or for a remote peasant to become a beacon of science, like Lomonosov, is certainly not easy. Seemingly nothing helped them. Everything was as if against them, and yet "Light conquers darkness!"

As children we liked the book *Martyrs of Science.* It is really necessary that there also should be published books on *Martyrs of the Spirit, Martyrs of Art, Martyrs of Creativeness.* The life dramas of Van Gogh, Gauguin, Rider, Vrubel, Mares, and many martyrs for the beautiful make one more unforgettable ordainment that leads the youth. "Gratitude is the virtue of great hearts." Let us not only remember the glorious names with gratitude, but let us arm ourselves with the whole of their experiences in order to confront all destructive forces of darkness. The experience of creativeness forges all those invincible "Armor of Light" of which the apostle speaks. Now is an urgent hour, when one must be armed with all the experience of the past in order not to surrender the stronghold of culture. Now is the time to be aware of the whole spiritual treasure of creativeness in order to repel with this "Armor of Light" the dark forces of ignorance and to move onward fearlessly! *Per aspera ad astra!*

It is not joyful that we can, notwithstanding varied parties, address every sincere artistic group with the hearty greetings: "Despite all kinds of disunity, the human spirit turns again to positive constructiveness, when every sincere cooperation is appreciated. Do not many kinds of different flowers grow upon the spring meadows, and are they not magnificent in their diversity? Does not this creative multiformity manifest in its fragrance the festival of the spring, which is celebrated by all people since time immemorial?"

Nothing can replace the divine multiformity. So also

in the earthly reflection of Divinity in art, multiformity means bountifulness of the people's spirit. Amid the disasters of humanity, we feel more the value of creativeness.

May constructiveness and the beautiful desire for the good—in other words, that which is to be laid at the foundation of all activities of a cultural man—resound. Everywhere man feels oppressed under conventional divisions, terrible in their insignificance; he is suffocated by the stench of ignorance, by the poison of nonculturedness, which poisons all existence.

All to whom human dignity is dear, all who strive toward truly preordained perfection must naturally work together, casting off, as shameful rags, the dictionary of malice and lies, remembering that in the dictionary of good, there are many non-abstract really vitally applicable conceptions. And now, undeferrably, these conceptions must be applied in life so that the word ceases being an empty sound but becomes the actual strengthening factor of creative thought.

Everyone striving toward the good knows how valuable are all the so-called obstacles, which for a virile spirit are only measures of strength, and which in their tension work out but a new and transmuted energy.

It is not yesterday that is being affirmed. One can affirm but the tangibility of the future. As long as we shall not be convinced in our hearts of the radiant constructiveness of the future, we shall remain in hazy abstraction. For the future trees are being planted along the roadside, and for the future the milestones are being erected. The builder would not put up milestones if in his heart he could not know whither this path leads.

We affirm—this path leads to knowledge, to the beautiful; but this knowledge will be freed from all prejudices and will follow the aims of the good. We affirm—this road leads to beauty, and not luxury or caprice; but everyday's necessity will impel the striving and realization of the beautiful on all paths. We shall not be afraid of the conception of reality. Those who strive in valor know all conditions of the path.

As the wise ones say: "Before leaving, one does not pronounce unkind words." The weak ones will say, "The heart became weary. But what lives in infinite love, leading toward realization in discipline of the spirit and in beauty, will not become weary and overfilled." By tension and burdening of the heart, we increase our experience. Let us be guided by the beautiful words of the wisdom of the East:

Tire Me now, load Me better, laying upon Me the burden of the world.

But I will multiply the strength.

Dost thou hear? The load will blossom with roses and, the grass will be garbed in the rainbow of the morning.

Therefore tire Me.

When I am nearing the garden of beauty, I do not fear burden.

In wisdom everything is real, and the morning is real and the beautiful garden is real; and the burden and the weariness of the world and transfigured attainment are also real.

THE HOUR

Awaken, O friend. A message has come.
Ended, thy rest.
Now I have learned where is guarded
One of the Sacred Signs.
Think of the joy if
One sign we shall find
Before sunrise we shall have to go.
At night we must all prepare.
Look at the night-sky. . . .
It is beautiful as never before;
I do not remember
Such another.
Only yesterday
Cassiopeia was sad and misty,

Aldebaran twinkled fearfully
And Venus did not appear.
And now they are all ablaze.
Orion and Arcturus are shining.
Far behind Altair
New starry signs
Are gleaming and the mistiness
Of the constellations is clear and transparent.

Dost thou not see
The path to that
Which tomorrow we shall find?
The starry masses have awakened.
Take thy fortune.
The armor we shall not need.
The shoes put tightly on,
Tightly girdle thyself,
Our path will be stony.
The East is aflame.
For us
     Is the hour.

CREATORS

BY the sign of beauty, the locked gates may be opened. With song, one can approach a wild yak so that she loses her fierceness and submits to milking. With a song one may tame horses. Even the serpents hearken to a song. It is significant to observe how healing and exalting is the touch of beauty.

Often we have had occasion to write of the importance of the so-called applied arts. Many times we compared the so-called higher arts with no less significant manifestations of all the branches of artistic industry. It is even dreadful to have to repeat again that the "button" created by Benvenuto Cellini is not only not inferior to but undoubtedly far superior to multitudes of average paintings and graveyard sculpture. These comparisons are old; and it would seem that reminders are no longer necessary, but life itself indicates quite the opposite.

In all fields of life, the sphere of applied art, which is blatantly stamped with some such shameful appellation as "commercial art," is abruptly separated from the general understanding of art. Instead of a gradual realization of the unity of the substance of creation, humanity seems to be striving to divide itself still more pettily, and to spread mutual humiliations. It would also seem absolutely apparent that the style of life is created not merely by great individual creators but by the entire body of artists in the applied arts. It is not always their hands that create a poster or a work of jewelry. By some inexplicable curiosity, the products of ceramics are considered inferior to sculpture in marble, although the charm of the Tanagra has given us ample evidence of a noble folk creation.

One may still hear the sorrowful exclamation of many young people: "I cannot live by art. I have to enter the commercial field," thus implying that by this act, the artist dooms himself to the inevitable disgrace that is presumed to accompany participation in practical art.

What material, what circumstances, could deprive an artist of his quality? What manner of demand would compel him to do anything artistic in any expression of life? What type of promoter would destroy the creative fire which gushes unrestrainedly through all materials? It is important for each promoter, even for the most elementary and inartistic one, that his product be clear, vivid and convincing, and easily assimilated by the masses in their daily life. After all, which of these conditions may be regarded as disgraceful? Raphael himself, after receiving his order, was guided by the condition of conviction. Truly the quality of conviction in no way contradicts the true artistry.

Gauguin, through sheer desire for self-expression, painted the doors and interior of his dwelling in Tahiti. Vrubel placed his "Swan Princess" on a platter. The number of examples is countless, in which the most diverse artists sought for expression through the most extraordinary materials. As we have previously noted, the material itself, by its very subtle quality, lends a special conviction to the object. Is there any need to repeat the identical examples that have been mentioned as often in widely varying circumstances? Not discussion but action should strengthen the attitude so necessary for culture. If we reach the expression of the unity of arts, we thereby affirm the need of the closest correlation of all branches of art in its various materials.

It would be difficult to indicate a defined order in which such workshops could be conducted side by side with sketching, drawing, and life classes. This order must be left to life itself. In each country, in each city, and even more, in each district of the city, there are special impressions of life. Hence to these problems one must respond to first. Near a large textile factory, it would be good to provide drawing and study of the technique of this industry. Near ceramic and porcelain factories, one could lend assistance precisely to this medium—thus expanding and refining the understanding that one should correlate in the immediate neighborhood, the practical expressions prompted by the closest possibility. Incidentally, one should not overlook the fact that the physical environment of three of these workshops will afford reciprocal assistance and provide unsuspected combinations that will afford new and fascinating possibilities. The open mind of an instructor, unhampered by prejudice, and the broad demand for creativeness from the students will result in that living vibration that, uncongealed by monotony, will afford to the craft shops an endless, practical variety and conviction.

Another gracious quality is gained through the manifestations of practical variety. They temper the spirit, freeing it from the sense of limitation, which so often constructs our dwelling of fear. But it is from fear, above all, that each aspect of creation must be liberated. In fear, creation cannot be free; it will bind itself with every chain, and forget the noble and victorious discipline of the spirit. Long ago it was said: "One must be cured of fear." One must pursue such methods consciously to liberate oneself from that fear of dusky pettiness and the creeping phantoms that caused even the stone that fell from heaven, aflame with a heavenly fire, to become opaque. Truly, opaque and veiled, when it could have been transparent for all, this Scarab of light!

The Egyptians called artists and sculptors *seankh* or "revivifiers, resurrectors." In this definition is manifested a deep comprehension of the substance of art. How immeasurably broadened this concept can become if we apply it to all manifestations of life, when we acknowledge that each adorner of daily life is an "artist of life." And this true "revivifier" of everyday life himself will be uplifted with new power, will become imbued with the creative spirit in ennobling each object of daily life. Then the shameful and hideous understanding of "commercial art" will be cast out of usage. We shall call this noble adorner of life an "artist of life." He must know life; he must feel the laws of proportions. He is the creator of the needed forms, the evaluator of life's rhythms. To him, numbers, correlations are not dead signs but the formulas of existence.

Pythagoras calculates and creates, sings praises in rhythms, prays in rhythm because numbers were not only the earthly but the heavenly rhythms—the music of the spheres. With Pythagoras, the mathematician, resounds also St. Augustine, the theologian: *Pulchra numero placent.* "Beauty enchants by number." This magnet of number proportions, correlations, and technical consonances, necessary for each of life's adorners, precludes all diminishing of disintegration of the great creative understanding.

Do not let us fear to speak in the highest terms of each manifestation of beauty. A solicitous, exalted expression is a shield for all practical art, which is often exiled to the obscurity of the cellars. A country that is mindful of the future should protect all—from the smallest to the greatest—for whose vindication it will be responsible at the great Judgment of Culture. Facilitating the destiny of these builders of life, the country of culture only fulfills the fundamental covenant of the Beautiful, so beautifully expressed by the poets of antiquity: *Os homine sublime dedit coelumque tueri.* "I gave to man a lofty forehead that he should perceive the summit."

With an exalted covenant the Bhagavad Gita confirms the multiformity of creation: "By whatever path you come to Me, by that path shall I bless thee."

STRUGGLE FOR THE BEAUTIFUL

EXHIBITIONS were lately held, demonstrating the idea of which I had already the occasion to write and speak several times. From the point of view of the history of art, it is always most important to reveal the so-called unknown artists. The names of great masters are very often in public judgment collective conceptions. When looking over the standard handbooks on art, we will find, in addition to the well-known celebrities, numerous names whose creations are not commonly known. And yet these artists lived to an old age, worked incessantly, and had as their teachers, great masters.

About an exhibition in Paris, the press reported the following: "An exhibition of sixty paintings, acclaimed by connoisseurs as the highest works of art but bearing the signatures of unknown artists, was organized in Paris under the patronage of Georges Huysmans, and was heralded to be the most remarkable of the series of thirty exhibitions of the Parisian season."

An exhibition of unknown artists reminded old collectors and critics of many episodes concerning mistakes of judgment committed by the best authorities on art.

One of them narrates: "Thirty years ago I got the idea of submitting to the jury of an exhibition a small Roman landscape painted in light-yellow and bluish colors, and also a pen drawing representing a peasant with a large hat. Both paintings were flatly refused. And yet the landscape was by Corot, and the drawing was nothing less than one by Rembrandt himself."

Another art critic added that paintings by unknown

authors were now and then acquired by the largest art museums and believed to be by known great masters. On a recent exhibition of old Italian art in Paris, there was exhibited the famous *Open-Air Concert*, previously catalogued by outstanding authorities as a Titian and now regarded as a masterpiece of Giorgione.

Such anecdotes remind us of the famous saying of Toulouse-Lautrec: "A painting should be perceived by the heart." In other words, a painting should be valued on its merit, and not because of the signature. This French artist adds: "What would it matter if an image of an Evangelist turns out not to be by Velasquez, if its high quality ranks it equal to the brush of the latter!"

We can remember many facts from life that prove on what quicksand conventional judgment is based. In the Metropolitan Museum of Art in New York, there is a painting attributed to Matsys, which is actually a painting of the very interesting but completely unknown master of the Netherlands, Hasselaer. His signature, which I and the well-known authority on art, Senator Semenoff-Tianshansky, have seen was evidently removed by its previous owner. On the market it is, of course, an entirely different thing to sell an unknown Hasselaer in order to have the opportunity to offer a famous Matsys.

I myself have seen a written certificate by a well-known authority stating a painting to be a Rembrandt. Yet from this painting there had just been removed the name of Jan Victors, a distinguished pupil of Rembrandt. I also remember a landscape of the eighteenth century, under which was visible an older signature of the seventeenth century. One may cite many stories that eloquently prove that a painting should be judged not by the signature but on its merit.

There are two types of collectors. One group requires, first of all, only the name. The other demands an artistic quality. For the collectors of the former type, there have been created innumerable fakes. A rather rude art dealer used to laugh: "A signature costs but a couple of shillings!"

If even today, before our very eyes, there disappears a signature from a painting, then evidently such sinister episodes also took place in the past. It is said about a well-known collector that he always carried with him a phial with alcohol, and while bargaining for a painting, he washed off the signature to decrease the value of the painting. Many tragedies indeed have taken place around art objects. We ourselves were once horrified at seeing how a restorer reduced a beautiful painting to a seemingly dilapidated condition in order to purchase it cheaply.

Everyone has heard of the destruction of masterpieces of Leonardo by religious fanatics and cruel invaders. I remember how a beautiful sketch by Rubens was used as cardboard for the binding of a book. An excellent portrait by Bryulov was covered by an ugly landscape. Under the excellent painting attributed to Ingres was discovered the signature of his collaborator, Carbonniere. In all countries there has always taken place intentional or involuntary shiftings of names and definitions. Together with revaluations and fashions, every century had its own conventionalities. Instead of true revaluation, new concealments are taking place.

But let us not dwell on old art only. The problem of contemporary art is still more acute. May the examples of the past teach our generation to open their hearts to young artists! And after all, who can affirm who are the unknown and the known artists, and to whom are they known or unknown?

I have been told of a most remarkable collection of "unknown" French artists of the recent period. A collector from Marseilles began to collect paintings of artists who died very young or who, in despair, discarded art. A large collection was assembled. A visitor who did not know the names might have thought that they were paintings by Degas, Monet, Manet, Rafaeli, Menard, LaTouche, and other celebrated French artists. This collection also contained some strongly individual conceptions. It became quite clear that at some time, an enterprising person may arrange from such a collection a most striking and significant exhibition. Besides paintings of artists who died early in life, there were those of artists who considered themselves *decouragés.* And it is yet another question whether they were all right considering themselves failures. Sometimes a terrible injustice brings people to this entirely undeserved self-estimate.

A friend of ours when saying "unknown" always used to add "unknown to me." And in this he was quite right. How can anyone say that a person unknown to him at the moment, and in a certain place, may not be greatly revered by other people elsewhere? Such a consideration should be understood by many people nowadays. Otherwise, in self-conceit, some people may imagine that if they do not know something or do not accept it, then all other people also do not know and do not admit it. Such is the usual vanity of the ignoramus. Besides, the question of being known or unknown is one of the most conditional. This definition is based on many casual circumstances, both conscious and unconscious. Many excellent geniuses received recognition only after their death. For some curious reasons people seem to value only the factor of death in their judgments.

Helas! Because of crass ignorance, so often the ugly Danse Macabre replaces the beautiful predestined Dance of Life.

May exhibitions of "unknown" artists remind us once more of the conventionality of human judgment, and may they create one more act of justice in the contemporary world.

We all know of the martyrdom of scientists like Copernicus, Galileo, Paracelsus, Lavoisier, and other innumerable sufferers for truth. There exist entire books dedicated to these martyrs of science, and next to them there should also exist volumes on "Martyrs of Art and Culture." However, once we know that artists are priests of the beautiful we also know all unavoidable attributes of attainments.

We know not only of ancient Herostrates who destroyed the beautiful. Even in our days, Sargent's painting was barbarously cut in the Royal Academy in London. A vandal slashed Millet's *Angelus* in the Louvre, and another brute in 1912 stabbed Repin's *Ivan the Terrible* at the Tretiakov Gallery in Moscow. Much has been written about vandalism. We introduced the Banner of Peace as a Red Cross of Culture to protect real treasures of humanity. And now let me mention another hidden but cruel vandalism that quietly existed in the life of many nations.

When studying Old Masters, we often find that many very good paintings were, for some reason, overpainted by inferior artists with entirely different subjects. It is obvious that the old paintings had become old-fashioned, and the artists simply used the wood as material for his modern and more fashionable creation. One should not think that only paintings of secondary importance were subjected to such barbarous manipulations. On the contrary, among the recorded cases we find some very important names which today occupy a place of honor in the history of art.

I have personally seen an old replica of the well-known painting by Correggio, which is in the National Gallery in London; and on this replica I could clearly see the outlines of an ancient portrait, and indeed the panel on which it was painted proved to be far older than the replica. Once we had occasion to witness how from beneath paintings of the seventeenth and eighteenth centuries, there appeared in good condition beautiful originals by Lambert Lombard, Rogier van der Weiden, Adrien Bloemaert, and other artists equally renowned.

Such examples show to us that vandalism is committed not only by the hands of an infuriated mob but also secretly, in highly distinguished dwellings for the sake of vanity and prejudice.

Beauty cannot be guarded by orders and laws alone. Only when human consciousness realizes the inestimable value of beauty, its power of creating, ennobling, and refining, only then will the real treasures of humanity be safe. And one should not think that the vice of vandalism belongs but to past ages, to some notorious invaders and conquerors. We see that vandalism of many kinds takes place even today. Therefore, the endeavor to protect and save beauty is not an abstract, nebulous move but is imperative, real, and undeferrable.

Verily, education in art and beauty is a necessity. And although it is a "beautiful" necessity, yet it is a necessity with all its duties and obligations. We always rejoice when we see that thoughts are being transmuted into action. Such transfiguration is manifested by a true *oeuvre*, a clear yet at the same time almost untranslatable word. One can say "creative work," yet something more profound and summarizing is expressed in this French concept.

About art in all its manifestations, people are accustomed to judge very light-mindedly. Some have read two verses and already speak with authority about the poet. Some have seen three or four paintings or reproductions, and already pass judgment on the artist. From one novel they fix the position of a writer. One book of sketches is enough for an irrevocable opinion over a cup of tea.

More than once it has been noted in literature that the celebrated "cup of tea" binds one to nothing. And perhaps the pronouncements at the dinner table likewise are not binding, yet they often have very profound consequences. In such conversations, over a "cup of tea," people do not think about the fact that the separate productions are only as the petals of the entire *oeuvre*. Even an experienced horticulturist or botanist would hardly undertake to form a judgment about an entire plant from a single petal of its blossom.

In all kinds of creativeness—in literature, in music, in the graphic arts, everywhere—an attentive and careful correlation is decidedly necessary. It is well known how much has been attributed to authors that which was entirely alien to them, based on incomplete quotations from some train of thought. You know that not only casual people take it upon themselves to pass judgment. In each domain dwells a self-appointed judge.

It is said that the valuation by critics changes three times in a century, that is, by generations. To observe these deviations of evaluations is very instructive. How many irrelevant considerations will influence public opinion! The competition of publishers or greed of the dealers in artistic productions, finally any of the various forms of envy and enmity are so complexly reflected in appraisals, that for the future investigator-historian it is often completely impossible to discriminate. A great number of examples of this could be adduced.

Let us not bring up certain episodes out of the world of collectors, when competition led these people to most unworthy conduct. It is only important to remember that appraisals of creative work are singularly tortuous and personal. We recollect how a certain music lover warned a well-known musician not to play on a particular day because an influential critic had a toothache. But when to all these mortal chances there is united the wish in general not to acquaint oneself with a man's entire work, then his situation becomes truly tragic.

Let us recall any prolific author. Can one form a judgment about him without knowing the sequence of all his works? One can, indeed, estimate separate productions of the author, but then this will be an opinion which concerns the production itself but not all the man's creative *oeuvre*. It is not alone the biography of a great personality, for it is still more valuable to follow the accumulation of creative power, and all the paths of its expression. Thus once again we see how significant in its meaning is the word *oeuvre*. It impels one to out-"oeuvre"-line the entire manifestation, and comprehensively to examine its influence and consequence.

History, passing from a personal *oeuvre*, appraises also the *oeuvre* of an entire nation, of a whole epoch. If the historian does not teach himself in the small and accessible, then by what means can he draw near to and encompass broad problems? Before thinking about such comprehensive tasks, it is necessary to reflect about the conscientious judgments of parts, of individuals. He who sets himself the task of always staying within the bounds of truths learns to discriminate in all fortuities and to compare causes and effects carefully.

Just now when there is so much destruction and upheaval, each clear, honest, exhaustive understanding of a subject will be an especially needed contemporary task. We have read how Stokowski has definitely expressed himself about the harm of mechanical music for true creativeness. Stokowski has justly reminded us that even between the very vibrations transmitted directly or mechanically there is an enormous difference. Certain instruments are generally imperceptible in mechanical transmission.

In a time when music and science design and the graphic arts have been subjected to mechanization, precisely then must the appraisals of creativeness be still more precise, profound, and well-grounded. At this very moment, when it is the modern practice to strive for the brief, the staccato, and the casual, it is especially necessary to aspire for evaluations on the basis of the entire *oeuvre*.

Greetings to all true lovers of the beautiful, who help to make the masterpieces known and revered.

FATE

"**R**EMBRANDT from the first steps of his activity surpasses the limits of a certain local significance, and his entire creativeness has a pan-human aspect. The grim tragedy of his life loses its routine and historical meaning, and becomes, like the tragedy of all great martyrs, a universal symbol. At the same time the symbolism of the art and life of Rembrandt carries a fatal character. Everything that happened to him—had to come, according to some higher laws. The horror of his life acquires a grandiose beauty precise owing to its enormous scope. This is a true Golgotha, a cross, unbearable for average people; a test, for which only the Great Ones are chosen.

"Studying this tragedy, which is so logical in all its details, one realizes its inner harmony. Witnessing the awful finale of Rembrandt's life, when one sees him as an ailing old man, forgotten by everybody, indulging in wine, living in deep poverty, one shudders, but yet understands that such an end was the most majestic, the most dignified for a genius. From the point of view of Highest Justice—it was more worthy and beautiful than the plague of the centenarian Croesus Titian, or the parting of Rubens from his beautiful wife or the over satiety of Velasquez with pompous court functions. Rembrandt was glorified by the crown of martyrs and contrary to reason, one sees in this the highest reward."

Thus the art critic, Alexander Benois, describes the apotheosis of Rembrandt's life in his essays. Alexander Benois found convincing characteristics for many artists, but this criterion of the life of Rembrandt—of the martyr's wreath, of beauty contrary to reason—proves his great understanding. "Contrary to reason"—this simple, convincing expression no doubt seems to many to be out of place and ill-fitting. The weary last physical days of Rembrandt or Franz Hals (who closed his life story as a watchman in an almshouse) may appear to many average minds an unworthy end.

The knighthood of Van Dyck at the Court with its luxurious garments will no doubt seem a more befitting consummation of the life of a great artist. But behind this ephemeral apotheosis, one may distinguish something far greater, the glimmer of which is so intensely saturated that not every eye can conceive it. Precisely in the same way, an electric spark in its greatest tension becomes imperceptible to the human eye.

Also, if you will try to substitute the tragically majestic fate of Leonardo da Vinci for the gorgeous fairylike end of Raphael, then again the highest harmony will be destroyed. Even the fact that the forgotten grave of Leonardo, near the monastery of St. Florentine, has forever been leveled with the ground, even this gesture of fate remained in the style of the great artist.

Beethoven in his Symphony *Eroica* deplored the fate of the consul Napoleon, but if instead of the tragic end, one would imagine the picture of a gradual decay of the Emperor, then the symphony would have lost all its grandeur.

And the great Boehme?—A shoemaker!

During a discussion of the fate of Joan of Arc, someone tried to visualize what final chord would have been the most glorious finale for the triumphant warrior-virgin. Many suggestions were advanced, and one even went so far as to propose crowning her the Queen of France. But after many long disputes, the decision was arrived at that the apotheosis preordained by the Highest Laws was undoubtedly the most magnificent. Of course, no one will vindicate the treacherous judges of Joan of Arc. Similarly no one will justify those quasi-connoisseurs of art who condemned the now-famous painting by Rembrandt, *The Night Vigil*, or his other painting, which was rejected by the municipality, but now is one of the greatest treasures of the Royal Museum at Stockholm.

The evil condemners, ignoramuses, and traitors will forever remain as such. They by no means intended to make the martyrs' crown. They, as true servitors of darkness, will remain in its sinister abysses. But quite above their machinations, beyond all earthly understanding, the Highest Justice transforms carbon into sparkling diamonds. No doubt everyone could add to the above-cited examples many others from all parts of the world. From the highest to everyday testimonials one may see how some unforgettably glorious crowns are being manufactured for some future cosmic needs.

Only to know the untold paths and to be aflame in their realization! Rembrandt could have closed his life as the owner of a curio shop, or as the head of the local Guild, or even as the captain of the society of musketeers. Many different bourgeois solutions may be found. Rembrandt was a collector, and such a great connoisseur could easily find a way to deal in art objects. He was a rich house-owner, and could have, in time, increased his real estate. He could have indulged in many things, and could have "peacefully" rested in his native city. But apparently, such a trivial end was not his fate. The great treasures that Rembrandt gave to the world were weighed on entirely different scales, unseen to the human eye.

Joan of Arc could have "peacefully" remained in her village as an esteemed prophetess and healer. She could have concluded her life as a venerated abbess or just as a respectable citizen. To everyone the path was open. But the Great Law expressed through her one more testimony of truth. The flame of her heart, the fire of the pyre—this flaming crown was far above all common laws. It was quite beyond human imagination.

People speak much about fate. But from what links is so-called fate forged? From a peaceful herd to a devouring fire. From the highest welfare to the greatest poverty. And by what human definitions can this Highest Plan be expressed? One cannot find words to express them, but one can feel them with one's heart. And one must acquaint oneself with such subtle feelings, because through them the new world is perceived.

Confucius, who was misunderstood and persecuted, ordained:

"When we study manifestations, we can achieve knowledge; when we reach knowledge, we acquire goodwill; when we reach goodwill, the heart is purified, and man becomes cultural; when man becomes cultural, order reigns in his home; order reigns in his country; when order reigns in every country, then peace will be attained in the whole world."

This also looks like an easy path—from everyday routine to the peace of the whole world. In this path, which looks so easy and obvious, is expressed the highest universal Law, which is not accessible to many. This law hints by some superhuman language at predestined fate. Every man, every member of the human family carries the responsibility for the peace of the whole world. No one has the right to refuse the beautiful duty of goodwill. No one has the right to burn Joan of Arc at the stake. Who has the right to bemean Rembrandt? In fates, which seem complicated to the earthly eye, resound the Highest Laws which demand extraordinary expressions.

The poverty of Rembrandt is majestic. The pyre of Joan of Arc is beautiful. The thorns of Confucius are great. The Thorny Crown leads the world.

For indefatigability let us remember an advice of Leonardo da Vinci:

"Patience is for the insulted ones, as a garment for the freezing ones. As the cold increases, dress more warmly, and you will not feel the cold. In the same way, during terrific insults, increase your patience, and the offense will not touch your soul."

ACADEMIES OF UNITED ARTS

WHAT we said about schools and cooperation refers first of all to our Institute of United Arts. Outside of the existence of various studios and classes in the different domains of art, we should think about the expansion of the Institute into outside fields of usefulness. Not by accident is the establishment called an Institute rather than a studio. The concept of a group of studios would consist precisely of the labors within them, whereas the Institute acts both within and without.

Our internal programs have already been spoken about in the proper place. They should be carried out within the limits created by circumstances. If something, on account of circumstances beyond the control of the Institute, cannot yet be brought to life, this still does not mean that it has been abandoned in general. Of course, it has not been abandoned; it merely awaits the nearest opportunity.

Now is the time to reflect still more systematically about the outside work of the Institute.

It has always been the cause for rejoicing to hear about the lectures of the director and deans of the Institute in outside institutions. In the archives of the Institute is kept a lengthy series of expressions of gratitude, inquiries, and proposals regarding such appearances.

Likewise it has been joyful to hear about the formation of student guilds and certain other internal groups united by useful ideas.

On the basis of what has already been done, it is particularly easy to bring the outside work of the Institute into a systematic development, which would be reflected both in current reports and in future plans of the institution.

Both from among the teaching staff and the former students should be prepared cadres of instructors. These mobile bearers of the fundamentals of creativeness in different domains of art and knowledge will appear in all kinds of educational, industrial, and business establishments with the living word about the tasks and problems of creativeness and of cognition. It is natural in those cases where the word can be accompanied by musical, vocal, or any other presentation that such will always be useful. The question of remuneration will, of course, be an individual one, depending upon the nature and circumstances of the inviting institution.

I repeat that much has already been done along these lines, and this only confirms the urgency of systematizing such outside work of the Institute. Such labor, aside from its absolute usefulness, can create all sorts of other constructive possibilities.

Among the existing classes is one in journalism. It is desirable that side by side with journalistic practice should be taught the fundamentals of public oration. Such training is absolutely necessary because those experienced in it acquire that convincing quality and enthusiasm that is so needed in personal appearances for enlightening people.

This outside work of the Institute, into which can also be invited people who do not figure either as instructors or students, can be made an important part of the Institute's program. To bear the light of cognition and to affirm the fundamentals of creativeness is always joyful work. Therefore, one can picture to oneself that through systematic work, this part of the occupations of the Institute will find its sincere enthusiasts.

During the years of the Institute's existence, besides the active cadres, there have been in its organization an important number of graduated students; precisely from these could be drawn useful workers for instructional outside activity. Whether in the public schools or hospitals or prisons or churches or remote farms—there will be those highly useful sowings that enter into our common obligation. Since we have already seen that physicians assist such activity with goodwill, since we have made many appearances in churches, likewise traveling to remote farmlands with the torch of creativeness should be welcomed by agricultural officials.

Outside of new acquisitions of knowledge, these discourses can lay the foundation for the revival of household handicraft, of domestic manufacturing. Each rural establishment has seasonal periods of time when any home-industry productions would be manifested as a splendid auxiliary. Entering the old home of a German or French peasant, we are struck by the distinctive style of the household objects. These old-fashioned works of rural homecraft have a great value just now among antique dealers. And, of course, these objects were created in hours of leisure time from farm work. In them has been incorporated an inborn feeling of creativeness and homebuilding. Its self-made, beautiful hearth was created in place of running into the empoisoned cities. One may easily imagine how much such artistic-industrial emissaries will be welcome guests on the work farms. So much refinement of taste and quality of labor can be brought about so easily and naturally.

When, then, we are concerned about preserving cultural values, such excursions through all parts of the state will be the living custodians of the traditions of Culture. Where instead of destruction born of despair there is awakened a living home-building, there blooms also a garden of beauty.

What has been said is no abstraction. These affirmations have been tested by many experiences in different parts of the world. Everywhere the human heart remains a true heart and is fed by the beautiful nourishment of Culture.

I recall a beautiful Persian story. Several artisans on a journey had to pass a very wearisome night in a wild locality. But each one had with him his tools, and in some ruins was found a fallen beam. And here, during the watch hours, each one of the craftsmen applied his own lofty art to dressing the piece of wood. A woodcarver executed the figure of a beautiful girl, a tailor fashioned a garment. Then she was adorned in every way, with the result that a spiritual person with them inspired life in the beautifully created image. As always, the tale ends in full happiness, at the basis of which lies craftsmanship in various domains.

Another story tells how one of the caliphs being taken captive and wishing to convey news about the place of his imprisonment wove a rug with conventional signs, as a result of which he was liberated. But for this means of rescue, the caliph had to be a skillful weaver.

Yet again I recollect a wise covenant of Gamaliel that "not having educated his son in arts and crafts, he prepared him for brigandage on the highway." We need not recall the multitude of other highly poetic and practical covenants, but we urgently direct the attention of the Institute to such possibilities of highly useful outside work.

FORWARD

RECOLLECTION is often considered as a way of looking backward, a check on the forward movement, and a damming up of the stream of fresh thought. If it arrests progress, then it would be better not to practice it; on the other hand, if it corrects error and, at the same time, inspires us to fresh quests, then it is desirable. Among the mass of our recollections, only those which inspire us to remain young, strong, and tireless are of any value. We cannot always love what was done in the past because, for the most part, it remained imperfect; and in so considering it, we are quite right, since this leaves open the path to the quest of beauty. Let us not regret the past, which is full of examples for the future. In every failure we can find the seeds of perfection, and for this it has been said: "Blessed are the obstacles, by them do we grow."

One need not cry over sour milk, but turn it to good use. Synthesis has been proclaimed so that cooperation and friendly intercourse can be initiated.

Specialization is useful if it leads to synthesis. No one member of the body can put on airs; even our most active limbs only exist by virtue of the other parts.

Synthesis, the sum total of forces, leads forward. Infinity sounds through such a proclamation, one not based on the absurd divisions of race or class, nor does it give rise to the quarrel of the generations. Generation is a distinction of old age and youth. Thought, however, is outside of time, and thoughts about good, about knowledge, and beauty cannot be senile. Senility is a matter of decomposition and can easily be recognized.

Malice and hatred and homicide do not belong to attainment. Forward! And in this impetuous command, all that is of decay or malignance must be left behind.

Should you encounter the old, then make it new by understanding what is imperishably beautiful. He who aspires forward always thinks of beauty, and longs to fly and create and merge his efforts with the common welfare. In selfishness there is no horizon opened up, no flight to regeneration. *Per aspera ad astra.*

Let us mention, at random, several artists worthy to be hung in the museum. Maso di Banco, Traini, Altichero, Stefano da Zevio, Michele Giambono, Pitochio, Benedetto Diana, Empoli, L'Ingegno, Lanini, Licinio, Marziale, Morett, Morando, Gerini, Buonaccorso, Ortolano, Orsi, Oriold, Pulsone, Stanzioni, one might name many, many others. They were excellent artists. Some of them occupied outstanding places. They were heads of academies and ateliers. Yet the ways of Fate are amazing. Many of their contemporaries outstripped them. More than once their works have been attributed to other masters, and the error has only been found out after a lapse of many years. The frescoes of the Campo Santo in Pisa were, in turn, attributed to Gozzoli, Nardo di Cione, and Traini. This often happens with works of art, and certain anonymous works of contemporary painters are cause for argument and discussion.

It is all the more difficult, then, with those remote periods when individual style was, as a rule, merged in some traditional method. It is not always easy to distinguish between the work of the more gifted pupils of Rembrandt, Rubens, and Van Dyck and that of their master. It is hard to discern the difference between the work of Lastmann and that of his great pupil, Rembrandt. Even Bramer is very often like Rembrandt. Later the works of Jan Victors and Fabricius, who lost his life in an explosion at Delft, came to be mistaken for those of Rembrandt. Think of the immense number of names in Wurzbach's catalogue of Netherlands artists, most of which were absorbed under the names of other artists. Signed pictures are relatively few, and an enormous quantity of anonymous paintings offer a wide field for conjecture. We have records of pictures by Titian, Durer, El Greco, and Velasquez that have disappeared from fire or vandalism, which is common to all epochs. Some of them may even be hidden away in a garret, somewhere or other, and in recent times we have seen masterpieces of Vermeer, Holbein, and Rubens brought to light.

Great names often cover the work of talented painters, while great works of art often remain unrecognized.

"This is for the future." (Sophocles)

Works of art have varied destinies. I have many times had occasion to note that pictures can completely change their appearance not only because of restoration, but due to chemical processes. It is not merely a matter of color but of all sorts of ingredients. Canvas can play all sorts of tricks, and so will wooden panels or composition. The transport of pictures to distant countries may have disastrous results, and every journey may be considered as an ordeal for a work of art. The artist is often accused of what he did not intend, in fact most artists have experienced this. On the one hand, exhibitions are necessary, and yet they damage the pictures. After standing the strain of fifty exhibitions my *Treasure of the Angels* even changed size. Every time the canvas shrunk at the edges and took in a part of the picture. So great are the risks that pictures have to run in traveling that even the colors sometimes change, or they will come back from distant parts in a damp condition—from Tibet, for instance. In Venice a picture was once covered over with dense mold. And then, paintings will darken in a storeroom or fade under the rays of the sun, so that it is impossible to determine the original colors except by the borders that have been covered by the frames. Anything can occur. I was told that one of my pictures was discovered in a custom house on an island. How did it get there?

I saw *The Summoning* folded up like a handkerchief,

Viking Song was lacerated out of all recognition. My pastel *The Three Magi* was disfigured. *Unkrada* disappeared during the war. Many pictures have been lost or cut up. Where is the *Cry of the Serpent, The Red Dawn, The Boundary of the Kingdom,* or *The Three Joys?*

In one Polish castle were many pictures and six of mine. In the retreat during the war, all were burned. In ancient catalogues we came across the names of sculptures and pictures that have long been lost. Vandalism of all sorts has raged over the face of the earth. Today, war is thundering in both east and west, and many treasures are being destroyed, and people are beginning to plant underground refuges and sandbag defenses.

Even the troglodytes were in a better position, since the drawings on the caverns at Altamira have lasted longer than those in the museums. We have just received a catalogue of Salvador Dali's American Exhibition. We were beginning to wonder whether any new craze would be possible after "Surrealism" and here it is. Dali himself proclaims that his art is derived from *paranoya,* which is a state of madness. This, of course, is new since none of the other modem crazes proclaimed that they were mad. Americans, attracted by the novelty of the ideas, flocked to buy his pictures. Dali, who appears to be a very astute sort of person, has explained that his pictures are kaleidoscopic; that is, each of them contains a variety of paintings. Whoever cares to purchase any of these masterpieces then gets half a dozen paintings for the price of one, since each picture will vary according to his changing mood.

There are, of course, always people who hanker after novelty. The latest craze among the "golden youth" of America is to swallow live goldfish. One of these amateurs, we hear, scored a record, and succeeded in swallowing eighty goldfish at a sitting, and also took first place among these "golden youth."

There is no dearth of innovation of this sort in the world today, and one has but to glance through a list of modern movements that have arisen in recent years to find a series of strange terms that have no meaning whatever. All of them publish lengthy manifestoes, drawn up in vague language, which pretend to overthrow or improve upon the existing tradition.

When we turn back to the innovators of past ages we find no such pretensions. After Bellini and his beautiful art come the splendors of Giorgione and Titian. They were all innovators in their time, but they did not label their work with some uncouth name nor set it up in opposition to that of their predecessors.

El Greco was a great innovator but never published a manifesto on his very original work. He worked in the way that suited him best, and the song that he sang was natural, spontaneous. And later when we come to the more modern innovators of the time of Manet, we find that they did not think it necessary to offer apologies for their innovations or threaten the timid bourgeoisie with their manifestations.

Manet, Van Gogh, Gauguin, Vrubel worked in the only way that came natural to them.

It has been said that Van Gogh was mad, and from a doctor's standpoint he might have been; but he himself never insisted that his own art was a product of madness.

But, of course, we have to progress! Dali's recent exhibition has shown that when an artist today can announce that his work is the result of madness, he scores a great success. Once again the bourgeoisie has been fooled, and so it goes forward.

Anatole France once remarked with a smile: "All that is valued for its novelty or exclusive fashion soon becomes old. Fashions in art soon fade out, like any other fashions. There are phrases that appear pretentious and new like the gowns of some famous dressmaker. But they only last for a season. During the Roman decadence, artists began to comb the hair on the statues of the Empresses according to the latest fashion. Very soon they looked ridiculous and had to be rearranged with marble wigs. A style which is combed, in this way, has to be replastered every year.

A good style, however, is like the ray of light that filters through my window, as I write, and owes its brightness to the fashion of seven colors."

A simple style has this pellucid quality.

GATEWAYS TO THE FUTURE

LET us inscribe on the Shields of Cultural Educational Institutions the covenants, ancient yet forever alive, because in them must be affirmed the unity of all creative forces leading to advancement. Let us say:

"Art unifies humanity. Art is one and indivisible. Art has many branches, but its root is unique. Art is the banner of the coming synthesis. Art is for all. Each one senses the truth of beauty. To all must be opened the gates of the 'sacred source.' The light of art illuminates countless hearts with new love. At first this feeling comes unconsciously, but later it purifies the whole human consciousness. And how many youthful hearts are seeking something true and beautiful. Then give this to them. Give art to the people where it belongs. Not only must museums be adorned, and theaters, schools, libraries, station buildings, and hospitals, but prisons also should be beautiful. Then it will no longer be a prison.

"There have been forthcoming before humanity events of cosmic magnitude. Mankind has already understood that what is taking place is not accidental. The time has drawn near for the creation of the culture of the spirit. Before our eyes has occurred a reappraisal of values. Amid heaps of depreciated currencies, humanity has discovered a treasure of world significance. The values of great art pass triumphantly through all the storms of earthly perturbations. Even "earthly" people have understood the effective significance of beauty. And when we affirm Love, Beauty, and Action, we know that we are pronouncing the formula of an international language. This formula, which now belongs to the museum and the stage, must enter into everyday life. The sign of beauty opens all the 'sacred gates.' Under the sign of beauty, we go forward joyfully. By beauty we conquer. By beauty we pray. By beauty we are unified. And now, let us pronounce these words not on the snowy summits but in the bustle of the city. And, sensing the path of truth, we meet the future with a smile."

Precisely, only by unity, altruism, and just affirmation of true values is it possible to build in good, in the betterment of life. Many primary concepts have become obscured in usage. People utter the word "museum," and remain far from the thought that museum is the *Museion*, in Greek, the House of the Muses. The dwelling of the Muses is manifested, first of all, as a symbol of Unification. In the classical world the concept of the Muses was not at all something abstract; on the contrary, in it was affirmed the living fundamentals of creativeness everywhere—on the earth, in our dense world. Thus, long ago, from the most remote ages have been affirmed the basis of unity. All human examples clearly speak about the fact that in union is strength, in goodwill and cooperation. The Swiss lion steadfastly guards the Shield with the inscription "In Unity is Strength."

When we think about the construction of the school of United Arts, with all the organizations formed in connection with it, we have in view precisely a living work. Any abstractness, any obscureness and groundlessness must not enter into the plan of construction. Obscureness is not for the structure. Light is needful for the structure in order to have in clear rays the possibility of discovering durable and beautiful materials. Each task must be well grounded. Its goal must, first of all, be clear to the creative worker himself. If the toiler knows that each action of his will be useful to humanity, then his forces are greatly increased and will take the form of the most convincing expression. Work is always beautiful. The more intelligently directed it is, the more its quality rises and creates still more for the general welfare. In toil is benefaction.

Each school is an enlightening preparation for vital labor. The more a school equips its students in the field selected by them, the more vital it will be, the more beloved it will become. Instead of a cold formal graduation from the school, the student will forever remain its friend, its faithful coworker. The basis of schools is a matter truly sacred. The pre-eminence of the Spirit is established amid true fundamentals, freed from prejudices. There, then, where arises steadfastly the primacy of the Spirit in all its great reality, there will spring up the best blossoms of regeneration, and there will be affirmed hearts illuminated by the inextinguishable Light of Knowledge.

The school prepares for life. The school cannot give only specialized subjects, not affirming the consciousness of the pupil. Therefore, the school must be equipped with all kinds of useful appliances, selected objects of creativeness, thoughtfully compared libraries, and even cooperatives. The last circumstance is enormously important in realization of the contemporary, general social order. From the youthful years it is easier to accept the conditions of rational exchange; it is easier not to sink into self-interest, into concealment and egoism. The school cooperative society is established naturally. Children and youth love it when to them is entrusted serious labor, and therefore according to each one's abilities must be widely opened the gates of future attainments. The principle of collaboration, of cooperation, can be vitally applied also in the structure of the school buildings themselves, these *Museia* of all the Muses. Can there be hostelries attached to the school buildings? Assuredly. It is even desirable that people who have gathered together for the good tasks of Culture should have between themselves possible greater communion. And if newly approaching people should wish to find themselves in such cooperatives, this must only be welcomed. He who unites himself to Culture must inevitably receive one or another of its gifts. In such a manner, the school building will not only be a direct source of light for youth but will also be made a wide disseminator of knowledge for all who wish to draw near. Of course, eternal learning is ageless. The acquisition of knowledge is infinite, and in this is eternal beauty.

All must be vital, and therefore must stand firm in a compact relationship. For this, all calculations of educational structures must be made with the utmost preciseness. If all cities are full of countless profitable houses, this means the construction, even in the worldly sense, is recognized as being profitable and correct. Even if without cultural functions, the houses are built only through a desire for enrichment; then, indeed, through accurate computation likewise will be profitable such enlightening structures, along with dwellings, schools, museums, libraries, and cooperatives. Not upon great knowledge but upon engineering and financing computation depend the correlation of the parts of such unifyings. All examples of our present times speak about the fact that profitable houses exist, publishing houses thrive, cooperatives flourish, means for museums and schools are to be found, galleries exist for the sale of artistic productions, lecturers receive fees, and there even exist rental libraries that pay their own way. We ourselves in our age have been assured how the matter of artistic postcards alone, in the space of the briefest period of time, yielded enormous incomes. We have seen the beautiful results of exhibitions. We have known how a school, by the payments of a part of its pupils, was able to give free instruction to six hundred indigent ones. We have seen how cooperatives have flourished within a very brief period. We can testify how the self-activity of useful institutions not only supported themselves but also made possible a widespread contribution to philanthropy. Culture cannot be something groundless, abstract. If Culture is the effect of the best accumulations of knowledge, if it is an affirmation of the primacy of the Spirit, if it is a striving for beauty, then it will be an affirmation also of all correct calculations—constructions.

Any feeling of selfish gain is already not Culture, yet earnings and payment for work is a legitimate right, a right based on life, on knowledge, on the worth of the individual. Conventional values will always fluctuate. It is uncertain what metal will be recognized as being the most precious. But the value of spiritually creative labor throughout the history of mankind has remained a stable and universal treasure. Whole countries live by means of these treasures. All revolutions, in the long run, merely confirm these values; people invite honored guests to these feasts of Culture. Entire ministries are instituted in the name of these immutable values. People sensibly try to preserve and care for such universal memorials of Culture. The Red Cross cares for health, but there will be a Sign which guards Culture! It will be a League of Culture!

It is urgently needful that steadfast beacons of Culture rise up amid world agitations and perplexities. If someone thinks there are already enough schools and all kinds of educational institutions, he is mistaken. If there were enough enlightenment, humanity would not stand on the threshold of terrible dissolutions and destructions. All have seen enough dark ruins. Every newspaper speaks about destructions and increasing misfortunes. It was long ago said that at the base of all terror and destruction lies ignorance. For that very reason, the bringing in of increased Enlightenment is the most immediate duty of humanity. Peace through Culture. And who then does not aspire in his heart for peace, for the possibility of peaceful and creative labor, for transforming life into a Garden of Beauty?

And again, no garden will blossom and be fragrant if there be not vigilant supervision over it. The earth must be made better; the best dates for sowing must be chosen, the best seeds selected, and the best day of harvesting calculated. Accurate computations should be insisted upon. The engineer, the builder knows these calculations in order that the foundations of towers conform to their summits. The human heart knows also another unfailing fundamental. It knows that public opinion must in every way be sympathetic toward cultural structures. If philanthropy is manifested as a sacred obligation of the people, the more so is enlightenment as the basis of healthy generations of all earthly evolution, manifested as the nearest and most sacred duty of every inhabitant of the earth. Culture is not the share of the wealthy; Culture is the property of all the people. Each one in his own measure and his own goodwill can and must resolutely bring his seed into the common granary. Cooperation as the basis of existence is manifested also as mutual aid. If one section suffers from disorganization, then the others come to its assistance.

Culture does not produce slander and malice. Evil is the coarsest form of ignorance. Evil, like darkness, must be dispelled. The inflow of Light already disperses darkness. Each cooperation in the name of Light by its very existence already opposes the chaos of darkness. The workers of Culture must in justice see to it that not one of those united to the work of Enlightenment should suffer. Sympathetically and heartily they must stretch forth to each other the hand of true assistance. Yet again this will be no abstract goodwill; each cooperative foresees the possibility and necessity for such assistance.

We have always stood for the social principle. In my stay in Russia, accepting the leadership of an extensive educational institution, I, first of all, applied as a condition the establishment of a Council of Professors, intrusted with the right of making decisions. A general matter must be solved in common. Likewise every financial problem found itself in the hands of a particular Committee composed of experienced financial experts. In addition, a very strict Auditing Committee was in control of all accounts. Seventeen years of work merely confirmed the fact that the social principle must lie at the base of a common task. Very recently I had happened to meet in different countries our former students. I find that in their opinion and recollection their past experience is heartily esteemed.

We also had a publishing house; there were exhibitions, lectures, and discourses; there were many workshops where the children of local factory workers received the fundamentals of their future work. There was also a medical section. There were discussions and conferences dealing with various questions of Art and Pedagogy. There was a museum—I shall always remember the enlightened director and founder D. V. Grigorovitch. Do you remember his tales of popular life? He also brought this love for the people within the walls of the Storehouse of Art, inspiring the accessibility and the wholesomeness of the sources of beauty. It is something to be remembered.

Thus, thinking about construction, we equip ourselves with an unbreakable spirit. We write upon the Shield words that we shall never disavow. We shall look upon coworkers, upon students, upon all those uniting themselves as upon the nearest workers and friends. We shall not be distressed by difficulties, for without difficulties there is no attainment. And we shall always steadfastly remember that all labors must be truly useful to humanity. Therefore, the quality of these labors must be lofty. Likewise lofty must be the mutual heart quality, for inseparable are heart and Culture.

BEAUTIFUL UNITY

COLOR, sound, and fragrance are cornerstones of great synthesis. From time immemorial, people have felt the great inner meaning of these expressions of the human soul. Quite recently people have again begun to remember how close are color and sound, and that the three are the basic remedies against human diseases. Thus he who thinks about the conception of color does not at all associate it with paint as such, but he has in mind one of the greatest concepts of our existence.

The color value of a painting, indeed, does not mean the mere value of paint but of its harmonic correlation, as the French say *valeur*. What does such correlation mean? Again we must say, that for him who is ignorant of the concepts of synthesis and symphony, such correlation will be an empty word.

Let us not dwell here on the deep significance of art for human life—this axiom should be clear to everyone. But nowadays we must especially stress the meaning of synthesis and the symphony of life. Synthesis will be understood by everyone to whom is close the concept of Culture. If human thinking were to remain but on the level of elementary civilization, then it would be too early to mention sacred synthesis; but where the human spirit has traveled toward Culture—that is to say, the Cult of Light—there one may already find cooperation and understanding on the basis of synthesis.

If civilization has not saved humanity from disunity and mutual hatred, then Culture has opened the beneficial gates of synthesis, behind which we can find a true cooperation.

The artists do not rest on primitive considerations of paint, but the very understanding of sonority of color leads them to such beautiful gardens from where may be seen superb vistas of the glorious future. When we speak of synthesis, and of the symphony of life, we shall not avoid powerful and enthusiastic expressions. All these domains of synthesis and symphony are uplifting and lead to the summits. Often the human eye can hardly stand the radiance of snowy peaks, and it is not for the human eye to judge the splendor of these summits. But we have not been called into this world to criticize, but to labor, to admire, and to follow these leading summits in continuous creation.

Create, create, and create! Create in daytime, create at night; for creation in thought is as essential as our physical expression. In this creativeness you shall overcome the most hideous habits of vulgarity, triviality, and quarreling. People sometimes think that creators are very selfish and conceited. But these ugly properties belong to the domain of darkness. When a person "climbs" to the Light, then such an abhorrent husk drops off by itself, and man becomes enlightened. His "I" is changed into the conception of "We."

On the same path toward the summits, man will understand the true meaning of *"Guruship."* From the depth of darkness one can hear at present disgusting cries: "Down with culture," "Down with heroes," "Down with teachers." It is a shame on humanity, but one witnesses such outcries of crass ignorance even nowadays. But he who thinks of such a refined conception as color and sound, culture and harmony, he will understand the infinite Hierarchy of Beauty and Knowledge; and having ascended the majestic stairs of achievement, he will lead also the pilgrims of life following behind.

It is splendid that you all are young. Some in age and some in spirit. Around creativeness there must be this perpetual feeling of youth, which gives incessant striving toward heroism. Countries measure their glory not by captains of industry but by artists and scientists. Such a requirement of history places upon us the duty of incessant perfectioning. He who never ceases in this ascension never becomes old.

I send you my heartiest greetings on this path toward the radiant summits, and I trust that you, forgetting all petty divisions and small human moods, will progress in continuous creation, cherishing the glorious traditions of your great Motherland, India!

Nolini Kanta Gupta writes in the *Triveni,* in the course of his article on the "Beautiful in the *Upanishads*":

"Art at its highest tends to become also the simplest and the most unconventional; and it is then the highest art, precisely because it does not aim at being artistic. The aesthetic motive is totally absent in the *Upanishads;* the sense of beauty is there, but it is attendant upon and involved in a deeper strand of consciousness."

Verily, Art at its highest does not tolerate any conventionality, nor violence. In the very foundations of Be-ness lives the concept of Beauty, in all its convincingness.

We, as builders, do not deny, nor reject.

> "In Beauty we are united!
> Through Beauty we pray!
> With Beauty we conquer!"

III

ROSSICA

"PODVIG"

THE Oxford Dictionary has legitimated some Russian words, which now find international usage. For instance, the words "Ukase" and "Soviet" are defined in the dictionary. One more word should be included—the untranslatable, significant Russian word *podvig*.

Strangely enough, not one European language has a word approximating its meaning. It is said that the Tibetan language has some similar expressions, and perhaps among the sixty-thousand Chinese characters, there may be something similar, but the European languages have no equivalent for this immemorial, characteristic Russian expression. Heroism heralded by trumpet blasts still does not fully interpret the ever-living, all-perfecting idea carried by the Russian *podvig*. "Heroic deed" is not quite it; "valor" will not cover it; "self-denial" again is not the same; "improvement" falls short; "achievement" is entirely different because it implies some conclusion, while podvig is unlimited. Collect from different languages many words that carry the best ideas of advancement, and not one of these words will be equivalent to the succinct but adequate Russian term *podvig*. And how beautiful is this word: it is more than advancement—it is podvig!

Endless and tireless work for the general good results in great progress, and it is this that has given Russia her glorious heroes. Great deeds are accomplished without great noise by simply going on and on, considering only the benefit of humanity.

Among the many noble concepts being fast forgotten is the especially neglected principle of humaneness. Ugly or not, the fact is that humans are forgetting about humaneness. Destruction, insults, belittling are taking its place. But, precisely, podvig does not destroy, does not insult, does not condemn.

Podvig creates and collects the good, perfects life, develops humaneness. Is it not wonderful that the Russian people have created this luminous, elevating concept? The man of podvig accepts a great burden, and he takes it up voluntarily. In this voluntariness there is not a trace of selfishness; there is only the love for one's fellow man, for whose sake the hero struggles along all thorny paths. He is a staunch worker; he knows the value of work; he feels the beauty of action; and in the tension of labor he welcomes every coworker. Kindliness, friendliness, help to the hardpressed—all this characterizes a hero.

Podvig is not manifested only among the leaders of nations. There are many heroes everywhere. They all work, they are eternally studying, and they advance the true culture.

Podvig means movement, alertness, patience, self-sacrifice, tolerance, tirelessness, vigilance, heroism, creative labor, knowledge, knowledge, knowledge!

If the foreign dictionaries have accepted the words "Ukase" and "Soviet", they should by all means include the best Russian word—*podvig.*

> "Glowing with rapture
> The boy brought a benevolent message—
> That all shall ascend the high mountain.
> Exodus of the people he was commanded to tell.
> A sacred message, but my dear
> Little envoy, quickly
> Change one word
> When thou farther hast gone
> Thou wilt call thy luminous
> Message, not an "exodus,"
> But thou wilt say,
>   "Podvig!"

UNDERSTANDING

I HAVE met all kinds of people during my excursions through the fields of culture. They can be classed in many ways, but I would like to deal with them in their friendly understanding of the Russian people. Some think that the Russians are without friends, others that they have many friends, but neither are perhaps, in the right. Friends there are, but they are difficult to discern. A disposition for friendly understanding cannot be decided mentally but is an innate quality, which, as history shows us, has no connection with racial understanding. Wars have been waged with friends, and stimulated civilities have been exchanged with enemies.

We know how Russia has helped other nations and, in the majority of cases, received neither gratitude nor friendliness in return. She has practically made a gift of large portions of her territory, but this has been forgotten. Some people through envy, ignorance, or atavism have shown no friendly understanding for the Russian people, A few have become sentimental and romantic about the cranberry trees or bears in the Moscow streets, while others have slandered the Cossacks and accused them of eating soap and candles or even babies!

Even today in the films one sees the most outlandish settings and little regard to truth. One cannot say if this be done intentionally or through ignorance because of hostility to the Russian people. Much is being done just now in sending Russian art around the world together with translations of Russian literature, and all who come in contact with these get a true picture of Russian life. So soon as anyone comes to understand the truth about the Russian people, he will understand them.

We will not speak of love, friendship or good intention, but understanding makes for good, for mutual comprehension, and a just estimate of a people's character. In Russian literature, we can see the reflection of the Russian soul from the earliest times until today. The main thing is to possess accurate information.

RUSSIAN SILHOUETTES

MUSSORGSKY

"DODONSKY, Katonsky, Lyudonsky, Stassensky"—these were the nicknames of the Golinishchev-Kutuzov sisters, which Mussorgsky used to hum as he worked on his compositions in their house. The mother of Elena Ivanovna was called Katonsky from her name of Katherine. There are many stories of his stay with this family and later with the Princess of Shakhovsky at Bobrovo—she being the one called Stassensky. Dodonsky afterward became Princess Putyatin, and Lyudonsky was Lyudmila Rizhov.

After Mussorgsky's last visit to Bobrovo and at the time he became seriously ill, a most unfortunate thing occurred. Piles of the rough drafts of his compositions were discovered there, but through negligence almost all of them were burned. No one really knows what was lost—complete works perhaps or many fresh inspirations. Ignorance and carelessness is responsible for such losses, and in many a warehouse and garret, valuable manuscripts are still being handed over to the mice.

There have been several biographies of Mussorgsky but all of them omit certain characteristic details. Had he not been the uncle of Elena Ivanovna, we ourselves might never have heard of certain episodes in his tragic career. This year the centenary of his birth is to be celebrated, and there is probably still much to be learnt concerning his life. We ourselves remember his name in connection with many events. We recall the choruses of Mussorgsky sung in the studios of the Society for the Advancement of the Arts, under the direction of Stephen Mitusov. It was at A. A. Golenishchev-Kutusov's house that Mussorgsky composed

The Great Captain. We can also recollect Stravinsky's sonorous rendering of *A Night on Bald Mountain.* We also remember Chaliapin, in Paris, teaching a Raskolnitsa to sing "Sin, Deadly Sin" from *Khovanshchina.* The poor woman was unable to render the weighty intonation of Feodor Ivanovich, and the passage had to be repeated over and over again. She almost burst into tears when Chaliapin shook his finger in her face, and insisted: "Now remember, you are singing Mussorgsky." In thus emphasizing the name, the great singer expressed the admiration that every Russian must feel for Mussorgsky. The only set design I ever made for *Khovanshchina* was that of the Chamber of Prince Golitsyn, which I painted for Covent Garden. And here in the far-off Himalayas, we can hear the strain from the "Streltsi Quarters."

In all Mussorgsky's work there is the primordial Russian spirit. Stasov was the first to call Mussorgsky to my attention at a time when people ignored him or thought that it was useless for him to continue his work. Stasov's circle, however small it may have been, was very influential, and all who attended the first Belyaev concert were admirers of the great Russian genius.

Perhaps if Mussorgsky had lived today, he would have been better understood; but one can never be certain, and perhaps recognition would again have been withheld for half a century. Many may think it a scandal that such misunderstandings can still occur; may the lessons of the past serve to enlighten the future.

It is a pleasure to know that Russia will celebrate this centenary and that *Khovanshchina* is to be produced.

They will realize that it is unnecessary to make cuts in the score or alter the text, and that this great masterpiece ought to rise up to its full stature.

The more complete and authentic the production of such a masterpiece, the more is it likely to prove inexhaustible.

Hail to Mussorgsky.

Stanislavsky

A good eye is rare. An evil eye very often can be found. Stanislavsky impressed upon his pupils: "Know how to find not the worst in everything, but the best." The great sensitive artist knew that the majority of people take pleasure in serving the cult of evil, not knowing how to approach that which brings joy.

People eagerly belittle what they do not like. They are ready to spend a long time around that which seems to them abhorrent. Often the meetings with something they dislike cause colorful expressions and vivid comparisons. Quick are then man's words. And expressive are the movements. And their eyes sparkle. But on the other hand, how dull are the words of praise and approval. People are afraid to find something and acknowledge it. The very vocabulary of good words becomes poor and trivial. And the eyes lose their glow.

Once we tested a connoisseur of art. I went behind with a watch and, without his knowing it, marked the time he spent examining paintings. It appeared that he spent twice as much time criticizing than he spent admiring. There was no need for him to look at what should have given him joy; he had to spend the time condemning. At last I said to him: "Now I know with what to attract you: you should be surrounded by objects that you hate."

But great masters always decree: If something seems bad, it does not deserve discussion. Life is too beautiful, too great that one should debase oneself by contemplating an unworthy sight. There is around us too much of the joyful that is so worthy of enthusiasm and admiration. But one must know vigilance and joy.

One must learn how to rejoice and to admire the uplifting and the beautiful. If people have besmeared their eyes and words, they must learn how to cleanse them. One must strictly keep away from contact with evil. And then the good eye will open.

These uplifting thoughts came into my mind after my meeting with Stanislavsky. He was not only a magnetic personality but also an untiring sower of everything encouraging and creative. One can say of him that he had indeed the good eye.

It was very sad to receive news here, in the Himalayas, that Stanislavsky is no longer on our earthly plane. But where he is now, he will be happier, because his unabating enthusiasm will lead him to new radiant summits.

Several great men have lately left us. Chaliapin is no longer. Gorky and Glazunov have gone. Trubetzukoy has passed away. Yakovlev has departed; the last mail brought the news of Kuprin's death. One remembers Anatole France's masterful story of how great souls meet beyond earthly borders and continue there to unfurl their ideas, which inspired them in life. How much wonderful enthusiasm Stanislavsky will spread everywhere, wherever he may be. And we gratefully retain in our hearts the memory of his unforgettable theatrical impersonations and that uplifting enthusiasm with which he imbued everyone who met him.

No doubt everyone who knew him was moved by the description of how even after death, he was placed in the mourning hall of his theatre—which always was for him a true Temple.

DIAGHILEV

A grandiose exhibition of theatrical art dedicated to Diaghilev was held at the Louvre. Organized by the famous dancer Lifar, it was an event for Paris.

A decade has elapsed since the passing of this remarkable Russian patron of art, with whom began a new era for the Russian Theatre. Chaliapin, Pavlova, Bakst, Stravinsky, Nijinsky, Benois, Sert, Picasso, Lifar—these artists in all fields of Art were connected with Diaghilev.

Who does not know the ballets of Diaghilev, which were renowned throughout the world? To friends in India, a memento about the great Russian leader of art will be of special interest.

Diaghilev has gone. Something far greater than an individual force has passed away with him. We may regard his achievement as that of the great individual, but it would be truer to regard him as representative of synthesis of the great moment when modern art freed itself from conventionality and superficiality.

Diaghilev's life was stormy, as is the life of every genuine artist. More than once our personal relations were severed and renewed. Diaghilev was first to show the faith in the value of my painting *Messenger.* At the time of Paris Exhibition of 1900, he requested my painting *The March*, for his section, but the painting had been promised, however, to the section of the Imperial Academy of Fine Arts, and this estranged him.

When I became Editor of *Art*, published by the Imperial Society for the Encouragement of Art, Diaghilev was taken aback, fearing that I would be associated with official circles. But life brought us together, thanks to Serov.

In 1906, Diaghilev asked me to design the "Polovetsky Camp" for his ballet. It was a joyous period when French critics, such as Blanche, heralded the Russian ballet and Russian art. I was no longer bound to the Academy of Fine Arts and its exhibitions and could partake in the exhibitions of Diaghilev and Mir Iskustva, of which I became president in 1910. From this time nothing clouded my relationship with Diaghilev.

Then came the productions of *Prince Igor, Ivan the Terrible,* and *Kitege* of Rimsky-Korsakov, and our last work together was *Sacre du Printemps* and a renewal of *Prince Igor* in 1920 in London when Diaghilev invited me there from Sweden. I met him for the last time in 1923 in Paris, and I recollect this friendly meeting, so full of memories.

One might often disagree with Diaghilev, and yet not feel it to be personal. Only questions of art or of vital activity can allow such friendly conflicts. Because of this, no one remembers his dissensions with Diaghilev, but remembers only this great constructive work for the benefit of humanity.

Diaghilev was not one to advocate a drowsy life. From childhood, he was a talented musician, and recognized genuine art. It was not superficial modern art, but Beauty.

I remember how, during the exhibition of Mir Iskustva in 1903, I completely changed my painting *The Building of the City*. During the process, Diaghilev arrived. When he saw the painting, he grasped my arm saying: "Not a stroke more! This is the right expression. Away with academic forms."

His motto "Away with academism" was not necessarily destructive. He understood the genius of Mussorgsky. He valued the best of Rimsky-Korsakov. Against contemporary pettiness, he evoked the power of Stravinsky, and it was he who so carefully fostered the art of Prokofiev and, the most interesting thing, French composers and artists.

Only those who knew him personally at the time of his indescribable difficulties could value his constructive genius, his refined sensibility. His partners may recollect how during one day in Paris, he was active as usual, and no one sensed any danger in the air. In the evening he said: "Now you deserve to have a quiet supper, because we were almost ruined. Only five minutes ago I received the news that all has been settled."

With a smile his great consciousness encountered the battles for art, taking on his own shoulders all its responsibilities. Never did he spare his name. He knew that the battle to beautify life was necessary.

It has been said that his enterprise was a personal one. Only evil tongues could have pronounced such a slander; he was a crusader in the service of beauty. Giving his own name liberally, he covered many responsibilities. I remember when during a most critical moment, he said: "Well, I alone shall sign. Please hold me liable for this." This was not the sign of egoism, but a great fighter who knows why he holds both sword and shield.

Was he narrow in his opinions? Only an ignorant person

could say that he only cared for the modern. In his historical exhibitions of portraits, he showed the whole history of Russia from its very beginning, with equal respect for modern as well as the old, even the icon painters. In his magazine *Mir Iskustva*, he showed the most modern artists as well as the discoveries of old masters. Being very sensitive, he felt the sources from which the renaissance arose, and showed the hidden treasures of ancient times and our hopes for tomorrow.

Could anyone think him one-sided in music? No! The Italian primitives and the most modern French composers equally attracted his attention. His productions were always festivals of beauty, feasts of enthusiasm, of faith in an enlightened future, where all the real values of the past were cherished as signs of progress.

Without vulgarizing art, he revealed what was genuine in all manifestations. To relate all the productions, exhibitions, and artistic enterprises of Diaghilev is to write a history of Russian art from the nineties to 1928.

Remember the quality of his magazine "Mir Iskustva"! Remember his work with Princess Tenishev! All the exhibitions—historical, foreign, and modern Russians! And innumerable productions of ballets and operas throughout the world.

Perhaps in time his name will be identified with many conceptions with which he did not agree, but he was generous and never niggardly with his name. When he felt that it would be useful, he gave it freely—his one and sole possession.

A refined nobleman, brought up under the finest conditions, he encountered war, revolution, and all life's hurricanes with the smile of the Wise Man. This wisdom is always a sign of synthesis. Not only did he expand his consciousness, but he refined it, and on this refined plane he could equally understand the past and the future.

During the first night of our *Sacre du Printemps*, and the outburst of public opinion, he smiled saying: "This is victory! Let them hiss! Let them cry! Because inwardly they already feel its value, and only the conventional mask is hissing. You will witness the results." And in ten years came the real understanding as a result.

The personality and work of Diaghilev is one of the greatest records of synthesis. His broad understanding, his virility, faith in beauty provides a beautiful, unique example for the young generation. From this can they learn to preserve the values of the past, to hold on the constructive victories for the future.

With great joy we recorded the glorious epopee of Diaghilev!

ROSSICA

I HAVE had opportunities to meet Russian writers of the last and present generation, and many of them were my close friends. Among them Maxim Gorky, Leonid Andreyev, Alexey Remizoff, Alexander Block were in specially close contact. I also had cordial meetings with Leo Tolstoy, Chekhov, Merejkovski, and with Grigorovitch. I fully understand why India is interested in all these authors not only as representatives of world literature but also feels drawn to their personalities. Fortunately, Russian literature at present is spreading widely in translations in many languages all over the world, and thus a correct understanding of the Russian people is being reached. Till recently, even in so-called educated circles, there were the wildest notions about this vast country. Let us not forget that in French literature there were descriptions of heroes of Russian stories sitting in the shade of a huge branchy *klukva*—apparently the author did not know that *klukva* are the berries of a tiny three-inch shrub. Let us further remember German stories about Cossacks eating children, candles, and soap; that a samovar is carried on the head, and that bears roam in the streets of Russian cities. All these absurdities are now vanishing with the spreading of glorious Russian literature abroad.

When we add to the above-mentioned Russian authors Dostoyevsky, Turgenev, Nekrasov, Gogol, and do not forget the great Russian poets Pushkin and Lermontov, and include further the father of Russian poetry Derzhavin (end of the eighteenth century) and Lomonosov, the scientist and writer of the middle of the eighteenth century, we have a fairly complete outline of the leaders of our literature. Of course, I mention above the literature of the last two centuries, but let us not forget that since the seventh century, Russia already had excellent literary gems such as the famous "Discourse (Slovo) on the Campaign of Igor," which just celebrated its 750th anniversary.

Derzhavin's famous ode to God written 150 years ago is one of the best poems of the Russian language. This poem has been translated into scores of foreign languages. I cannot refrain from quoting the first verse of this ode because it so beautifully represents the spirit of the poet:

O thou eternal One! whose presence bright
All space doth occupy, all motion guide;
Unchanged thru time's all-devastating flight;
Thou only God! There is no God beside!
Being above all being! Mighty One!
Whom none can comprehend, and none explore;
Who fill'st existence with Thyself alone;
Embracing all, supporting, ruling o'er;
Being whom we call God—and know no more!
In its sublime research, philosophy
May measure out the ocean deep, may count
The sands or the sun's rays—but God! For Thee
There is no weight nor measure! none can mount
Up to Thy mysteries, Reason's brightest spark,
Though kindled by thy light, in vain would try
To trace Thy counsels, infinite and dark;
And thought is lost ere thought can soar so high;
E'en like past moments in eternity.
Thou from primeval nothingness didst call
First chaos, then existence; Lord, in Thee
Eternity had its foundation; all
Sprang forth from Thee—of light, joy, harmony,
Sole origin, all life, all beauty, Thine.
Thy word created all, and doth create;
Thy splendor fills all space with rays divine.
Thou art, and wert, and shall be! Glorious, Great,

Light-giving, life-sustaining Potentate!
Thy chains the unmeasured Universe surrounds,
Upheld by Thee, by Thee inspired with breath,
Thou the beginning with the end hast bound,
And beautifully mingled life with death!
As sparks mount upward from the fiery blaze,
And as the spangles in the sunny rays
Shine round the silver snow, the pageantry
Of Heaven's bright army glitters in Thy praise.
A million torches lighted by Thy hand,
Wander unwearied thru the blue Abyss!
They own Thy power, accomplished Thy command,
All gay with life, all eloquent with bliss,
What shall we call them? Pyres or crystal light,
A glorious company of golden streams,
Lamps of celestial ether, burning bright,
Suns lighting systems with their joyous beams?
But Thou to these art as the moon tonight.
Yes! as a drop of water in the sea,
All this magnificence in Thee is lost—
What are ten thousand words compared to Thee?
What am I, then? Heaven's unnumbered host,
Tho' multiplied by myriads, and arrayed
In all the glory of sublimest thought,
Is but an atom in the balance weighed
Against Thy greatness—is a cipher brought
Against Infinity! What am I, then—naught
Even to the eternal throne of Thy divinity,
I am, O God! and surely Thou must be!
Thou art directing, guiding all, Thou art!
Direct my understanding, then to Thee;
Control my spirit, guide my wandering heart;
Tho' but an atom midst immensity,
Still I am something fashioned by Thy hand;
I hold a middle rank 'twixt heaven and earth,
On the last verge of mortal being stand
Close to realm where angels have their birth,
Just on the boundary of the spirit land!

The chain of Being is complete in me;
In me is matter's last gradation lost,
And the next step is Spirit-Deity!
I can command the lightning, and am dust!
A monarch and a slave; a worm, a God!
Whence came I here, and how? So marvelously
Thy light, Thy love, in their bright plenitude,
Filled me with an Immortal Soul, to spring
Over the abyss of Death, and bade it wear
The garment of eternal day, and wing
Its heavenly flight beyond the little sphere,
Even to its source, to Thee, its author there.
O thought ineffable! O vision blessed,
Though worthless our conception all of Thee
Yet shall Thy shadowed image fill our breast,
And waft its homage to Thy Deity.
God! thus alone my lowly thoughts can soar;
Thus seek Thy presence—Being, wise and good;
Midst Thy vast works admire, obey, adore!
And when the tongue is eloquent no more,
The soul shall speak in tears its gratitude.

When we speak of Fyodor Dostoyevsky he often is
represented as a stern psychologist of suffering humanity.
The very names of his works *Crime and Punishment*, *The Idiot*,
The House of Death already seem to point in this direction.
But let us not forget that precisely Dostoyevsky proclaimed
that "Beauty will save the world." Besides this, in his *A
Writer's Diary*, he gave many prophetic provisions.

Ivan Turgenev gave an entire epopee of Russian country life, and Dmitri Grigorovitch was one of the first to
describe Russian peasantry. For me, Grigorovitch is like
the godfather of literature, because he blessed me and
introduced me into this domain. My first meeting with
him dates back to 1897. The sufferings and aspirations
of the Russian people are also expressed in the poetry of
Nicholas Nekrasov, which culminates in his poem: "Who
can live happily and freely in Russia?"

Leo Tolstoy, more than any other Russian writer has been translated into many languages. His famous *War and Peace, Anna Karenina*—and let us not repeat the whole suite of his remarkable works—show that amid moralizing writings, he dreamed about a wonderful country that would give a real happiness to the people.

Anton Chekov, whom I met now and then in Moscow, was an unusually striking personality. Whereas he himself was extremely modest, his sweeping scope of writings covered the entire period of his time in Russia. In his sad smile at certain manifestations of life, he expressed his sensitiveness and love to his motherland.

In 1934 the Nobel Committee, intending to give a prize to Russian literature, had four candidates: Gorky, Merezhkovsky, Bunin, and Remizov. The committee decided in favor of Bunin. But public opinion was surprised that the palm was not bestowed upon Gorky or Merezhkovsky. As regards Remizov, he is very highly revered in the circles of the intelligentsia because of his genuine, old Russian style of writing.

Gorky worked at the same time as Leonid Andreyev, and they were often regarded as rivals although essentially they are quite different. Gorky was a psychologist of the masses, whereas Andreyev in his profound writings evinced the qualities of a prophet. Let us remember his *Man's Life, King Bunger, Red Laughter*, and *Anathema.*

We all remember and cherish that the recent Centenary Celebrations of Alexander Pushkin turned into a world event. On February 10, 1837, the greatest Russian poet died after receiving a fatal wound in a duel! The name of Pushkin is known all over the world. The sad centenary of his violent death was reverenced in the whole world by all true lovers of literature. Not only in the immense vastness of Russia but in all countries, there were held solemn celebrations, exhibitions were opened dedicated to the poet, and many new editions of his famous works were published. In Russian and foreign theaters his immortal dramas were produced in the musical interpretation of the best Russian composers.

The commemorative event resulted in a great Day of Russian or, rather, world culture. The immortal creations of Pushkin, equal to Shakespeare, Dante, Goethe, Balzac, will forever remain a vital inexhaustible source of spiritual enrichment of the present and future generations of humanity. *Eugene Onegin, Poltava, The Bronze Rider, The Captain's Daughter, Ruslan and Ludmila, The Queen of Spades,* and hundreds of other works of Pushkin will live as precious evidence of radiant thought, as expressions of the feelings of true, noble inspiration.

Pushkin's poems, written over a hundred years ago, move the hearts of mankind as deeply now as they did at the time of his contemporaries. Only now has the glory of Pushkin become a truly universal glory. He has expressed the inner life of the country in unprecedented, evoking artistic images. For Pushkin the poet, there were no geographical nor historical boundaries. Ancient Hellas Rome, Italy, Spain, and the ancient and new East, all Slavonic thoughts, were reflected by him with the same deep comprehension.

No one has before or after Pushkin enriched Russian culture to such an extent as this greatest poet of his motherland. He was the true creator of the Russian literary language. He has conquered for Russian literature a place of honor in world classics. The poems, stories, and essays of Pushkin prove the inexhaustible wealth of human expression. Pushkin was the creator of a magnificent, flexible, expressive Russian literary language. He imbued Russian literature with the spirit of the people; he magnified the language with innumerable words taken from the very depths of folklore treasury. He introduced real poetical gems of national bards. Pushkin's contemporaries used to say about him that he was ever restless, that his spirit was rebellious, and, as such, he died.

The great Russian critic, Belinsky thus defined Pushkin's poetry: "What a style! Antique plasticity and stem simplicity were combined in him with the charming play of romantic rhythm. The entire acoustic wealth, the might of the Russian language were revealed in him in extraordinary perfection; he is delicate, sweet, tender, like the murmur of the waves; he is rich as soil, brilliant as lightning, transparent and pure as a crystal, aromatic and fragrant as spring, strong and mighty as the sword in the hand of a hero. Should we want to describe the verse of Pushkin in one word, we would say that it is *par excellence*, a truly poetic, artful, and artistic verse; and this would solve the mystery of the majestic pathos of the entire poetry of Pushkin."

Gorky, usually severe in his judgment, says of Pushkin: "Pushkin is for Russian literature what Leonardo da Vinci was for European art. We have before us a great Russian national poet, the creator of poetical tales, which charm with their beauty and wit; the author of the first realistic novel, *Eugene Onegin*; the author of our best historical drama, *Boris Godunov*; a poet, who up to now is unsurpassed in the beauty of his verse and in the mighty expressions of emotions and thoughts; a poet—the father of great Russian literature. In the person of Pushkin, we have the example of a writer, who being imbued with impressions of life, was striving to reflect them in verse and prose with the greatest truth, with utmost realism, and in this he succeeded as a real genius. His creations are a most valuable testimony of a clever, wise, truthful person about customs, habits, and conceptions of a certain period—indeed they are the true records of Russian history by a genius."

As befits every great man, Pushkin suffered great injustice from his contemporaries. The great poet was exiled, and for a long time there hung upon him the threat of evil suspicions. This cannot be avoided—without these torches of savages no great achievement is possible. Thanks to his all-containing heart, Pushkin joined all advanced movements, was a friend of free thought. We find him among the *decabrists*. We see Pushkin as a mason, and to this society belonged all the foremost thinkers of Russia. The poet was seeking everywhere for Truth; and listening to the fairy tales of his old nurse, he was enchanted from his very childhood by the beauty of Russian folklore.

During the short span of his life (1799–1837), he, while studying historical chronicles, yet remained ever in the defense of the new, carrying in his heart the vision of Russia's great future. When still in the Lyceum, Pushkin already astonished everyone with his sonorous verse, and the great Derzhavin blessed him and foretold his glory. Seldom can one's heart embrace simultaneously both the East and West. Every reader in the Orient will understand Pushkin's *Ruslan and Ludmila, The Captive of the Caucasus,* or the *Fountain of Bokhchisarai,* whereas *Eugene Onegin, The Queen of Spades* or *Dubrovsky* will resound in Western hearts.

Boris Godunov, the drama in which Pushkin, with astounding depth, unfolds the tragedy of a ruler "who has attained the highest power," now attracts the attention of the whole world. Recently *Boris Godunov* was staged in Berlin; in Praha—*Eugene Onegin*; thus, in the most diverse and even contradictory audiences, the splendor of Pushkin's creations calls forth equal admiration.

As we see, Pushkin simultaneously proceeded by all creative paths. During the twenty-seven years of his literary career, Pushkin became a great poet, a great prosaist, a great dramatist. In his works we have examples of all literary styles. Every new creation of Pushkin was not only a real *chef d'oeuvre* but became a new chapter in the history of Russian literature. In his immeasurable artistic might, in his extraordinary multifacetedness, in his unusual alacrity of mind are expressed the potentiality and genius of the great nation in which he was born. Let us remember his Self-characteristic poems "Echo" and "The Prophet," which are significant as describing the view of the poet upon his mission in life. Let us not attempt to translate them into poetical verse, but try to render the poet's thought:

ECHO

Whether beasts roar in forests deep—
Whether the horn sounds, or thunder storm,
Whether a maiden sings on hillocks far—
To every voice
An echo in the empty air
Resounds at once.
Thou heedest to the thunder's roar,
The calls of storm and waves,
To shouts of shepherds
You an answer send,
But you get no response. . . .
This, poet, is your fate!

In the other poem "Prophet," a six-winged Seraphim appears on the cross road to a wanderer and, touching his lips and ears, opens to him his prophetic vision. The tremors of heaven and mysteries of earth and sea are revealed to him. The Seraphim tears out his tongue and replaces it with the wisdom of the serpent; for his heart he substitutes a piece of glowing coal. The poem concludes as follows:

"Alone as lifeless corpse in deserts I remained,
And God's voice called:
Arise, though prophet, behold and hearken!
Be filled with my glory,
And, faring seas and distant lands,
By word the hearts of men thou set aflame!"

Thus the poet foresaw his glorious mission.

THE GREAT NOVGOROD

LET us grant that our North is poorer than other lands. Let us grant that its ancient image has vanished. Let us grant that in general very little is known of its true character. But, the tales of the North are found enchanting. The winds of the North are vigorous and joyous. The lakes of the North are dreamy; full of reverie are its rivers. The dark forests exhale wisdom. Its green hills have witnessed the passing of many a century. Its grey stones are full of miracles. Even the Varangians come from the North. We are ever quoting beautiful, ancient Russia.

"What rough habits they have!" records Nikons' ancient Chronicle about the inhabitants of Novgorod.

Princes were afraid to go and rule the vigorous and restless Ilmenians.

But Marfa Posadnitza prophesied well: Great Novgorod has become one of the most inconspicuous, the most silent, of the Russian towns.

It has become secluded.

It has lost its former aspect. Nobody now can imagine how the once mighty, picturesque, and busy Hanseatic city extended many miles out to the Yurievsky Monastery, to Nereditza, to Liadki. Nobody now can realise that the bare hills and hollows—the present environs of Novgorod—were once the vital habitations of the city.

It is even difficult to imagine that in the past, the inhabitants of Novgorod dominated practically all Pomorya up to the Arctic Ocean and along the rivers of Pechora and Vym, and the high impenetrable mountains in the country named Siberia along the great river Ob to the mouth of the white river, the haunts of wild animals and sables.

It is hard to understand how those Novgoroders came to the Caspian Sea and the Sea of Venice.

Unimaginably broad was the grasp of the "youth" of Novgorod. The youthful free man perpetually aspired and dared. The success of the freemen was the success of the big city. If they failed, the elders did not mind, since it was a venture of "youth." How wise!

Wherever there was something worthwhile—the Novgoroders were there. From everywhere they bore all that was worthy into the treasury of Novgorod; it was kept, carefully hid.

It is possible that these treasures are lying buried for us there.

In the very Novgorod—in each hillock, mound, and hollow—gleam traces of an incalculably distant, vast existence.

Its black earth is saturated with charcoal, chips of pottery, bits of stone and brick of all ages, chips of tile and all sorts of metallic fragments.

Walking along its streets and alleys, one can pick up, underfoot, pieces of broken glass of the tenth or twelfth centuries, bits of old Venetian smalt beds; here a coin, a piece of a small cross; there, fragments of lead seals.

While looking observingly at the rich layers of the past epochs, it seems that the statement of V. Peredolsky is not exaggerated when he says that the inhabited strata of the soil of Novgorod is over seven *sajens* (forty-nine feet) deep.

You feel you walk here on an ageless graveyard, an ancient, inhabited spot, sacred, but superfluous to life.

Any contemporary life upon such a sacred *kurgan*—tomb—seems out of place, and very likely Great Novgorod, not without reason, is sunken in the sound sleep of time.

It is time to turn again seriously to old Novgorod.

I love the region of Novgorod. I love all its hidden aspects. Everything that lies there is ready for us.

Why is it necessary to travel distant parts, to search the

distant deserts, when right here in our own soil are buried such worlds of treasure? The province of Novgorod has experienced everything.

Past is its valor, past is its culture, past is its confidence. Undiscovered stretches of treasure, it is actually difficult to choose where to begin.

We have such many-sided proofs. But from which shall we proceed? Investigation of churches, exploration of old buildings, or excavation of cities, and the most ancient remains beneath them.

The most stirring to our imagination is the authentic view of old churches and excavation of ancient ruins, where each stroke of the shovel may reveal a magnificent discovery.

The Rurik site, the place of the oldest settlement, where in later times the ruling princes were accustomed to live with their families, is full of potential discoveries. In the gardens along the shore, one often discovers the most varied objects from the most recent to the Stone Age, inclusively.

One senses how after vast settlements of the Stone Age in the lower region of Kolomtzy, at the mouth of the Volhov river in the Ilmen (a lake), life expanded toward more elevated regions through Gorodishche. Nereditza, Laidka to Novgorod proper.

In the regions of Gorodistche are likely to be discovered the remains of the princely *terems*, foundations of churches, of which only one remains—the one built by Mstislav Vladimirovich.

What illuminating tablets of the strata of life might not be excavated from such an ancient place!

Besides the Gorodishche section, a number of suburban sites vie with each other concerning the importance of their ancient history.

Kolomotzy, where Peredolsky obtained a great many of his objects of the Stone Age, Liadka, Lipna, Nereditza, Seltzo, Rakom (where Yaroslav had his palace), Migra, Zverintzi, Viajishtchi, Radiatina, Kolopgorodok, Sokol mountain, Volotova, Lisitchia Mountain, Kovalevo, and many other sites and cemeteries await their explorer.

But the chronicled and legendary places are not the only ones filled with their hidden treasures.

First of all, the city itself is filled with them. Even if we do not know what filled the deserted hillocks through which human habitations formerly extended, yet in the boundaries of the existing city are known many places that must have left their traces.

The court of Yaroslav (1030), the court of Petratino, Nmetzki court, Pluskowsky court, Gotzki court, the Prince's court, the Gridnitza Piteinaya, Kleimanya Seny, the courts of Posadnik and Tysiatizky, the grand passage, the courthouse, the chapels of the foreign believers, granaries of lords and princes, and finally the courts of wealthy boyars and burghers—all these places noted by historians could not disappear without a trace.

In the foundations of all these places still lie the prehistoric strata of life.

This is all unexplored.

Strange to say, even the Detinetz of Novgorod is unexplored, with the exception of a few local excavations.

However, Detinetz is very noteworthy. Its present appearance means nothing. It has been greatly changed.

But we should bear in mind that Detinetz is an ancient place, as is its square, and on the Lord's side, St. Sophia, which witnessed too much.

We have records as early as 1044 that Detinetz was built of stone. The southwest part was built by Prince Yaroslav; the northeast, by his son Vladimir Yaroslavich. They were princes of great culture!

Undoubtedly they left some worthy treasures.

We were going to Kolometz toward Ilmen:

From the direction of the Yurievs Hermitage blew a "rolling wind." The waves lashed against the side of the boat. A wave broke overboard and flooded the boat.

The municipal boat was shaking. We beckoned to a large fishing craft. Thus we sailed down to Kolometz.

An old fisherman held the rudder. His daughter manipulated the sails. In her copper-colored face glittered white teeth.

We asked her, "How old are you?"

"How do I know that?"

"How is it you don't know? Think it over! Remember."

"Don't know. Maybe over twenty."

And there sat the hardy fisherman. Such people die, but have no ailments.

At Kolometz, the old man hurried us back. "Listen to me. I'll leave you. The boat shakes too much."

We hurried. We got in at the stern of the fisherman's sailboat, while the city boat with its oarsmen could not get away from shore.

Three oarsmen could not move it.

"Shall we help you? Sit down!" And the sturdy girl of Novgorod waded through the deep water.

She took hold of the boat and with all the oarsmen easily pushed it into the deep water. She got out of the water on the stern.

A real Marfa Possadnitza.

Next to her, on the poop of the boat, sat her father—a sturdy man with an aquiline nose; sharp, deep-set eyes; thin lips; and a beard in two curly tufts. And thus, he looked sharply at the waves, trying to conquer and chastise them.

A real Ivan the Terrible.

Marfa Possadnitza! Ivan the Terrible! Everything became confusing. The meeting with primitive fishermen was evidently necessary for our impression.

Such folks still live along the lakes. They seldom go to the towns. Like the soil, thus they know how to guard the words of ancient times. As with the soil, it is difficult to know when and where to begin with these people.

All is untouched. Everywhere the luring ways of creation. Everywhere rich discoveries.

After us will come others. They will find new ways,

new approaches. But no one can say that we searched in empty places. It is worthwhile to work.

It is not in distant deserts nor behind tall mountains that all is rich in discoveries, that everything awaits the hands that will gather them, that everything needs help. No, it is right here within our reach, only three or four hours from the center of the country. And the poor man in this case is not some unknown tramp; no, it is himself—Novgorod the Great.

Lately it has become the fashion to talk about antiquity. Everyone seems interested in it. During the past two years three societies of the lovers of antiquity have been founded; the Museum of Old Petersburg, the Pre-Petrian Museum of Art and Folklore, and the Society for safeguarding the monuments of antiquity, whose first and excellent task it was admirably to restore and maintain the historical village of Grusino.

So much is being written at present about antiquity that we, who inaugurated this movement, are actually frightened.

Perhaps this has become merely a fad—simply an accidental, quickly passing fashion, or is it the result of cultural development?

Only the future can give us the true verdict. Only the future will disclose the ultimate motives of those who are now preoccupied with antiquity.

Empty, unnecessary talk is one thing; an entirely different matter is that which requires knowledge, effort, outlay, and love.

Let us hope that our society has approved antiquity in the dissection of sincerity and enthusiasm, of a vital study of the past in order to build a more beautiful future.

We learn to believe:

"Those who are unaware of their past are incapable of planning their future."

KIEV

WALKING through the plains beyond the outskirts of Rome, one is unable to imagine that it was just in those now empty places that Caesar's capital was unfolding itself, giving gorgeous shelter to some ten million inhabitants. It is equally unbelievable to imagine the gorgeousness of Kiev (The Mother of Russian Towns), where Prince Yaroslav the Wise entertained foreign guests from East and West. The remnants of the wall paintings in Kiev's cathedrals, all those large-eyed, serene figures of world-wise men, interpreted by the brush of real artists, give us a glimpse of what art actually meant to the Russians of those times (about 1000–1200).

A few years ago, there were excavated in Kiev some remnants of ancient walls, frescoes, tiles, and ornaments; these are believed to be fragments of the Princes' court-yards. I have seen some of the exquisite frescoes, and I found them bearing the features of art of Asia Minor. The structure of the stone walls in itself indicates a special quaint manner of technique, which usually marks the periods of great love for architecture. I think that the Rogere Palace in Palermo gives an idea of the palaces of Kiev.

It was really a combination of North and South: the metal sheen of the Scandinavian style, beaded with the pearls of Byzantium, made the ancient city that place of beauty that led brothers to fight for it. The astounding tones of enamel, the refinement of miniatures, the vastness and dignity of the temples, the wonders of metal work, the mass of handwoven textures, the admixture of the finest laws of the Roman style—all these melted into one in giving Kiev its noble elegance. Men of Yaroslav's and Vladimir's times must have had a highly developed sense of beauty, or the things left by them would not have been so wonderful.

Note those paragraphs from the heroic epos where the people's mind dwells on the details of ordinary life, leaving for a while the achievements of heroism. Here is a description of a private house—a *terem*:

Around the terem—an iron fence;
Its spikes—topped with carving;
   Each of them crowned with a pearl.
The gateway—floored with whale tooth.
Over the gateway—about seventy ikons,
In the middle of the court—the terems do rise;
The terems with their gilt domes;
The first doorway—in wrought iron work.
The middle doorway—in glass;
The third doorway—latticed.

One can trace in this description a likeness to the images on the Aegean structures and Trojan columns.

And, here is a description of horsemen:

Their clothes are of scarlet cloth.
Their leather belts are pierced with wrought metal
    clasps. Their caps are black and pointed
In black fur, with golden crowns.
Their feet are shod with precious leather,
Titled at the toes like awls;
The heels are pointed too;
There's room enough for an egg to roll around the
    toes,
There's room enough for a sparrow to fly around the
    heels.

This is an exact, although poetic, description of the kind of garments that can be seen in the Byzantine wall paintings.

And, here again is the picture of the hero himself:
The helmet on his cap shines like fire.
His plated shoes are in seven shades of silk.
Each has a golden tack in it;
On his shoulders—a coat of black ermine,
Of black ermine brought from over the seas,
Covered with embossed green velvet.
Each buttonhole has a bird woven in,
And each golden button—a furious beast cast in.

I would suggest in regard to such a description, not from the viewpoint of philological curiosity, but as a piece of direct realistic information. The details are archaeologically true evidence. Thus in this quaint statement, we can see a fragment of a great culture—one that was not enforced, not strange to the simple people; the unsophisticated folk obviously had no objection to it whatsoever; they spoke of it without the scorn of the (lower) classes for (the elect) but freely expressed a genuine pride in what was beautiful and elegant to their own senses as well. In those days, the elaborate arrangements of the Princes' hunts; the merry feasts they gave, in the course of which they would put a number of wise questions before their foreign guests; the nobility in the construction of new cities—all this blended together in harmony. Such life did not jar on the poetic mind of the simple people; and it is evident that wise initiators of art have inhabited and ruled the Mother of Russian Towns.

Here is a quotation from the first historical annals (the exact language of which remains untranslatable, being a mixture of Russian with the Old Slavonic, which in itself makes it a piece of poetry of the eleventh century).

"Yaroslav founded Kiev the Great and its Golden Gates with it. Also the Church of St. Sophia, also the Church of Annunciation upon the Golden Gates, also the Monastery of St. George and St. Irene.

Loving the laws of Church and being a master in books, he read them by day and by night, and wrote them too, thus sowing book-words in the hearts of true men, which we now reap. For, books are rivers that carry wisdom throughout the world, and are as deep as rivers. Also, Yaroslav lovingly embellished the churches with gold and silver vessels, and his heart rejoiced upon it."

Yaroslav's exulting over the gorgeousness of the St. Sophia temple is immeasurably removed from the exclamations of our contemporary savages at the sight of bright colors. Yaroslav's was the exultation of a man who sensed in his creation a monument of art that would live for ages. One can envy and admire the modes of life where such art was in demand.

A question may arise: How could Kiev have become a center of culture at the very start of Russian history?

But, do we possess any knowledge about the foundation of Kiev?

That city tempted Prince Oleg the Varangian—a man of the world, a man of experience. Before him, the Princes Askold and Dir coveted Kiev; so did many other Normans.

(And many Varangians forgathered and came into possession of the Slavonic Land).

It should be noted that there are no indications anywhere in the lines of the annals about Askold and Dir being uncultured. Thus, the facts about the foundation of Kiev are really pushed back into the depths of the legendary times. Let us not despise tradition either; it says that the Apostle Andrew had visited Kiev: Why should an Apostle come to virgin forests? But his appearance in Kiev becomes quite comprehensible if one thinks of the secret cults of Astarte, which have been recently traced near Kiev. These cults take us back to the sixteenth–seventeenth centuries B.C. A large center of mental interest ought to have existed already in order to shelter such cults.

It is a comfort to know that all of the Great Kiev is still resting within the ground in peace, unexcavated. There are glorious discoveries yet to come. They will open almost the only gate into the depths of the past of our land. Even the Scandinavian period and the Bronze period will have a light thrown on them through those gates.

There is no doubt that the joy of art has grown in Kiev side by side with the neighboring Scandinavian culture, without being engendered by the latter altogether. Why should the birth of the Russian Scandinavia be attributed entirely to the legendary Prince Rurik? The ancient annals mention a fact which is of great significance, yet it has never been picked up as a key:

(The Russians pushed the Varangians beyond the sea and would not pay duty to them). Now, if the expulsion of the Varangians took place before Rurik's name came in at all, when did their first appearance in the Russian land take place? It is quite possible that the Russo-Scandinavian era may have been rooted in the depths of the ages.

We have a startling illustration of carelessness the (historical) textbooks on the subject:

The famous phrase attributed to the old Russians, which is meant in the textbooks as a wholesale invitation from the Russian land to the Varangians (from over the seas) runs thus:

"Our land is large and prolific, but there is no order in it. Come and rule over us". What is usually given as a sequence to this invitation are the following lines: "There came the Varengian Rurik with his brothers Sineus and Truvor." (862).

Now, in the Scandinavian annals, the words *sin huus* and *truver* mean "his household" and "his true guard." Therefore, I would suggest, a different explanation of the famous phrase: very probably it has found its utterance, not on the part of the ancient Russians themselves but among the Scandinavian colonists, who inhabited the banks of the northern river Volhov. It is they who must have asked Rurik from behind the Ladoga Lake (which is very much like a sea, where he, most likely, used to come from Scandinavia for hunting) to come and organize a military force for them. And that man—with his household and his guards, with his means and his probable love of adventure—came in response to the asking of his compatriots. By and by, his kind of (princes) the warriors hired in the North of Russia were attracted by the Kiev principality where the role of a (prince) was more than that of a warrior and included the position of a statesman.

Going further into the depths of the ages, we find the last frontier of realistic entities. Apparently, only dust seems to be left beyond those frontiers, and an amateur is put hard to believe that it is not merely a theory of dull archaeology that we are asked to adopt. But in reality, there survived some atoms of fascinating gorgeousness that did live in the past. Now it is time for everyone to realize that art has existed not only where this is obvious to all, but that much, much is hidden from us by the veils of time. And what seems dull now will appear one day lit up by the joys of penetration. The onlooker will become a creator. Herein lies the fascination, both of the past and of the future.

The fantastic bas-reliefs on the northern rocks, the tall hillocks among the trade routes, the long daggers, and the attire, so rich in design, make one love northern life; they awaken respect for the primitive forms of beauty beyond which our imagination sinks in the depths of the bronze patines.

A great deal of art can be sensed even in the mysterious and dusky periods that stand back furthest from us. Can the animal Finnish phantasmagoria be strange to art? Do the bewitched forms of the Far East escape artistic penetration? Are the first adaptations from the antique world hideous in the hands of the Scythians? Are the ornaments of the Siberian nomads merely coarse?

No. These finds are kindred to art, and one can envy the clarity of conception of the ancients. They incarnated symbols that meant so much to them, and created well-defined, distinct, and manifold artistic forms.

It is in the mysterious cobweb of the Bronze period that we have to look around. Every day brings with it new conclusions. We can discern a whole pageant of people.

Beyond the shining, gold-clad Byzantines, we see the motley crowds of Finno-Turks pass by. Deeper still in time, majestically come the gorgeous Aryans. Still deeper, there are only the extinguished bonfires of unknown wanderers; these are numberless.

It is the gifts that all of these have left for us that are nowadays building up the neo-nationalism. The younger generations will heed it and will become strong and sane through it. If the blunted modern nationalism of art is to be turned into a neo-nationalism—the foundation stone of the latter will be the great ancient world in its genuine conceptions of truth and beauty. This truth and beauty will one day find its equal in the great future.

COLLECTING

FROM ancient times, collecting has been a sign of stability and introspection. It is very instructive to survey the various means and ways of collecting, and of studying art from our days down to the heart of antiquity. Again, as in all the spirals of accretion, we see almost completed circles; yet, at times, an almost elusive heightening of consciousness forms another step which is reflected in many pages of the history of art. We see how specialization and synthesis alternate. Collecting formed by the inner consciousness of the collector and united by one general idea is replaced by a classification almost pharmaceutical, sometimes destroying completely, by its pedantry, the fire of new discoveries. Not so long ago the combining of Gothic primitives with ultra-modern aspirations would have been considered a proof of dilettantism. It would have been regarded altogether taboo simply to have a collection of beautiful medals and coins. Pedantry was wont to confine its scope of vision to a certain epoch, limiting it to objects of a certain type and character. Thus icons and primitives glowing with color, were turned into iconography, in which the descriptive part obliterated the true and artistic meaning.

Thus, not very long ago, the history of art was taught as a collection of anecdotes of painters' lives, while the exposition of sculpture and the technique of painting were reduced to a summary of proportions and to the mechanics of construction, diverting and distracting attention from the essence of creative work. Peculiar textbooks began to appear in which one would come across such chapters, for instance, as: "How to paint a donkey," in connection with which grey paint—which does not exist—was recommended. I remember that my attention was arrested on a boat by the typical argument between a mother and her little girl, in which the mother earnestly asserted that the mountain in the distance was black, while the child affirmed candidly that it was blue. It seems to me that the mother's eyes must have been dimmed by some textbook she was studying about the way to paint donkeys.

What a joy it is for children when, from their tenderest age, they see objects of art and serious books in their homes. Of course, it is necessary that these artistic objects do not cease to "live" and do not find themselves in the pitiful situation of remaining upside down, sometimes for an entire decade—which means that the soul of the collector has long departed for the cemetery, and that his heirs have for some reason become morally blind.

During the very recent years we have had occasion to rejoice many times over the synthetic system of collecting that has again come into existence. Not afraid of being called eccentrics or dilettantes the sensitive collectors have begun to group their treasuries of various objects according to an inner meaning. Thus, the most modern pictures could be combined with those masters who, in their time, burned with the unquenchable fire of bringing new ways to creative work.

In the newest collections one sees such giant pathfinders as El Greco, Giorgione, Peter Breughel, and all the noble galaxy of those who were not afraid to be considered the seekers and innovators of their epochs.

And how convincing among modern paintings are the forms of Roman art and the collaborators Giotto and Cimabue, and the icons of Novgorod and ancient Chinese artists.

As all conventionalities of division and demarcation vanish, the combined creative and spiritual findings shine before you like beacon lights, outside the conventional boundaries of the nations. If circumstances do not permit the bringing of originals into the homes, then sketches and even well-reproduced copies could permit one to entertain happy dreams about the future.

I have had occasion to write the stirring story of those collectors who began their activities when still at school. Probably many painters have had experiences like mine of having little boys, coming to one of my exhibitions, who would bashfully hand me a dollar, asking to be given a sketch in return.

Another still more moving case was when public school pupils raised a collection in order to purchase a painting. That meant that within them ardor was stirring and taking shape, and they wanted to transmute meaningless words into facts, into conscious action. Without such an imperative impulse to action, how many lightwinged thought butterflies singe themselves in their flutterings!

In various countries we can help by experience and advice in the question of how to begin collecting. To open the door to those who knock timidly is one of our immediate obligations. And not only to open the door but also to explain that they should knock with a firm hand, without entertaining the prejudice that the use of art is a privilege only of the rich. No, first of all, it is the privilege of bright and courageous spirits, who long to beautify their existence and who have decided—instead of taking to the deadly hazards of gambling—to strengthen themselves by the manifestations of the spirit of man which like an infinite dyanamo breathes life into everything made by it. Great joys are to be found at this feast of creative impulses. And many dark places in life can be so easily brightened by the brilliant rays of admiration. It is our sacred duty to help in this.

We are speaking about collecting. Someone smiles wryly: Is it timely? Is it timely to speak of artistic values when even the richest countries are horror-stricken by the general crisis? Let us answer him firmly, and with the realization of the import of our words—Yes, it is timely!

According to the latest reports, in spite of the tremendous

business depression in America, the prices for art objects have not suffered any depreciation, and this does not surprise us in the least; on the contrary, we consider this to be a characteristic sign of the existence of the crisis.

We have seen that during the most acute upheavals in Russia, Austria, and Germany, the prices of art objects did not fluctuate noticeably. In some cases it happened that the objects of art were instrumental in bringing an entire state out of financial difficulties. We preserve this irrefutable fact as proof of the true value of the spirit of man. When all our conditional values are shaken, the consciousness of man instinctively turns to that which, amidst the ephemeral, proves to be relatively the most valuable.

And the spiritual, creative values that have been neglected during the triumph of the stomach again become a shelter of refuge. Therefore, it is always timely to speak of the growth of spiritual creative power and to lay stress upon collecting and preserving; and this is especially needed when evolution passes through difficult moments and does not know how to solve the actual accumulated problems. To solve them, however, is possible only in spirit and in beauty.

In my address on the significance of art, I gave formulas that have become the motto of the International Art Center of the Roerich Museum. I said: "Humanity is facing events of cosmic greatness. Humanity already realizes that all occurrences are not accidental. The time for the construction of a future culture is at hand. The revaluation of values has taken place before our very eyes. Amid heaps of valueless currency, humanity has found a treasure of world significance. The values of great art march victoriously through the storms of earthly commotions. Even the 'earthly' people have understood the vital importance of beauty."

And I closed the address with the following: "Not on snowy heights but in the turmoil of the city, we pronounce these words. And realizing the path of true reality, we greet with a happy smile the future."

These words were based on thirty years' experience. Ten more years have since elapsed. Have the formulas then expressed changed during the period? No, the experience of many countries confirmed and even strengthened them. And we must base our conclusions on experience and on nothing else. Theory for us is only the consequence of practice. And that same practice brings forth the happy smile with which we greet the future. May the smile of knowledge and courage become the banner of our meetings. We unite to make application of knowledge, and may each crumb of knowledge add spirit to our smile.

COLLECTORS

HOW are we to bring art into everyday life? Where are these blessed paths? Perhaps they are inaccessibly difficult. Or they may require countless wealth. Or only spiritual giants may venture along these paths of beauty?

All assurances will be unconvincing. These doubts can be answered only by a page out of real life.

I shall take the portraits of four of my friends. They have all left us now. Only one of them was rich in money; the other three were rich only in the brightness of their spirits.

The rich collector was the Moscow merchant, Tretiakov. There was nothing in his family to dispose him toward art. Rather did that old merchant family look with suspicion on the art it did not understand. But unexpectedly, young Tretiakov was drawn into a new path. And gropingly guided by personal feeling, he began to collect pictures of the Russian school. He went his way alone, only now and again listening to the advice of some artist friend. And it was not by chance that the now-famous Tretiakov Gallery in Moscow began to come into being. With the true intuition of a picture-lover, Tretiakov understood that the government generally filled its museums mostly with official productions, passing over the best work of the artists. And this official physiognomy of the museums could not reflect the evolution of the national school. So has it ever been. So far, it will be in the future.

Art has always blossomed with an ardent personal urge, which will comprehend and find and preserve and give to the whole nation. And so the merchant Tretiakov grasped the national task of art. And he found out fresh artist powers and lightened their path. And he preserved their work, surrounding them with pure delight. But he made his joy a national joy, and while still alive gave the whole of his remarkable collection to the city of Moscow. And the task that he had set for himself was no small one. He had not simply gathered together a mass of valuable pictures but made his collection reflect the whole of the Russian school. Everything that was new, brilliant, important came under the eye of Tretiakov. This taciturn, gray-headed man, in his large fur coat, indefatigably visited all exhibitions, and nothing could hold him when he considered a picture important. He would mount the steep stair leading to the studio of the young beginner in art. He was first to see a picture finished. He was first at the opening of an exhibition. But he was also first in the possession of the best and most characteristic work.

It came to pass that the prizes given by the highest art institutions were considered as naught compared with the purchase of a picture by Tretiakov. And the destiny of the beginner in art was decided not by the Academy but by this sincere and taciturn man. When there was no more room on the walls in his house, Tretiakov built another beside it. If this was needed it had to be done. And art was not to suffer any loss.

Of course, it may be said that with Tretiakov's great wealth it was possible to collect on this vast scale. He was able to choose the best and could gather enough to represent the whole of the Russian school in his collection. It was true that his wealth made this scale possible, but the quality of the collection, his love of the work, and his living creative work in the choice itself of pictures and of men—all this proceeded not from the amount of his means but from the countless riches of his spirit. Thus did one man, strong in spirit, do an infinitely important national work. And now, should the government seek to have a new Tretiakov Gallery, it would find itself powerless, for it was the urge of the spirit that created that inimitable combination of beauty.

This is an instance of ideal creativeness within national limits.

Now for another spiritual portrait. Here we have the same power of spiritual urge along with a mighty struggle with means. It was Count Golenishchev-Kutuzov, a well-known poet and worker in the sphere of culture, and chamberlain at the Imperial Court. In his case family traditions conduced to the development in him of the love of art. His historical knowledge was great; special deep poetic gifts were his.

His collection consisted of pictures of the old Dutch, Flemish, and Italian schools. Its fundamental characteristic was not the search for conventional names but the truth shown in wonderful creations. The collector understood that the names of Rembrandt, Rubens, Van Dyck are purely collective names, that only the lowest type of collector seeks in the dark for that which to him is but an empty sound. But a better knowledge of art shows us a countless number of artists engulfed in so-called great names. And the task of the cultured collector is to distinguish among these forgotten names for truth's sake. If on an excellent picture attributed to Rembrandt, we find the signature of Karel Febricius, his pupil, is a fine picture any the worse for that? Or again, could Van Dyck paint two thousand portraits in one year? Of course not, but he had up to two hundred pupils.

I know how grieved the Count would be to learn that one of his favorite pictures, by an unknown Flemish painter Hasselaer, now hangs in the Metropolitan Museum in New York under the name of Joachim Patinir.

In the name of truth, Count Golenishchev-Kutuzov sought to discover the real names of painters, and remedied, as far as he could, the sins of mercenary human history. And what loving intimacy breathed from his choice collection. Every picture, too, had been obtained with difficulty, with privation. Every new member of the collection was greeted with the disapproval of numerous relations who grudged the money spent on it. And money was so scarce. His small Court salary was not enough to live on. And this collector departed this world surrounded by his real friends, his pictures. And he willed that his collection be dispersed to give new joy to new seeking souls.

Golenishchev-Kutuzov was the type of the refined collector, who, working and rejoicing in new beauty and truth, sends it forth again to serve for the ennobling of the human spirit.

Now for the type of a young collector—an instinctive collector from his school days. Instead of the joys natural to his age, the boy develops a love for works of art. From childhood, without possessing any personal artistic capacities, he is distinguished by education and developed taste. He is attracted by all that is beautiful. His spirit seeks to rise.

"What pleasure it was to pass the time with young Slepstoff." While yet a pupil of the Imperial Lyceum, he began to collect pictures. His purchases were not chaotic, not accidental. He knew what he was doing. And all the money given the boy by his mother for pleasures was spent on his noble pursuit. And if sometimes he was short of money, his enthusiasm for his general task never suffered from this.

And this general task was a fine one. The boy developed a love for certain very subtly selected painters and decided to have specimens of each of them in all the periods of their work to preserve and to hand on to posterity a complete picture of the creative human life of each. The youth dreamed of the future; each painter was to have a separate room, and the whole furnishing of the room was to correspond with the character of the art represented in it—the furniture, the embellishment of the walls and ceiling, the character of the lighting, and floor covering. From this we may gather what subtlety of perception lay in that young soul, and what deep love and care surrounded each of the artists represented. In these special rooms choice singing and music were to be heard at times. Or suitable passages were to be read aloud. In a word the dream of harmony of the unity of art was to be realized.

It was a joy to hear how a new work of art was selected for the collection. What subtle and truthful considerations were expressed for discovering and bringing out a new and worthy feature in the creative work of an artist. And you could see in this treatment of art no mere fancy but a real cultural need. And this subtlety of culture infected those surrounding him. Both thought and speech were purified by this bright ascension of the spirit.

Slepstoff dreamed of handing over his collection to the nation, without any care for his name. But he left us too early to do so. And he left us in an unusual way. He went out for a ride and did not return. He passed over unexpectedly, in the midst of Nature, listening to the harmony of the Cosmos. An enviable passage—a passage to new beautiful labors.

This was the type of a sensitive soul with ingrained feelings of a future harmony and unity.

Now for one more touching type of a collector.

A very poor officer in a line regiment, stationed in a distant provincial town, reaches out to art with all of his soul. Depriving himself of many things, Colonel Kratchkovsky, always pleasant in manner, always active, burning with enthusiasm, seeks to gather a collection of specimens of Russian painting. Of course, he is unable to collect large pictures. So he collects small pictures, sketches, studies, drawings. But in its essential value, his collection becomes a very considerable one. He seeks for the best painters; he understands that often the sketch is more valuable than the picture itself. He seeks to bring out the character of the artist in its most typical features. This is not a buyer of cheap pictures. This is a true collector, and therewithal he himself is often in want of ten rubles (five dollars), and for him it is a matter of the greatest consequence whether he has to pay ten rubles more or less for a picture. And he asks the painter to let him have the picture, and persistently persuades him to accept a lower price. And his words produced their effects, and the sketches were given to him. And he would rejoice with the bright joy of a child, and would write enthusiastic letters about his new treasure. How he loved art, and with what lofty meaning he surrounded the conception of true creative work!

In his will he bequeathed the whole of his collection for public use. More than that, he commanded that all of his modest property, all that he had in daily use, be sold, and the proceeds applied to the purchase of more works of art that were to be added to his collection.

This is the type of an outwardly unnoticed but deeply important worker for the culture of the future. His example drew the attention of many. And if you could see his letters written from the battlefield! His was a pure soul. Colonel Kratchkovsky left us during the late war.

I might show you many more characters, full of noble seeking in different spheres of art. But even these four types show the level of those cultural aspirations which are so necessary for humanity.

So do things happen, not in dreams but in real life —sincerely and actively. And such pure labors are accompanied by a smile of joy. How near are the seekings of art to the attainment of the spirit.

It is time to understand, to note, and to apply to life these wondrous channels.

And when art has entered actively, irresistibly, and simply into all the spiritual development of public life, then it will also be brought into the whole of modern life.

And it is through these channels that the true paths of blessing will draw near to every human heart.

RUSSIAN ART

LITTLE knowledge—brings dusk with it; great knowledge—brings light. Spurious art—brings the commonplace; genuine art—creates joy of the spirit and that power on which the building of our future rests.

We should now firmly establish everything that can lead Man along a new road. As in pre-historic times, Paleolithic was replaced by Neolithic, so in our days the mechanical civilization is about to be replaced by culture. The Druids secretly cherished the laws of wisdom; similar to that, in the engendering kingdom of spirit, attention is tending toward knowledge and beauty, and many a home is already lighted up by that sacred fire; many are united, each of them a creative atom in the new construction. The same thought springs up in different countries simultaneously, like a strong plant sending forth many new shoots from the same root.

Friends, would you like to hear about art in Russia? You seem to be interested in it and kindly expectant. You are right. The Russian nation has always been closely attached to art. Since the times of yore, all its modes of life have been saturated with the self-expression of true art. The ancient heroic epos, the folklore, the national string and wind instruments, laces, carved wood, icons, ornamental details in architecture—all of these speak of genuine, natural artistic aspirations. And, even at the present moment, all exhibitions, concerts, theatres, and public lectures are invariably crowded. In Moscow, ten-thousand people out of two million inhabitants visit every exhibition (whereas, by the way, the same five-thousand is the average of visitors to an art exhibition in London out of her ten million inhabitants).

It was but a short while back that Kuprin wrote:

"Russian villages welcome the intellectuals. They have become more kindred to the peasants' conception. A newcomer from among the students, man or woman, is trustfully asked to teach small village children, while their elder brothers and sisters are keen on learning not only music but foreign languages as well. Wandering photographers are met with lots of orders. A painter who is able to produce on a piece of canvas an approximate likeness to a human face can rely upon a long life of safety and comfort in the country. I say safe because the village bestows its sincere guardianship upon these strange artists."

I, too, could point out numberless instances of love of art and of enlightenment among the simple Russian people.

It would be impossible to cover in one article every section of the vast horizon commanded by Russian art. But it is possible to point out the milestones, and to map out the main roads that will lead us from our day into the depth of the ages.

Besides the modern Russian masters—Serov, Trubetzkoy, Vrubel, Somov, Bakst, Grigoriev—you have shown your appreciation of our outstanding nationalists, such as Riepin and Surikov, Nesterov and Levitan. You have also come across the names of old masters: the classic Brulov, the religious genius Ivanov, the interpreter of national life Venezianov, and our great portrait painters Levitzky and Borovikovsky. But it is necessary all the same to point out the characteristic national features and movements of Russian art from a bird's-eye point of view, as it were.

What shall we cast away from our art in marking each successive step of development? What shall we adopt? Which way shall we turn? Toward the new interpretation of classicism or to the antique sources? Shall we sink into the depths of primitivism or find new light in neo-nationalism—with its fragrance of Indian herbs, its spells of the Finnish land, its inspiring thoughts of the so-called Slavophilism?

We are deeply excited over the question: Whence is coming the Joy of Art? For it is coming—although it has been less perceptible of late. Its resounding, approaching strides are tangible already.

Among the recent achievements, one is notable and bright; the understanding of the decorative, of the adorning nature of art, is growing rapidly. The original purpose and meaning of art is again coming to the fore, rightly understood as the embellishment of life, which makes the artist and the onlooker, the master and the owner join in the ecstasy of creation and exult in its enjoyment.

We have reasons to hope that these modern aspirations will fling away the dead-weights forcibly attached to art in the last century. Already the word "to adorn" seems to be acquiring its renewed meaning among the masses.

Very valuable is the fact that the cultured part of society is just now keen on studying the birth springs of art: it is through these crystal-like springs that the great value of embellishing human life will be realized again. It may acquire quite a new style and lead to a new era beyond the limits of our present imagination; but one thing is certain, that that new era in its intensity of exultation will be akin to the first human ecstasies.

But flowers do not grow on ice. In order to mold that new era, it is necessary that society should follow the artists; people should become their coworkers. The public mind assisting art work by prompting its creations through the demand for exhibitions, art galleries, and private collections will be that warmth without which no roots can produce plants. Happily, as I say, the interest of the cultured public is veering round to the dusk of the past ages, in the midst of which gems are sparkling: either costly or modest gems but equally great in the purity of thought that has given them their material form. We are trying to discern what we would see if we were transferred into the depth of those times: would we be amazed at the wisdom of an innate artistic instinct, or would we find just gifted children around us? No, we would find not children but wise men.

We are not going into the details of various ancient art creations; such measurements and explanations might offend both their masters and their modern possessors. It is the impression of harmony that is essential in art; and that what still bears the fascination of beauty and purity, of nobility and of singularity, should be counted as art and need not fear any libel. As it is, judging art creations of our days, many of us are given to dwell on their flaws and drawbacks. This is a sign of youth with a country where it is done.

Let us look at the thirties of the last century and further back still. Much of it stirs our heartstrings: the noble bloom of the epoch of Alexander I, the truly decorative sparkle of the times of Catherine the Great and of Elizabeth (XVIII) and the amazing conglomerations of art in Peter the Great's time. Happily, a great deal of it all has escaped ruin and vividly speaks for itself.

What are by far less known and understood are the 'pre-Peter' times. Our conception of these had been out of gear for a long time due to the admixture of "self-made" knowledge—which is always the result of little knowledge. The safest way to study the homes and churches of the pre-Peter epoch is to transfer into it in our minds the treasures from our museums, the objects of jewelry, textures, icons, etc.

Almost the highest place among the ancient Russian art creations should be given to the icons—applying this definition to a large scale. The faces on these "wonder-working" paintings are magically impressive. There is a great understanding of the effects of the silhouette painting in them, and a deep sense of proportion in the treating of the backgrounds. The faces of Christ, of the Virgin, of some beloved Saints—they seem actually to radiate the power attributed to them: The Face of Judgment, the Face of Goodness, the Face of Joy, the Face of Sorrow, the Face of

Mercy, the Face of Omnipotence. . . . Yet—still the same One Face, quiet in its features, fathomless in the depth of coloring: The Wonder-Working Face.

No one dared until recently to regard the icons purely from an artistic point of view, and only then a powerful, decorative spirit has been discovered in them at last—in the place of naiveness and crudeness which were hitherto supposed to be their characteristics. A genuine decorative instinct gave their unknown creators, in their days, complete mastery even over the largest surfaces of church walls. We are still in the dark about the proximity of that instinct in regard to actual technique and knowledge, but the "specialists" indifferent descriptions of these walls and canvas icons often call forth feelings of pain and offense for those works.

Is it not sufficient to sense the exulting audacity of color in the wall paintings of the churches in Yaroslavl and Rostov? Just have a good look at the interior of St. John the Baptist in Yaroslavl.... What harmonies of the most transparent azure with bright ochre! What atmosphere of ease and peace in the grayish emerald of the verdure, and how well it blends with the reddish and brownish ornaments of the figures. Serene Archangels with deep yellow halos round their heads, flying across the warm-looking sky, their white robes looking only just a shade colder against it. And the gold: it never hurts your eye; it is so perfectly placed and so perfectly balanced. Truly, these paintings are the daintiest, the finest silk textures befitted to clothe the walls of the Forerunner.

In the labyrinth of the church passages in Rostov every one of the tiny doorways startles you with the unexpected beauty of color harmonies. Softly outlined human figures are discerned looking at you through the strangely transparent, pale ash-gray of the walls. In some places you seem to feel the heat of the glowing red and chestnut chords; in others, peace comes breathing from the greenish-blue masses of color; and, suddenly, you stop short—as before a severe word from the Scripture—faced by a shadowy figure in ochre.

You feel that all this has been created consciously, not casually, and that you have been brought to that house for some reason, and that hence you shall keep the impression of its beauty and benefit by it more than once.

These works—to quote from an old book of the seventeenth century—have been painted "with honest mind and decent purpose, and with noble love for embellishment, for the people to see themselves here as standing before the face of the Highest."

When later on, the famous "wonder-working" icon of the Virgin Iverskaya was to be painted, the planks for its foundation were bathed in consecrated water; an exceptionally arduous service was held; the paints were mixed with petrified remains of some Saints; and the painter, while at that work, consumed food only on Saturdays and Sundays. The ecstasy of painting an icon was great in those days, and it was a real happiness when the lot befell a true artist, elated by the eternal spiritual beauty that he was to embody.

Some splendid laws of the great Italians can be traced in the Russian wall paintings, applied from a purely decorative point of view. On the other hand, the Far East has poured, through the Tartars, a tinge of willfulness into our old art works. Toward the Tsars' period of our history (16th), the decorative element in everyday life came to its highest. Whether temples, palaces, or small private dwellings, they all clearly reflected a perfect sense of proportion through which the structure itself blended with its ornamentations into one. Looking at them, you will find nothing whatever to argue against.

The noble character of the arts that flourished in Novgorod and in Pskov—on "The Great Waterway" leading from the Baltic into the Black Sea—was saturated with the best elements of Hansa culture. The lion's head on coins of the Novgorod Republic is extremely like the head of St. Mark. . . . Was it not the northern giant's dream of the distant southern queen of the seas, Venice? The now whitewashed walls of Novgorod—the "Great Town that was its own Master," to quote its ancient name in full—look as if they could very likely have borne on them paintings of the Hansa character. Novgorod, famous for, and wise with, the incessant raids of his "freemen," might have turned his face away from a casual wanderer—but only through willfulness and not from shame: there is not one stain on the fame of the famous old town; it kept many of its old features even until the nineteenth century.

It is different with the influences of the Far East. The Mongol invasions have left such a hatred behind them that their artistic elements are always neglected. It is forgotten that the mysterious cradle of Asia produced these quaint people and has enwrapped them in the gorgeous veils of China, Tibet, and Hindustan. Russia has not only suffered from the Tartar swords but has also heard through their jingling the wonder tales known to the clever Greeks and the intelligent Arabians who wandered along the Great Road from the Normans to the East.

The Mongol manuscripts and the annals of the foreign envoys of those days tell us of an unaccountable mixture of cruelty and refinement with the great nomads. The best artists and masters were to be found at the headquarters of the Tartar Khans.

Besides the adopted viewpoint of the textbooks, there can be another one:

It was the Tartars' contempt and cruelty that taught the Russian Princes to give up their feuds and to rally against their mutual oppressor; it was the Tartars that taught them the omnipotence of merciless victors; but, at the same time, those nomads brought from Asia ancient culture and spread it all over the land that they had previously devastated.

It is more painful to think of the ancient weapons of the Russians themselves with which they ruined in their quarrels each other's towns even before the Tartars invaded them. The white walls of the Russian temples and towers—"shining as white as cheese," to quote from the ancient annals—suffered many a hard blow from kindred clans.

GORKY

THE great Russian writer Maxim Gorky passed away in Gorki, near Moscow, on June 18 [1936].

During the last months, three great Russians have left this world: the great physiologist Pavlov, the composer Glazunov, and now Gorky. All three were known to the entire world. Who has not heard of the famous experiments in the field of reflexes, conducted by Pavlov? Who next to Tchaikovsky and Rimsky-Korsakov did not also admire Glazunov? And who has not read among other Russian classics the works of Gorky, who has recorded unfading images of Russian life?

Over half a million people went to pay homage to the remains of the great writer, and over seven hundred thousand accompanied the funeral procession. The representative of the Union stood as a guard of honor and carried after the cremation, the urn to the Kremlin Wall, where it is immured. The entire diplomatic corps was present. Gun salutes thundered in honor of the great writer. Some French papers were amazed at the way a whole nation paid tribute to its national hero. There were wreaths from the French and Czechoslovakian Governments. The foreign Press unanimously hailed the achievements of Gorky.

It had been resolved in Moscow to erect monuments in honor of Gorky at the expense of the State at Moscow, Leningrad, and in Nijny-Novgorod, the latter already bearing his name now.

The Municipal Council of Praha decided to name a street in the Czechoslovakian capital in his honor.

Benes, the President of Czechoslovakia, sent the

following telegram to Moscow: "The death of Maxim Gorky will compel the entire world, and Czechoslovakia in particular, to remember the progress of the Russian people during the last fifty years and of the Union since the revolution. The participation of Gorky in this process was in the spiritual respect and convincing. For me, personally, Gorky and all other Russian classics were my teachers in many respects, and I remember him with gratitude."

H. G. Wells sent a hearty message from England,and Romain Rolland telephoned from Switzerland to Moscow the following letter: "At this painful hour of departure, I remember Gorky not so much as the great writer, nor even his colorful path of life and mighty creativeness. I remember his full, saturated life, which like his motherly Volga, flowed richly in streams of thoughts and images. Gorky was the first among the world artists of the word, who cleared the path for the people who gave them his strength, the prestige of his glory, and his wise life experience.... Like Dante, Gorky emerged from Hell. He brought out with him and saved his friends in suffering."

The Paris papers, which have reached the Himalayas, record many signs of a worldwide esteem to the deceased. He was honored not only by friends but by all sections of cultural life. Even the most reluctant obituaries highly comment upon Gorky's works, such as *The Lower Depths, Mother, Letopis, Childhood, Artomonov's Business, Chelkash, The Town of Okarov*, and conclude: "a man and an artist has passed away, whom we all loved." Thus art has united both friends and foes.

From the very beginning of his vivid literary career, Alexis Maxim Peshkov, whom the whole world knows better by his pen name Maxim Gorky, achieved an exclusive position amid Russian classics. About every great ma there are many legends; also around the name of Gorky, there was woven much truth and invention. Some tried to represent him as a severe cold-blooded materialist; others based themselves on single abrupt words, by which it is impossible to judge a man and his work. But uncorruptible history will depict to the full extent his great image, and people will find in him many unexpected traits.

About his last minutes, Dr. L. Levin writes in the *Izvestia* of June 20th: "Alexis Maximovich died as he lived, a great man. In these painful hours of illness, he never once spoke about himself. All his thoughts were in the Kremlin, in Moscow. Even in the interval between two oxygen cushions, he asked me to show him the newspaper with the project of Stalin's new constitution. During the short periods of relief from his illness, he spoke about his beloved subjects: literature and about the possibility of a future war, which worried him very much. The last day and night he was unconscious. Remaining constantly at his bedside, I discerned the following abrupt phrases that he said: "There will be war.... One should be ready.... Fasten up all buttons!"

N. Berberova writes in the Paris press of a characteristic episode in the life of Gorky:

"This was on the day when the current issue of *Sovremennye Zapiski (Contemporary Review)* was received with the concluding chapter of Bunin's novel *Mitia's Love.* Everything was put aside: work, correspondence, newspapers. Gorky locked himself up in his study and was late for lunch and absentminded. Only at tea it became clear: A remarkable work . . . truly remarkable—in these words he characterized *Mitia's Love.* . . . It is difficult to believe that Gorky could cry with real tears when reading the poems of Lermontov, Block, and many others. . . . "

Further, N. Berberova quotes from a letter she had received from Gorky, in which his devotion to poets and poetry was expressed: "I am deeply enchanted by the broadness and multifacetedness of themes and subjects in poetry. I consider this as a real quality, as a good sign. It shows the broad outlook of the author, his inner freedom, the absence of chains with any conventional moods, with any preconceived ideas. It seems to me that the definition: 'the poet is the echo of world life' is the most correct. Of course, there are and should be ears that perceive only the bass tones of life, and souls who hear but the lyric of life. But Pushkin heard everything, perceived everything and, therefore, has no equal. Can there be anything higher than literature—the art of words? Certainly not. It is the most astounding, mysterious, and beautiful in this world!" Those who do not know the groups of Russian literary thought should be told that Gorky's praise of Bunin shows his broad judgment, for Bunin belongs to another camp.

Many valuable traits of Gorky will reveal themselves in the course of time. I happened to meet him on many occasions in private talks and at numerous committee meetings, gatherings, etc., and I cherish his friendship. On all occasions I could trace some new remarkable details of character, which very often did not correspond to the outwardly austere appearance of Alexis Maximovich. I remember, how once during the organization of a great literary enterprise, when an urgent decision was required, I asked Gorky for his opinion. He smiled and said: "There is nothing to argue. You as an artist will feel what is needed. Yes, yes, precisely you will feel—you are an intuitivist. Often above reason, one should reach the very essence!"

I also recollect how once at a friendly gathering, Gorky revealed, quite unexpectedly for many, another interesting side of his character. We spoke about yogis and various psychic phenomena whose home is India. Some of the guests looked suspiciously at Gorky, who kept silent, and they apparently awaited his severe criticism. But his resumption amazed many. Filled with an inner radiance, he said: "The Hindus are a great people. I will tell you of my personal experience. Once in the Caucasus I met a Hindu, about whom many remarkable stories were circulating. At the time I was rather inclined to doubt. At last we met, and what I will tell you, I saw with my own eyes. He took a long thread and threw it up into the air. And to my surprise, it remained hanging up in the air. Then he asked me whether I would like to look at an album and what picture I would like to see. I said I would like to see pictures of Indian cities. He gave me his album and looking at me, said: 'Please, look at these pictures of Indian cities?' The album contained polished brass sheets, on which were reproduced beautiful views of different cities, temples, and other views of India. I looked over the entire album, attentively studying the pictures. Then I closed the album and returned it to the Hindu. He smiled and said: 'Well, you have seen views of India. Then he blew at the album and returned it into my hands inviting me to look at it again. I opened the album and to my surprise found only polished plates without any pictures whatsoever. These Hindus are indeed remarkable people. What refined thought!"

Does not this characteristic trait of Gorky prove his all-containing and broad consciousness?

He very much wanted to have my painting. He selected from those that I had at the time, not a realistic landscape but one of the so-called pre-war series, *The Doomed City*. This painting precisely corresponds to the mood of a poet. Indeed, the author of *Storm-Finch* was a great poet. Coming from the depth of the people, Gorky fearlessly walked across all obstacles of life—he went the path of the Russian people, encompassing its multifacetedness and the richness of the Russian soul.

The Moscow newspapers of June 21st, under the title "Gorky in the role of Harun-al-Rashid" tell the following story accompanied by a photo of Gorky dressed as a tramp: "This was in 1928. Gorky wanted to see what goes on in public bars, what kind of people visit them, whether he would find there any types similar to his old novel *The Lower Depths,* what became of them, what the new visitors are like, etc. But how to arrange such an expedition? Gorky decided to disguise himself as a tramp. With a huge beard, well he entered into intimate talks with the people there and as a result wrote a new novel, which forms part of his *Across the Soviet Union.*

"Those who know Gorky will understand that this episode is indeed typical of him. Being a true realist in the broadest sense, he considered it necessary to convince himself in life, not so much in order to enter into his diary leaves sketches of new types, but in order to affirm a synthesis for an actual expression of his consciousness.

"He was trustful and he trusted. He loved to trust and he was often cheated. . . .

"Once he came out from his study singing and his face expressed utter joy, so that everybody was amazed. It turned out that he had read a newspaper report that somewhere, somebody has discovered some new microbe. Gorky thus expressed his enthusiasm at the prospect of helping humanity through combating yet another disease.

Once I met Gorky in business relations when the publishing company of Sytin in Moscow and the Niva were merged into one big concern. A colossal, unifying program in the literary and educational field was in project. It was interesting to witness how every conventionality and formality tortured Gorky, who wanted to overcome all formal obstacles without delay. He knew how to build on a broad scale. Take, for example, the three mighty cultural institutions outlined by him: The House of World Literature, the House of Scientists and, the House of Art. All these three gigantic ideas show the creative scope of Gorky's thought, who was striving to find across all difficulties the eternal words—words of enlightenment and culture.

He carried his chalice of service to humanity throughout life unspilled.

In the name of the League of Culture let us offer our sincerest, heartiest thought to the great memory of Gorky, which will remain forever radiantly affirmed in the Pantheon of World Culture.

GLORY

"WHY did I go into thee Russia?" German prisoners sang, while trampling along the streets of Stalingrad. Thus we heard on the Moscow Radio. Victory, a grand victory! I recollected my Diary Leaf entitled "Do not outrage" (*Nezamai*), written before the present war. Verily, do not outrage Russia. Everyone who attempts against Russia will perish in utter disgrace.

History records stupendous examples of how the enemies of the Russian people have been defeated. Manifold have been these defeats. Some bore effect instantaneously; others gradually reacted upon the disintegration of the countries that had risen against Russia. A very instructive volume could be written about this.

And yet another book should be written of how magnanimously and heroically arose the Russian people in the defense of their Motherland. Countless enemies of the Russian land have been defeated by the unbreakable spirit of the Russian warriors, by the sacrificing self-denial of the people, Alexander Nevsky, Sergi Radonnigsky, Dmitry Donskoi Minin and Pojorsky, Suvorov and Kutuzov—how many glorious milestones, how many victorious ascents!

"The conflagration of Moscow served to beautify it." Every national trial infused new inexhaustible forces into Russian hearts. After the storm, the Sun shone all the brighter. Indeed great is grief, but "grief is passing while joy is imperishable." The Russian people know the sacred joy of devotion to one's country. They know the indefatigable labor of achievement. The Russian people are quick to grasp and full of creativeness. They remember that "delay equals death." They remember that "blessed are the obstacles; through them we grow." There shall never be found another madman who will dare to take up arms against the united family of peoples, who have come together in brotherly union on this sacred plough-field. From the warrior to the leader, everyone labors. New forces are born. Strengthened is cooperation. The predestined glory of the Russian people is being fulfilled.

There have been those lacking in faith, those cowardly turncoats, and there have also been ignorant negators, but all this dusty dross disappeared when the bright and happy sun of the people's achievements arose.

We have argued with many wavering and doubting ones. False prophets prophesied all kinds of calamities but we always asserted "Moscow will stand. Leningrad will stand. Stalingrad will stand." And they stand today!

To the amazement of the whole world grew the invincible Russian army. Self-sacrificingly the Russian people bring all they possess to the glory of their Motherland. *Glory, Glory, Glory.*

IV

PAX PER CULTURA

GUARD THE CULTURE

CULTURE is reverence of Light. Culture is love of humanity. Culture is fragrance, the unity of life and beauty. Culture is the synthesis of uplifting and sensitive attainments. Culture is the armor of Light. Culture is salvation. Culture is the motivating power. Culture is the Heart.

If we gather all the definitions of Culture, we find the synthesis of active Bliss, the altar of enlightenment and constructive beauty.

Condemnation, disparagement, defying, melancholy, disintegration, and all other characteristics of ignorance do not befit culture. The great tree of Culture is nourished by an unlimited knowledge, by enlightened labor, incessant creativeness, and noble attainment.

The cornerstones of great civilizations support the stronghold of Culture. But from the tower of Culture, there radiates the jewel—adamant from the loving, realizing, and dauntless Heart.

Love opens these beautiful Gates. As with each true key, so also must this love be true, and Culture self-sacrificing, daring, fiery. Where we find the sources of Culture, they are fiery and issue from the very depths. Where culture has once been born, it cannot be killed. One may annihilate civilization, but Culture, the true spiritual treasure, is eternal.

Therefore, the field of Culture is a joyful one, joyful even during labor, joyful even during the tense battles with the most obscure ignorance. The flaming heart is without limitations in the great Infinity.

The Festival of Labor and Constructiveness! A summons to this Festival means a reminder of eternal labor, of the joy of responsibility and of human dignity.

The labor of the worker for Culture is like the work of a physician. The true physician is acquainted with more than one disease. And not only does the physician cure that which has already occurred, but his wise foresight anticipates the future. The physician not only eradicates the illness, but he labors to improve the health for the whole of life. The physician descends into the darkest cellars in order to carry light and warmth there. The physician is not forgetful of all the amelioration and beautification of life, in order to give joy to the understanding spirit. The physician not only knows of the old epidemics, but he readily acquaints himself with the symptoms of new diseases, which have been induced by the decay of the foundations.

The physician has sage words of counsel for the young and for the old, and is ready to give everyone encouraging advice. The physician does not cease to extend his knowledge, otherwise he could not answer the needs of the present. The physician does not lose patience or tolerance because a restraint of feeling would repel the suffering ones against him.

The physician does not fear the sight of human ulcers because he is concerned only with their cure. The physician collects various curative herbs and stones; he knows the research for their benevolent application. The physician is not weary of hastening with and for the suffering ones at all hours of the day or night.

All these qualities are also inherent in the worker for Culture. He is equally ready at all hours of the day or night to contribute his help. The worker for Culture always beneficently answers: "I am always ready!" His heart is ever open to everything in which experience and knowledge may be useful. Helping, he himself continually learns, because "in giving, we receive." He is not afraid, for he knows that fear opens the gates of darkness.

The worker for Culture is always youthful, for his heart does not wither. He is movable because movement is force. He stands vigil on the parapet of Bliss, Knowledge, and Beauty. He knows what true cooperation is.

All coworkers for Culture are united by rays of the heart. Mountains and oceans are no obstacles to these flaming hearts. They are not dreamers but constructors and smiling plowmen.

In sending this Greeting of Culture, one cannot do so without a smile, without the call of friendship. Thus we shall meet, thus we shall gather together and labor for

Bliss, Beauty, and Knowledge. And we shall do this undeferrably, without losing a day, nor an hour in blissful constructiveness.

THE RED CROSS OF CULTURE

ONE reads in newspaper cables from New York a reporting of eight hundred thousand unemployed in this city alone; and in the whole of the United States; their number exceeds nine million. And one remembers such a multitude of personally known, intelligent workers, who are, of course, not included in number but who experience no less poverty from unemployment. Such figures are indeed a misfortune. They show that the crisis not only entered all classes but already has become a destructive factor. In the same mail one reads that the very existence of the Metropolitan Opera is endangered. The Art Institute in Detroit, of which Ford himself is the President, is to be temporarily closed because of a deficit. The capitol of Kansas City, formerly one of the richest towns, was sold at auction. Letters announce not only new cuts in the budgets of educational institutions but also losses of a million such people, who were considered unshatterable rocks of financial wisdom.

When before our very eyes, the foundations of this highly experienced "wisdom" is shattered, then is this not a sign that materialistic principles have reached their limit and are already dying out? And is this sign not one more proof that the time has come when one has to raise from the dust and ashes the forgotten Banner of the Spirit in order to counteract the evident-to-all destruction by eternal values?

When, if not now, should children's hearts be kindled by the best testimonials of past achievements of true education and untiring realization. Perhaps there has not yet been such a time when, in a most urgent way, one has to help in the hardships of family life, and based on all historical examples, to point out by what means all sorts of crises frequently arising in history were previously conquered.

One can no longer hide the fact that a crisis has taken place. One can no longer calm oneself by an erroneous idea that some new one-day collection will feed all the unemployed and starving. It is quite clear that what has happened is much deeper.

Long, long ago, we had already heard the saying of wise people: "When money is lost, nothing is lost; but when courage is lost, then all is lost." Today one has to think of this wise proverb because it has now become peculiarly fashionable to speak about the crisis. And those who suffered and those who lost little, both equally refer to the crisis as equally destroying all initiative and creative striving. Thus if some definite counteraction will not be undertaken then beware that this crisis does not turn into the prelude of some calamity still more terrible.

We optimists should first of all avert every panic, every despair, whether this be in the stock exchange or in the holiest sanctuary of the heart. There is no such horror that having called into life a still greater tension of energy, could not be transmuted into a positive solution. It is especially shocking to hear, when some people who have suffered from the crisis—people who may not even be so bad in themselves—in panic begin to state that now is not time to even think about Culture. We have already heard such voices, inadmissible in their timidity and despair.

No, my dear ones, especially now we have not only to hasten to think of Culture as such, but we must also apply this life-giving source to the young generations. One can easily imagine into what will change the budding consciousness of youth if in schools and at home they will hear only of narratives about calamities and horrors of despair. Imagine what will happen if youth are infected with the notion that they should deprive themselves of everything life-giving and that they should forget all sources of renaissance and progress.

This terrible "no," "It is not the time," "impossible" pushes the young consciousness into a darkest prison. And with nothing, with nothing in the world, can one enlighten the sinking twilight of these hearts if this darkness has once been admitted. And not only of the youth must we think but also of the infants. Every educator knows that the foundations of consciousness, which give a direction to the whole life, are formed much before the age of a youth. Often the silent look of a child expresses that the surrounding circumstances are to him much more understood than the conceit of the grownup presupposes. How many basic problems are solved in the heart and brain of a four-year-old or six-year-old youngster!

Anyone who has watched the development of children will of course remember the remarkable definitions, ideas, and advices that were uttered quite unexpectedly by the child. But besides these verbal expressions, how many sparks of consciousness radiate in the silent look of the child! And how often youngsters divert their eyes from a grownup, as if wishing to guard some definite thought, which according to their opinion, the grownup will not understand anyhow.

It is this penetrating mind of the child that one should nourish, especially now, with the most radiant, glorious thoughts. One should not feed with empty hopes because idealism is not in misty emptiness but is in that immutable reality, which can be proven by historians as the most accurate mathematical problem.

Is it not the very time now to come to the schools with the most calling, inspiring messages about human achievements, about the most useful discoveries, and about all the Bliss that is predestined but which due to our negligence has been overlooked.

Another clipping just to hand says: "Today Berlin is described as a dead city, and it is said that only half the possible number of taxis are on the streets, while most other forms of traffic have dwindled amazingly. People are finding it more difficult to pay their rents and, in consequence, are moving in vast numbers to the poorer quarters of the city." Thus from everywhere come signs of distress.

We began with news from New York, struck by the latest newspaper clippings, struck that in this richest city, the municipality requires many, many extra millions, only to prevent starvation. We mention these clippings because it is not only true but in essence does not even reflect the whole problem. To some extent this news from New York refers of course to all cities, not only of America but of the whole world. Often such problems are hidden either by conventional expressions or by the impenetrable dust of volcanic eruptions. Also now, newspaper reports are coming from South America, bringing information of an aerial survey from regions affected by eruptions and earthquakes: "Visibility nil." Indeed, in many places of the globe the visibility *is* nil. And when the dust of the eruptions scatters, we will witness a still greater commotion of the human spirit.

A picture of civilization that is "rapidly going to pieces" was recently drawn by H. G. Wells when addressing the London School of Economics. He stated: "Just as in the time of Noah, we must build an ark amid the wastes and ruin around us. If the efforts to save civilization fail, we may take heart in that perhaps we are laying the foundations for another and far better one." Truly, one should not dance on a volcano.

He who asserts just now the crisis—material and spiritual—he is by no means like the Cassandra of Troy in her ill-omened prophecies (which in her case unfortunately became true). He who signals about the crisis is simply like a railway switchman, who having noticed the imminence of a disaster lifts the flag to warn the engine driver, hoping that the latter is alert and will take heed to his signal. Let us be like this railway switchman.

Let us unfurl the Banner of Protection of Culture! Already last year, we suggested a World Day of Culture, a special day in schools, when instead of routine class work, a narrative about the best achievements of humanity should set aflame the young hearts by its radiant message. If last year we thought of the League of Youth and of even one day to manifest the Beautiful Garden of humanity, then now we see that the urgency of this need has multiplied. One day is already not enough to strengthen the consciousness upset by social and family misfortunes. One must speak oftener of the saving, creative, inspiring principle.

To educate does not mean to give only a number of mechanical data. Education, the upbuilding of a world consciousness, is reached by synthesis, not by the synthesis of calamities but through the synthesis of the joy of perfection and creation. If we shall cut off every influx of such joyful enlightenment of life, then what poor educators we shall be! What education can give the teacher who spreads around himself sorrow and despair. But not far from despair is also pseudo-joy and, therefore, every forced smile is correctly called "the smile of a skull." Before inspiring others, we too convince ourselves of the vital need and undeferrability of the Program of Culture, as a healing principle, as a life-giver.

From medical science we know that even the best life-givers cannot act spontaneously. Even the best life-giver requires a certain time to penetrate into all the nerve centers and not only to excite them mechanically (every excitement calls forth reaction) but actually strengthen and rejuvenate the nerve substance. If we have such a multitude of examples that a certain time is needed for the process of healing, then how undeferrable is it now to think and to begin to act under the Sign of Culture, similar to that of the Red Cross.

Humanity is accustomed to the sign of the Red Cross. This humanitarian symbol penetrated not only in times of war but purified life with one more beautiful conception. Just the same humanitarian conception so needed from the small to the great will be derived from a Sign of

Culture, similar to the sign of the Red Cross. One should not imagine that one may think of Culture only at leisure, digesting the food of a tasty dinner. No, just during starvation and cold, as the sign of the Red Cross shines to the heavily wounded, just in the same way the Sign of Culture will inspiringly shine to the spiritually and bodily starving.

Verily, now it is not the time to disseminate, to obstruct, and to attend to pettiness. When a Red Cross car drives along the street, then the traffic is stopped for it. In the same way, one should also for this greatly needed Sign of Culture give up at least some of one's daily bad habits, of the vulgarity and of many other dusty conventionalities of ignorance, from which sooner or later one has to cleanse oneself.

To people who have not come into close touch with questions of education, the Sign of Culture may appear as an interesting experiment; but thus they will show their scanty knowledge of history. But even if for someone the Sign of Culture is only an experiment, anyhow even crass ignoramuses will not dare to say that this Sign and the thoughts about Culture could be destructive and decomposing. The constructiveness of thoughts about Culture is so evident that it is even ridiculous to argue about this.

In case of serious danger on a ship, the order is given: "Act to your best ability!"

In the same way now, thinking of Culture, one should address everybody with the advice to act to the best of his ability, that is to say, to apply all his strength and experience to the glory of the life-giving creative conception of Culture.

DINOSAURS

MR. H. G. WELLS, in a recent talk, said that in the long tale of the ages great races of creatures "like the Dinosaurs, the Dinotheria, and so forth, have lorded it over the earth, and passed." They passed because conditions changed and they were unable to adapt themselves to them in time.

Has man, Mr. Wells asks, any prospect of escaping a similar fate? In Mr. Wells's view, he has. Because of his brains. "He is able to think and forestall what is happening to him. He can learn and change himself, as no sort of animal has ever been able to do." And Wells defines the changes to which the human race must adapt itself as (1) the annihilation of distance brought about by modern methods of communication; (2) the enormous increase of material power, and; (3) the way in which the unskilled work of "slaves" and drudges "can be and is being largely superseded by power-driven mechanism." He sees as the common denominator for resolving the problem of world peace, that "the governments of the world should surrender their sovereign right to practice economic and political aggression against one another." And he emphasizes that *"that is all* they need surrender, more than the power of mutual destruction."

Indeed, during recent years we have become convinced that it is not at all only the official wars that threaten the irreplaceable creations of human genius; not only war but insidious barbarism and savagery threaten, perhaps to a great extent, the best monuments of creativeness.

Not in the skins of cavemen, but in smoking jackets sit

these "gentlemen" who shamefully exclaim: "To Hell with Culture!"—unpunishable in their destructive arrogance and ignorance!

There is many a Herostratus! We set down the name of an insane as a most shameful stigma but not to burden the pages of history. Criminal savagery turns first of all against the most exalted and perfect creations. Ignorance attempts to disfigure the greatest—therein is the hideous seal of darkness.

Verily, the most penetrating universal measures are needed in order to renew the traditions of Culture. Let us hope from the depths of our hearts, that the World League of Culture will truly enlighten universally all the embittered, bewildered, obscured hearts with a new and benevolent life.

A criminal hand will reach everywhere if the brain and the heart are intent upon criminality. But from the earliest years of childhood, it ought to be taught in the home and in the school wherein lie the true universal and spiritual values. If we realize that ancient China and Egypt revered creation more than we do, it will seem a very unfortunate realization.

Only recently we learned of the destroyed Goyas in Spain, and about the peril of a valuable library in Shanghai and of many other barbarisms. People say it is a national fury. But why does it strike the beautiful and not the ugly? Shame!

In the entire world, the "Days of Culture" are being celebrated. This is well. Let them constitute a true homage to Light, Beauty, and Knowledge, which will make the hands of barbarians fall before the creations of the Beautiful.

Should one speak of the significance of Knowledge of Beauty? Is it not a truism? But reality in all its ugliness forces one indefatigably and continuously to implore the affirmation of cultural foundations. Instead of the repast of labor, in all its solemnity and constructiveness, there may come the night of the conflagration of destruction. You yourself see that it may occur in spite of all the "Olympic Games" which, unlike the ancient games, sometimes finish with a wild fist fight.

Let all the leagues, institutions, museums, societies, institutes, conferences, and conventions grow and multiply in order through enlightenment to expel all the horrors of ignorance and darkness.

"If you have built castles in the air, your work need not be lost; that is where they should be. *Now* put foundations under them." (Henry David Thoreau)

THE GREAT IMAGES

WHEN great images reach us from remote antiquity, it is somehow very simple to accept them. Even if they are veiled in myths and legends they are very convincing. During a long lapse of time anything is possible. Writers and painters of all the ages apply their best inspirations to these distant images. Many generations are guided by these inspiring distant heroes and heroines. Nobody is jealous of them, nobody is interested in the manner of achievements—what is preserved is purely a monument of human ascension.

Entirely different are images from the recent past, to say nothing of the present. Take the description of great people recently deceased. So many unnecessary, non-characteristic traits are emphasized, which only shows that the exact nature of their lives has not been considered and not evaluated. The most doubtful, entirely unproven details are brought up, and the conclusions, even though they are not necessarily negative, are at best belittling. Of course, with passing ages the scales will be balanced. The judgment of the people eventually will remove such of the dirt and dust as fills the eyes of the contemporary observer. The justice of ages does not belittle. Even within the expanse of a century, we see that many things attain their own balance. The printed sheets on which great characters were disparaged and despised are still in existence. In the time of our forefathers, the people laughed cruelly and unjustly at certain manifestations that in less than a hundred years became the pride of their country and even of the whole world, and we may witness now the same.

We shall not discuss separately the many writers, poets, scientists, social workers, and leaders whose names and whose very images have been transfigured in people's minds within the shortest time. Everybody knows many of such cases. Although our contemporaries severely condemn the ignorant prejudices of yesterday, they themselves often repeat such mistakes. It has been suggested that the dictionaries and encyclopedias alter their evaluations with every new edition. We may recall a number of great names who at first were described in dictionaries and encyclopedias as charlatans and agitators but later were considered most noble and honorable. Such a metamorphosis happens sometimes within one generation. Is it not remarkable for the history of human thought?

It is difficult to say what causes this, although the fact remains. Is it wickedness, envy, ignorance or perhaps plain stupidity and laziness?

Someone is responsible for the most peculiar proverb: "Angry words do not hurt." Probably this strange saying is attributable to some bully who wanted to justify his peculiarity.

Sometimes people reach such absurdity that a mere attempt to give a friendly opinion, even a very reasonable one, is considered as something untimely and unacceptable; while at the same time any criticism that is scandalous and perverted will be taken calmly and even with hidden approval.

Meanwhile, so many beautiful, truly great images have been coming to teach humanity, and not in ancient times, but right here, very near. It seems that these images, being so real, so concrete, should have inspired many people. But this happens so rarely.

We find these unforgettable, inspiring images sparkling not only in ruler or leader roles but also in ordinary daily life. Only the few can realize their deep significance for humanity. In this also, somehow and sometimes the scales of justice will be balanced. However, it is strange that people are using so little of what already has been gener-ously given to them and which could be widely applied.

Beautiful, heroic, exemplary men and women are liv-ing in our time; they are true creators of culture, and it would seem most desirable to know something about them immediately instead of leaving the construction of their images to the exaggerated imagination of people of some future day.

Let us consider a great feminine image. From early childhood the girl likes to retire secretly with a large heavy book. With an effort she carries away the large vol-ume and secretly admires the pictures; later on, she learns to read all by herself. From the same bookcases of her father, she takes philosophical treatises, and unusually early, in spite of the noisy, distracting surroundings, she enters into a deep contemplation of the world as if it were a familiar realm discovered a long time ago. The constant search for truth and justice and the love for creative work changes the whole of life around the young, strong spirit. The whole house, the whole family, everything seems sup-ported on the same beneficial foundation.

The family bears all difficulties and dangers under this same firm leadership. The girl's accumulated knowl-edge and aspiration toward perfection bring unconquer-able solutions of problems, which lead all the others to one luminous path. Ignorance, obscurity, and wickedness are painfully sensed. Wherever it is possible, a physical and spiritual healing takes place. From early morning till night, life becomes full of true labor, and all for the bene-fit of humanity. A large correspondence is built up, books are written, extensive essays are translated; and all this is done in a remarkable tirelessness of spirit. Even the most difficult circumstances are conquered by true faith, which becomes a straight knowledge. Wonderful accumulations were necessary for such wisdom. Such an unwearying life of labor, with daily great deeds, benevolence, and con-structiveness should be the ideal of all youth.

When facing innumerable difficulties, it is particularly

valuable for the youth to learn about these achievements through untiring labor. Often one may think that certain things are insurmountable, that evil cannot be conquered by good. This is the kind of delusion that the confused human mind likes to tolerate. And as a countermeasure, the true examples of the heroic life are particularly fitting. We may rejoice that we have these beautiful examples, so encouraging to all beginners in constructive work. The constructive principle must be affirmed. It is necessary to replace doubt, negation, and retreat by inspiring encouraging work.

Some may consider themselves retired and useless, not suspecting that here, not far from them, over all obstacles, all the impediments of obscurity, the unsplashed chalice was carefully carried. If one would realize this, how much new vigor and, combined with it, new possibilities would come! How much dark absurdity would be replaced by the thoughts about creative, constructive work, which is possible in all stages of life? Is it absolutely necessary to be burned at the stake like Joan of Arc? Will the scaffolds still be necessary when we realize the true value of moving, guiding words and exemplary work? Sooner or later humanity will have to give up everything that holds back, impedes, and hardens. The one who will be able to find a maximum of good indications will complete a most noble marathon. The true marathon has no occasion to stand on one leg! But only to find the maximum of good constructive indications! In these indications will be found real peace for which all churches are praying ceaselessly.

To achieve this true peace, it is necessary to exercise much care and much benevolence. Is it possible to talk about benevolence or about something abstract and inapplicable? Is it possible that there are such brutal hearts as could oppose every constructive benevolence? It is impossible. In every living heart, there must be some tolerance and kindliness. With such a kind approach, the great images will be distinguished and their work will be justly evaluated.

REALM OF CULTURE

"IN WHAT country would you prefer to live?"
"Naturally, in the country of Culture."
"To what would you dedicate your best thoughts?"
"To Culture."
"To what would you offer your enlightened work?"
"To Culture, of course."
"With what would you restore your consciousness?"
"With the victorious Light of Culture."
"Are you not agitators?"
"In constant labor, we have no time for agitations. We construct. In positive affirmation and realization, we aspire to make earthly life more sensitive and more beautiful."

Thus would the Light-bearers of Culture answer the questions of outsiders, or those who are simply unknowing, those who are fundamentally ignorant, or those who are envious of Light. He who knows the sacred foundation of Culture evaluates also the Great, the only Light. He is convinced of the Hierarchy of Benevolence beyond which there is no created path.

The one who serves Culture ceases to be a dreamer, but becomes incarnate with the greatest and brightest dreams in life. For what can be more resplendent and majestic than the service and realization of the enlightened elements under the shade of which are created great nations? It is necessary, by all means, to strengthen consciousness, that the thoughts of Culture be not abstract but a constructive affirmation. The one who understands the positive beauty of Culture does not remain asleep, nor does he remain inactive and uncreative. No, he who has immediate perception will bring his contribution to the harmonious, conscious labor.

The worker of Culture understands real collaboration—that vital, cordial cooperation by which even the smallest deed grows. He who has broadened his consciousness by the understanding of Culture would also understand his coworkers, not coercing them, but wisely transmuting the treasures of human experience. And fearless will be he who perceives Culture; because looking with sensitive and benevolent eyes, he would see that fear is inherent in darkness. As he is beyond superstition and prejudice, the servant of Culture understands that the only happiness of thinking man is in ceaseless labor, in creation, for all of existence may be created in beauty. Knowing the value of Culture he would begin to prize the quality of thought and would wisely apply this greatest creative power. From the qualities of the Light-bearers of Culture are eradicated condemnation, slanderous gossip, and speaking about that of which one is ignorant!

What a terrible scourge of ignorance it is to talk of that which one does not know! And how many apparently civilized people err in that regard. The bearer of Culture feels deeply all the divergences between fundamental, spiritual culture and the aggregations of materialistic civilization.

Valuing the luminous cumulations of nations, the servant of Culture would distinguish between the accidental transition and real existence. Understanding this great responsibility of human existence, the Light-bearer of Culture brings to both his thoughts and actions a high quality. He intelligently analyzes the miraculous strength of nature, remembering that without exception, everything that exists may be beneficially utilized for our well-being. In the name of this well-being and Light, you discover in yourself a precious language of the heart—a vocabulary that is fuller and more beautiful than any dictionary. What bright convictions the language of the heart carries with it, and how effectively does its victorious testaments destroy even the darkest gates of lies and ignorance! Certainly we are convinced that lies are foolish and futile; for in the Spirit, a lie finds no refuge. Wisdom rests in reality that renounces neither spiritual nor physical existence. And in the State of Culture, lies do not exist. It is impossible to remain static; you must either advance or retract. The standards of true Culture do not know of retreat. The real bearers of Light do not know disappointment because the magnet of Light is great.

The great nations—in whose name you are gathered here, and by whose symbols one may discover a creative heritage transmitted in the history of their great migrations—give us instructive examples. We meet here heroism, renunciation, and unselfishness, the martyrdom for Light, and the noble deeds for creation. These discoveries do not burden those who study them; on the contrary, they inspire them to similar incessant effort. The great immigrations of the nations are not accidental. There can be no accident in the constant phenomena of the world. By these characteristics is tempered the living strength of nations. With the contact of new neighbors consciousness widens and develops the forms of new races. Therefore, vital migration is one of the signs of wisdom.

On the steppes of Asia—in this cradle of all spiritual and creative migrations—in ancient times, migrations were considered the completion of education. Even now we meet with remains of traditions of these beginnings of education. In those far-distant lands, the gift of books or sacred objects is considered to be the highest sign of a noble spirit. The great voyagers carried along such remarkable covenants and on their way created great styles of art and living. We remember the "Alan" heritage and the beautiful "Romanesque style." We also remember the characteristic monasteries both in the Slavic lands and on Asiatic frontiers. Without astonishment we recall that the sword belts of the Himalayan Mountains and their fibulae are found in the Caucasus as well as in the Southern Russian steppes and scattered through Europe. On their fibulae, on the breastplates, we find many images that have become the symbols of whole nations.

Let our breastplates also bear the word Culture—the same universally evocative symbol. And let every Light-bearer of Culture be reminded of all the enlightened heritages and of the high responsibility for the quality of his creative work. We shall not think about luxury. Culture is found in Beauty and in Knowledge. Immense wealth is not necessary in order to exchange and mutually strengthen the language of the heart.

I believe in the indestructibility of our common creations. In the name of Light and of the Heart, in the name of Beauty and Knowledge, in the name of the vital, fundamental evolution, I greet you from the snow-white heights of the Himalayas!

CIVILIZATION

HOW proud we are of our Culture! In what lofty terms we praise our civilization! With what hopes we look forward into the future!

Meanwhile our reason assures us that Culture can exist provided it is founded on a widening of consciousness; that civilization can flourish provided it be based on certain healthy principles.

A better future must be based upon a renovation of life itself.

In the past, man's efforts seem to have evolved into opposing directions. On the one hand, he has striven to obtain mastery over the wonderful energy known as thought; on the other, his efforts have ended in suffocation from poison gas and bombs, or poisoning from the fumes of furnaces and factories.

In some of his recent essays on atmospheric dangers, V. Tartarinov has called attention to the many ailments due to negligence on the part of those responsible for the public welfare.

Quite apart from the quality of their foods, which may be good or bad, city dwellers are being systematically poisoned, and the danger would seem to come from the air itself.

All day long, whether in the house or in the street, we are breathing that deadly gas carbon monoxide, the imperceptible and odorless character of which makes it all the more dangerous. It is the gas that emanates from our stoves, that which is often resorted to by suicides; and when formed in large quantities, it is responsible for mine explosions and the death of colliery men.

There is a whole series of industries—chemical, metallurgical, glass, etc.—that suffer in this respect, and the danger exists in all industrial plants where carbon monoxide exceeds the ratio of 1 in 90,000.

Portable stoves, slow combustion stoves, and the kerosene and gas heaters of our bathrooms all constitute a danger and should be carefully regulated.

In the opinion of Prof. Piavo, who has made a special study of this question, the central heating of all houses over fifteen years ought to be carefully overhauled to see if any noxious gas is being emitted.

Dr. Fesange describes two cases of a mysterious ailment in which the patient complained of headaches, fainting, and asthenia, and in which no treatment proved of any avail.

The doctor, then, had an architect called in to repair the central heating, after which the patients quickly recovered.

The closed car, which is all the fashion today, is a real danger. However perfect its construction, it is impossible to prevent a leakage of gas, and this is why women, who are generally more sensitive than men, often complain of dizziness, nausea, and fainting.

The danger, however, exists out of doors as much as within, since the smoke from the city chimneys mixes with the exhaust gases of the motor traffic; so when the streets are narrow and the buildings lofty, the result is particularly harmful.

An analysis of the air in the busy quarters of New York shows that carbon monoxide is present in the proportion of 1 part in 10,000, that is, five times more than is admissible from the hygienic standpoint.

And what is the result of such a poisoning? The greatest danger resides in the fact that its evil effects are hard to trace. In the first place, it has a tendency to aggravate all the ailments of diseases from which an organism may suffer, even those that are latent. Those who suffer from dyspepsia begin to vomit. People troubled with insomnia soon find that their case has become chronic, and those afflicted with rheumatism that their pains are on the increase.

One of the most striking symptoms is a swelling of the stomach, which shows that the organism is striving to protect itself by the deposition of fat. The general effect, then, is so varied and far reaching that we are apt to overlook the cause, which, more often than not, emanates from a badly regulated stove.

Prolonged poisoning by carbon monoxide, however, will produce very serious consequences such as general anemia and angina pectoris, cases of which have already been detected in France and Germany.

In December 1930, all northwest Europe from Finland to the Danube and from the Netherlands to central France was enveloped in a dense fog formed by the mingling of moist sea air with the cold low-lying atmosphere of the Continent. Trains were behind time, radio was held up, and as the visibility did not exceed fifty meters, vessels were tied up in port.

In the happy valley of the Meuse, near to Liege, the situation was tragic. Farmers working in the fields beheld a dense wall of black fog bearing down on them, and many were soon seized with pains in the throat and violent coughing.

Terrified by the sight of this gigantic wall of fog, the people rushed for their houses and many died in violent pain as if they had been burned alive.

The population, seized with panic, remained at home, the windows barricaded with cushions and mattresses. Medical relief services were organized, oxygen tanks placed in the houses and gas masks distributed.

After the fog had gone, trained specialists, with the help of local magistrates, began their investigations. Similar phenomena had already occurred near Liege in 1911 and

1913 when some of the more aged among the miners and many domestic animals succumbed.

On a cloudless spring day in 1925, in the district of Wipperfurth, in the Rhineland, a dense black fog appeared, temperature suddenly dropped, and an odor of sulfur and chlorine filled the air. Scores of people suffered from spasms, and two men who had been gassed in the war succumbed. Many birds died and thousands of fish floated to the surface of the rivers.

All sorts of theories arose to account for this "asthma." Some considered it to be an inflammation of the lungs, although such an epidemic was unknown; others held that it was due to malignant bronchial diseases brought on by dust from the Sahara; while there were many who imagined it arose from poison gas that had been let loose by malevolence.

Whatever be its density or temperature, fog, in itself, is never likely to cause death; but, in this particular case, it had mixed with the poisonous miasmas rising from hundreds of metallurgical and chemical factories in the Meuse valley.

As a rule, such gases are volatile and disperse in the atmosphere. On this occasion, however, a sharp fall in temperature caused them to precipitate and the dense fog that prevented the zinc oxide, sulfur and hydride from evaporating proved fatal to those who breathed it. One should remember that sulfur and hydride mixed with moisture can precipitate sulfuric acid on the earth.

The discharge of poisonous fumes from the Meuse valley is no worse than that of the London industrial zone, but in London the atmosphere is usually warmer so that the warm currents carry off the poisonous gases.

The case of the Meuse valley is, of course, exceptional, but unfortunately, the dwellers in all of our great cities live in the very worst conditions, which, if not so fatal as those of the Meuse valley, are, all the same, highly pernicious.

"Danger from the air" is, as a matter of fact, a very real

danger. Sunspots are not so much to blame as the spots on a man's conscience. The experienced teacher will tell you not to give dangerous playthings to children and the same may be said of the gases and energies that we handle so irresponsibly.

These warnings are not issued by conservative and reactionary minds, but by those who consider that the only progress is that which promotes the health of humanity.

Whole cities are being destroyed today without any declaration of war. As Eden has recently remarked, the time is approaching when people will seek refuge like troglodytes in their caves. They now propose to safeguard museums and churches with sand bags which, in addition to sand, will also contain the disillusions of humanity.

People often speak of hiding art treasures underground and in primitive times we find the same tendency to bury treasures.

Despite all our modem progress it is astonishing that we have to revert to the condition of cave-dwellers and the days of buried treasure.

What is likely to happen to civilization? And why be indignant for the crimes of the past when such revolting practices are going on today?

"Danger from the air" there is no doubt about that! "Danger from hearts of stone" there is much in that too. But where is our Lady of Civilization? Why does she keep silence, why does she tolerate all such horror and destruction?

We should not blame the sunspots, for those on man's conscience are much more dangerous.

"Quicker quicker"—*per aspera ad astra*—to the gateways of Culture."

One of our gifted collaborators writes: "Generally speaking I should like to see everything grievous and difficult for humanity which lies ahead take place more rapidly, so that the united spirit can clear the way for greater speed and enable us to progress to the utmost of our forces. There is so much terror around us, so many signs of evil that I am urged to exclaim 'quicker.' More and more the impatient spirit is dissatisfied, although I am not sure whether this is good or not."

His wide outlook allows him to detect all those accumulations which are beginning to stifle mankind and he wishes to accelerate things.

He tells us that "Diseases are reported to be on the increase and dentists are surprised at the number of cases of inflammation. Snow fell in Paris at the end of May, and in Tokyo there were hailstones of the size of a two shilling piece. A simple peasant some time ago told a friend of mine 'to go abroad,' his instinct told him that it was necessary to get away."

Everywhere today there is confusion. And not only dentists but eye, throat, and lung specialists speak of the increasing number of inflammatory diseases, and cases of heart and tension are common enough.

Our collaborator asks if we have received a book on the Apocalypse. We have not seen it, but all that is taking place today is highly suggestive of the Apocalypse.

We have but to read the articles in our daily papers to meet with apocalyptic signs.

Only those who are blind or deaf are unable to realize the intense nature of the times, so even a simple peasant is urged to emigrate.

All those who are conscious of this not only wish to be on the move but are urged to increase their efforts for the general welfare, to go quicker.

They realize that without extreme measures abscesses cannot be cured, otherwise the infection will only grow all the more serious and finally infect the whole organism.

The experienced surgeon, when he finds that an organism is dangerously infected, wishes to hasten with the operation since he knows that the decomposition that has set in ought be dealt with immediately.

If the simpleminded are urged to abandon civilization, you may be certain that the same sort of depression is present in others.

Many are ready to let everything go, but our collaborator, whose character is naturally constructive, is not willing to lose all, and his desire is to go on with the work of renovation as fast as possible. Let the operation be over and done with so that we can think of the future and strive toward it with strength renewed by danger.

People, when confronted with danger, generally fall into two categories. Some are afraid of thunder and lightning. They stop their ears and after drawing the blinds hide themselves from the magnificent spectacle. Others are too exhilarated and enraptured by the beauty of the storm to care whether the lightning strikes them or not, whereas all who hide themselves away are no doubt concerned about their "precious life."

Imagine these sorts of people in battle and you will find the same evasiveness.

They will shelter themselves behind all sorts of considerations; they will be unwilling to advance, not having had time to decide whether it is really necessary for them to expose themselves to danger. They are never on time and, in fact, will always discover reasons for being late and for evading great achievements.

Tortuous are the ways of evading what is good, and the most sacred principles will not be spared. Just as a madman will show extraordinary resourcefulness and endurance, and a lunatic will be able to cross an abyss on a narrow plank, so will fear drive people to acquire fresh resourcefulness.

Such people are hardly those who cry "quicker, quicker"; on the contrary, they will seek all sorts of pretexts for delay.

They never, as a matter of fact, recognize their own true motives but invent all sorts of excuses and are even ready to abuse those who call out "quicker," all those who are not afraid of lightning.

With such people, this may be due to their natural character or is the result of their remote past; or again, it is the outcome of what weak-willed people have experienced during their lifetime. Perhaps their parents were afraid of thunder and lightning, or the child may have seen others struck down with terror.

From childhood such nightmares must have been making their way into the innermost folds of the spirit; and if there are no examples of courage, valor, and fairness to counterbalance these tendencies, then the spirit succumbs to what is negative.

All this is nothing but the formation of bad habits.

Education should, before all else, aim at eradicating bad habits; and for this, there is nothing like personal examples. Sometimes insignificant bad habits result from serious mistakes, but daily example can drive out these seeds of decadence and even an ailing organism can be cured.

In his later years, Pushkin remembered with gratitude his old nurse for the fairy tales she had taught him. Such tales are wonderfully stimulating because they carry with them an air of adventure and wonder that extends the bounds of the possible.

When you are told, "Do not regret delay," it means that what seemed a delay to you was not so in reality. There can be no harm, however, in wishing to accelerate everything that tends to the general good, but we must remember that we are not the only ones who have difficulties, and that constant vigilance should be our device, since vigilance alone gives that sense of joy that overcomes all the dark ways of life.

When someone exclaims "quicker, quicker," then it means that despite all difficulties ahead of him, he is devoted to the general good.

His cry is not one of despair; it is not one of the sheep that sees the knife held over him; rather is it the lion-like roar of achievement. It is the song of songs, the aspirant cry of "quicker, quicker," the song of the heart, which on earth as in heaven, responds to the same august call of daring.

The post has just brought the newspapers of August 27.

On the first page, there is a message from Reuters: "Japanese using poison gas. Two battalions wiped out on the Kiukiang front. The Chinese Ambassador has informed Lord Halifax that the Japanese are using poison gas on the Kiukiang front and wiped out two Chinese battalions with that on August 22."

And so after all the conferences and treaties on this subject, we have again poison gas and vandalism in all its hideousness. And yet the vandals are not alone responsible, for all those who look on through timidity belong to the same clan.

Our Lady of Civilization! Is it possible, then, that poison gas is allowed in your domains?

HRIDAYA

Carozon, Kokoro, Sin, Al-kulub,
Del, Cor, Njing, Dzuruhe.

IT sounds like an invocation! But thus people call the Heart. India, Spain, Japan, China, Arabia, Persia, Italy, Tibet, and Mongolia.

Heart, Coeur, Herz, Serdze

In all their writings, preserve the memory, shout, and whisper to each other the precious word of the heart.

The three hundred tongues of India and as many in the rest of Asia, and again as many in the Russian vastnesses, and again as many in the Americas, in Africa, and on all the islands proclaim the same concept of fire, love, and heroic achievement. Words fail to describe all the infamies that have spread all over the earth. The wheels of life are covered with mud. And yet, across all trenches, over all obstacles and pitfalls universally resounds the word which signifies the heart—the treasury of Light.

People have come to heartaches. People have covered their hearts with dust and their hearts have grown hairy. Their hearts shriveled in fear and horror. And yet they have not forgotten the word, that will remind them of the heart—the center of life.

At times it seems that all treasures have been desecrated by man. People have slandered the most sacred. The Highest has been belittled, but they have not forgotten the heart—the cradle of love.

People have become enshrouded in darkness. They have blackened their tongues with evil treason. The most valuable vessels have been broken. They have become choked by the vilest malice. But they have kept the memory of the heart—as of the last refuge.

*   *   *

"Coming into a new country, first of all ask, what is the name for the heart? Meeting new people, if even you do not know the sound in which they express their thoughts, point from your heart to theirs. Almost everybody will respond to this testimony of sincerity; only a few will be surprised or perhaps will feel ashamed, and only very few will become indignant. Remember that those who become indignant are in their actions evil people. Do not expect friendship or goodwill from them—they are already decaying."

*   *   *

There is as yet no institute devoted to the Heart. There are, of course, entire large institutions dedicated to the fighting of the various scourges of humanity, but there are no special institutions that study this most important moving factor of life. Gradually very important experiments on the heart are being achieved. News has just been received from Italy that a heart, which had stopped beating, has been brought back to life. At Milan on February 21, a person whose death had been attested by the medical personnel of the Milan Hospital was brought back to life by an injection of adrenalin. All newspapers are full with the particulars of this case.

The patient suffered from a complicated form of heart disease and was treated by all means available to science. But in spite of all precautionary measures, he died. Although the physicians were fully convinced that death had actually taken place, yet one of them made an injection of adrenalin by way of an experiment. After thirty minutes, the heart began to beat feebly, and in a few hours it was working normally; and at present, the physicians are in a position to state that the patient is out of danger.

Similar actions of adrenalin were known before; it remains to investigate how, in itself, this powerful substance will react upon the function of the organism. Many cases are known that when a fatal issue was prevented by an injection of adrenalin, it brought but a short postponement of death. And it was noticed—I speak in this particular case of children— that nervousness increased and, at times, became difficult to control. This perhaps was due to entirely different causes, but the above-mentioned makes us think over the use of this radical remedy.

Folk medicine often reports cases of cures by most unexpected means. And usually these unforeseen and at times strange remedies remain without proper investigation and are lost in the realm of anecdotes.

I recall how in the family of a priest, a child died from suffocation following croup. The priest in despair took the body of the child and ran with it into the church, toward the altar, where he began praying in frenzied exaltation. It so happened that the child had its head hanging down and his father, not knowing it, was shaking the child violently by its feet. Suddenly a large clot of hardened mucus came out of the child's throat, and it coughed and began to breathe. The heart had slowly returned to life.

Think how many multiform manifestations of apparent death may take place! History reports infinite cases of reawakened dead. Various forms of lethargy have been observed and, after all, cannot be properly determined. Why does the life functioning suddenly stop? Why do the dead again return and, even under such unbelievable circumstances, often after burial? Of course, there are many explanations to this. But until the world of the heart will be properly investigated, until then, these will be only fortunate or sad occurrences.

Of course, the profound life of the heart is perhaps the most difficult one to be described in words. Precisely the heart must be studied, not only in pain and anguish but in its healthy state. If the nervous system of plants reacts to the most minute changes of temperature, to distant clouds, to the slightest touch, then how many more beautiful and remarkable resoundings and pulsations take place in the heart. Besides, it is difficult to say what is a healthy and what is a diseased state of the heart. It is known that many die quickly from heart attacks, having yet a so-called sound heart; whereas others, long ago given up as cardiac catastrophes, live long, very long.

The pulse does not express itself only in a number of beats but first of all in its quality, and this quality of heart-beats is but little examined and explained. When one says: "Guard your heart," that means, first of all, not to become irritated, not to get angry; and on the other hand, do not feel sad and do not fall into despondency.

Every minutest detail of life will resound first of all not in the brain but in the heart. Precisely the heart realizes and responds to the most distant earthquakes, as the best seismograph. But it is not customary to consult one's heart. It is not customary to consider it as the receptacle of the most High. And when people read direct advices about the importance of such aspirations, they are being condemned as being abstract, abstract, as being invented by some inaccessible ascetics and as being inapplicable. And yet it can be always applied to that which is taking place in the heart, if only one would listen to it frankly and sincerely.

A man who is confident that he does not notice many quite realistic manifestations, first of all does not wish to notice them. He presupposes, in his haughtiness, that nothing will take place, that he will hear nothing and that nothing will disturb his peace. Precisely conceit prevents man from perceiving reality. At times the heart beats like a sledgehammer upon a darkened consciousness. A man is ready to pour upon his heart all kinds of poisons in order to stifle it. And he will not think what may be the cause that his heart is so excited, what bad or good has taken place, what usefulness or what harm has caused the knocking.

The smallest to the highest—all is contained within the heart. It resounds to everything that lives. Touching and wise are the ancient remindings of the great significance of the heart.

"The spirit, which is in my heart, is smaller than a

grain of rice, smaller than a grain of barley, smaller than a mustard seed, and smaller than the smallest seed of grain. And yet the same spirit that lives in my heart is greater than the entire earth, greater than space, greater than heaven, and greater than all the worlds.

"The messenger of all action, all desire, all perception, smell, taste, all-embracing, silent, distant—such is the spirit that abides in my heart. This is Brahman Himself. He who says, "I follow him who exists from this world," truly there is no doubt for him."

Thus says the *Chandogya Upanishad.*

YOUTH

THE youth is attacked from many sides. It is whispered: "Youth is absorbed by sport"; "It has turned away from humanitarian sciences and is engrossed in materialistic technicalities"; "It neglects the purity of language and spoils the speech with horrible slang"; "It has deserted its family"; "It prefers jazz"; "It avoids lectures"; "It does not love the book and does not like to read." A lot of awful things are said about the youth. Of course, in every single case there has been some reason for such accusation. Even in the daily press, one may find facts as if supporting them. Let us even admit that to some extent, this is so. But if we look at the causes, we find that, before accusing the youth, we must first call to answer the elder generation.

Is there much sincerity in the family? Is the home life always attractive? Is it possible to express serious striving under contemporary conditions? Is there much upliftment and high aspiration in the routine housework? Does the elder generation devote itself to humanitarian ideals? Who laid the first path toward materialism? Who filled the home with poisonous tobacco smoke? Was it the youth that introduced alcohol into the home? Has the family time to listen to the quest of the youth? Does the family strive into the future? Where is born indifference to good and evil? Where is the birthplace of slander, bad language, and gossip? Where has the youth heard for the first time blasphemous jokes? Where did they hear for the first time of destruction and not of upbuilding and creativeness?

Hence, instead of accusing the youth, let us realize where the hotbeds of this misfortune are hidden.

Let us ask ourselves: "Do we know the really hardworking youth?" Of course, we do.

"Do we know the self-sacrificing youth who gives to the family all of his earnings?" Of course, we do.

"Do we know the youth who is sincerely and ardently dreaming of a beautiful future?" Of course, we do.

"Do we know the youth who craves for serious books and inspiring discussions?" Of course, we do.

"Do we know the youth who knows how to live in harmony and mutual trust?" Of course, we do.

"Do we know the youth who has consecrated himself to the service of the Beautiful? Of course, we do.

Thus pondering over the best heights of humanity, we shall also find on every summit some of the best young souls. And this radiant ascension of youth takes place not only in one country—they symbolize our present age all over the world.

Greetings to all young coworkers! We rejoice to witness many most enlightened associations of youth, who struggle toward Light in strenuous efforts. How heartily they strive toward the highest aims of mankind. We know what hardships they have to overcome. We know how they have to rise above local and family circumstances and yet they find inexhaustible strength to go by the higher path. And on all their trails they affirm blessed milestones. And all this common good is accomplished amid indescribable difficulties. And still attainment takes place; and when one wishes to think of something touchingly joyful, one recalls these affirmations of the young generation.

Another instance of harmony among youth comes to mind. I remember how in a huge, stern city, the young, after hard work for their daily bread, gathered gaily in the evening, dressed in their best, hastening to partake of the living water of philosophy, science, and art. They were so accustomed to joint activities that they even tried to live in small communities.

We recall three rooms. In them live eight girls. All of them are hard workers. One is a shopgirl, one a secretary, one a stenographer and, the others work in factories. We asked them:

"For how long have you already lived together?"

—"For three years."

"And how often did you quarrel?"

—They laugh. . . . "Never!"

It is not a miracle! People of various professions can live harmoniously together, can after the day's difficult work, despite being tired, gather together; and they do not fight, but they revive and enrich each other through an exchange of lofty ideals. What inspiring and convincing affirmations one can hear from the youth. Who strives in highest enthusiasm to truth and is indignant at injustice if not young hearts! For thirty-two years at the head of schools, I am connected with the youth and no unhappy recollections have marred my contact.

If we shall judge the young without prejudice, we shall find many beautiful signs of self-sacrifice, striving toward knowledge, love, and beauty. Those who are in the habit of condemning youth should beware of senile babbling. These desperate condemners see that life today is in confusion and ugly misunderstanding. But when they try to find the guilty, they usually, excusing themselves, look for the easiest scapegoat. They see only the results but avoid thinking of the causes. These causes are quite curable if properly treated by the entire society.

If every unprejudiced observer would find the many numerous, beautiful, and touching examples in favor of the youth, then it would not be difficult to arouse public opinion to appreciate precisely these manifestations of good. The young people, even though inexperienced, yet courageously and self-sacrificingly oppose the dark forces; and, therefore, those who consider themselves wise should sincerely support every noble effort of the youth. But one can support only through examples in life. No abstract nagging will give a harvest. Only actions and deeds, living examples, can convince.

If youth itself realizes the joy of work and inspiring

communion, then the more so should the wise elders encourage exactly this joy. One should not coldly condemn that which has given such beautiful evidence. If because of our times, everybody finds it difficult, then one should jointly try to transmute these difficulties into joy. The young hearts understand this. Therefore, let us help in every way that the youth may meet on the path of bliss and inspiration.

One may equalize everything by the lowest, but such equality is tantamount to degeneration. But, every equalizing by the highest will be true progress. In many parts of the world, there exists a legend that because of one righteous man an entire city was saved. This legend, which is so beautifully and multiformly expounded, shows that in everything, quality is valuable and not quantity. Consequently, every good example outshines the negative suppositions.

The seal of the age is created by all nations and, therefore, the easier it is to gather good signs. In various languages, in various customs, these hieroglyphs of good are highly inspiring.

A child tries to reach a postbox to push a letter into it. A passerby wants to help him, and notices on the envelope, which was obviously made by the child itself, the scribbling: "To Saint Nicholas," and asks: "What is this?" —"Mummy is dying and nobody wishes to help her."

In such an amazing way, the heart of the child prayed to Saint Nicholas and received a response and help. Thus the young and youthful find the way to the highest.

CHAUVINISM

CHAUVINISM is a dangerous epidemic, which is unfortunately spreading throughout the civilized world. In many countries today, nationalism is only another name for chauvinism. Everything good and bad immediately makes its influence felt in the domain of culture. Nationalism, which has become chauvinism, must eventually lead to the decay of art and science. We are even told that every country ought to have its own culture and science, as if art and science, which are universal, could be fitted into the narrow frame of nationalism.

But who would undertake to deprive art and science of their universal character? As a Russian, I can speak for Russia, which has never known of chauvinism either in the past or present. We should always remember how hospitable Russia always was, not only in the great days of Kiev, but in the post-Petrian period, and always ready to assimilate foreign cultures.

In the Tretiakov Moscow Art Gallery, there is an important foreign section.

The Hermitage, which contains a splendid collection of old masters, is one of the treasure places of the world. The collections of Stchukin, Morozov, Terestchenko, Princess Tenishev, and a host of other Russian collectors contain many masterpieces of foreign art. No one ever objected to this influx of foreign art. On the contrary, the younger generation rejoiced at the opportunity to study foreign masterpieces from both East and West.

Nor did Russian art suffer from this abundance of foreign art. Where the soul of a people is strong, there is little danger of imitation or loss of character; for being in itself creative, it is able to assimilate almost anything.

Like a healthy organism, it will come to digest everything that is given it and, at the same time, express the soul of its people. On the other hand, chauvinism must be considered as the hallmark of envy or timidity.

The name of Siam has recently been changed to Maung-Tai, because Siam is a foreign word. Perhaps the new name carries with it magical powers for the good. Maps are now altered almost every year, and students have a hard time keeping up with all the changes that are going on. Greece may come to change its name to Hellas, and if this could produce artists and philosophers as in classic times, we should not object. If such changes are due to chauvinism, then they are deplorable like so many other manifestations of our time. In ancient times Paris was known as Lutetia, and many English cities bore Roman names. We cannot imagine, however, the name of Paris being changed to some ancient Gallic name just to satisfy some political prejudice.

Fortunately, the word "chauvinism" has never been much in honor, and like those other "isms"-alcoholism and narcotism-it always arouses a sense of shame.

It would be interesting to discover in what circumstances, and by whom the word "chauvinism" was invented. We have heard that the guillotine was invented for the sake of mercy. Perhaps chauvinism was created then, in order to promote the triumph of culture.

DANGEROUS DISEASES

THE *Chinese Hospital Dialogue* advises:
"Doctor, when I have formed a habit, is it hard to break?"

"I think if you are in earnest, it can be done. As the proverb says: 'There is nothing difficult in the world except the fear of an insincere heart.'"

It is most touching to see that a modern hospital book closes on such a wise proverb. Verily, remove fear and insincerity, and at once the heart will recuperate. How many dangerous diseases have been caused by ignorance and its children: fear, covetousness, and malice. As the next progeny of these, we find the creeping asp of slander.

Slander is the transmission of a lie. It makes no difference whether the lie is transmitted in light-mindedness or malice or ignorance—its seeds will be equally destructive. I recall the remarkable reply of Kuindji, who himself was against every form of lying. Kuindji was on bad terms with Diaghilev. A certain artist, knowing this and probably anticipating that Kuindji would enjoy a bad report about Diaghilev, told Kuindji some ugly gossip about Diaghilev. Kuindji listened patiently and then interrupted the artist with a thunderous exclamation: "You are a slanderer!" The man who had transmitted this gossip, after such an unexpected defeat, tried to justify himself by saying that he did not make up that gossip, but that he only transmitted it "for information, without even a bad thought." But Kuindji was adamant, he continued to look grimly at the unfortunate informer and repeated: "You brought me this vile news. Consequently it is you who are the slanderer!"

How many of such self-justifying slanderers intrude upon an atmosphere of creativeness. They scatter the most poisonous seeds and try to cover themselves with the shield of non-responsibility. They, as if, did not think of any consequences; they only repeated it for information, as if every slander and lie is not being repeated "for information" only.

It is not sufficiently emphasized that slander and lies are ugly. It is not pointed out that these fragments of darkness encumber and poison space. It would seem that people should know well how anger and irritation poison the system, but then every liar and slanderer in some measure sinks into lethal hatred and first of all poisons himself. Hatred also lives around jealousy and ignorance and around that same perversity of the thinking apparatus, which is so difficult to heal. A child may be unsociable, queer, suspicious, but it is not born hating; this evil quality is taken up from the many examples set by the elders.

"Slander, slander—something will always remain!" What malicious care is expressed, in order that something hateful should remain. In this manner certain people are more concerned with the preservation of evil than of good. The good in some measure will always be selfless; whereas evil, first of all, is egotistic. And if a man will begin to assure that he has committed something evil for the sake of good, believe him not; undoubtedly he wanted to justify his selfhood or tried to distinguish himself selfishly in the eyes of a superior.

One has to be surprised how weak are the laws that punish slander. In some countries the persecution of slander is almost impossible. One can convince oneself only, that not by laws that persecute slander but by preventive measures, one may considerably weaken this poisonous asp. This also may be attained in schools; but still more so, this can be achieved in home life. Exclude from the family circle all trifling gossip, and you will save the younger generation from committing great slander. If youngsters do not hear from childhood any mutual accusations nor any seeds of gossip and slander, they simply will not respond to this type of "recreation."

If at home there is no card playing, then the first foundations of their character will form themselves without the necessity of murdering the most precious time. The future of family life very much depends upon the parents themselves. Perhaps precisely now one is led to remind of the hereditary possibilities of the family, for very often instead of an attractive principle, the family creates but a repulsive element. And there, wherein lies repulsion alone, there—because of the absence of attraction—lies the beginning of chaos.

Gossip and slander—what an infamy!

There are many epidemics. It has gradually become evident that not only the generally accepted scourges, such as the plague, cholera, and the other infectious diseases, but also many other illnesses are contagious. And what if slander also represents a contagious manifestation and moreover an epidemic one? There are many forms of very contagious psychosis. History continuously mentions facts of mass psychosis, which at times took really threatening dimensions.

If one were to investigate the sources of slander, one would no doubt find that in a pure, worthy, and cultural atmosphere, slander does not thrive. Observe the home as well as the social atmosphere of notorious slanderers, and you will find the real seat of this dangerous psychosis. Even ordinary falsehood is not pronounced everywhere. There are such places in the world and such persons in the presence of whom the slanderer and liar feels himself so uncomfortable that he will not dare to resort to his favorite *mal* parlance. But where slander is pronounced lightly, there look for an old, established evil. The microbes of slander feel themselves there greatly at home.

Let us not feel astonished if among works on psychic diseases there will appear real medical treatises on slander, on its causes and methods of propagation and, let us also hope about preventive measures.

One thing is clear—that, if life is in need of newly affirmed foundations, then first of all, all fatal epidemics must be overcome. Among these scourges of mankind special attention will be paid to the multiformity of psychosis. Curing drunkards, drug-addicts, thieves, and all criminals in the field of sexual perversity will no doubt lead also to the cure of one of the worst perversities—the vice of slander.

It will be noticed how different perversities manifest themselves simultaneously. When observing a slanderer or a notorious liar, you will find that the rest of his life is not pure. Undoubtedly he will be subject to other forms of criminality. In the future, state hospitals, besides the wards for drug addicts, drunkards, thieves, and other criminals, there will be one for the most dangerous infectious disease—the ward for slanderers.

And old English law provides that precisely slanderers are punishable by flogging. But let us leave it to the *psychiaters* to decide, what measure of healing is best suitable for such a dangerous and abhorrent disease.

When one acquaints oneself with the Pasteur Institute, one will probably be asked not to remain too long in one of the laboratories. You will be warned: "Here are especially dangerous microbes." In the future, psychiatric hospital visitors will be asked to leave a certain ward more quickly, and it will be added: "The microbes of slander are very contagious!"

LAUDABLE ENEMIES

IN the American monthly *Inspiration*, there has appeared an article under the thought-provoking title "I Was Kicked Upstairs by My Enemies." The author tells us how his actual success in life was due to his feud. The story begins:

"Have you ever noticed how opposition sometimes is the making of a man? How enemies sometimes succeed only in 'boosting' the man they try to 'break'? As president of a successful company in the office equipment field, I am what I am largely because some business enemies of mine hatched a plot to throw me out of their way and start me 'on the toboggan.' It is all very pleasant now to contemplate serenely the course of events, from my vantage point in the president's office; but it was a far cry from pleasure during the miserable years I spent when I was their near-victim. I was a half-demented man for a few months, while I thrashed around as helplessly as a trout caught squarely on the hook of a beautifully colored fly. Yes, beautifully colored fly is a good parallel. My enemies did a very good job of it. They won their game with me in every way for several years. But, as I say, I can now sit here serenely and ask: 'Where are they?' They got what they wanted and found it different from what they expected; whereas I got what I didn't want and have made a lot out of it—more than I had ever hoped for." And the author concludes his instructive narrative: "I regard these 'enemies' simply as chessmen in the game of life, who, by attempting to checkmate me, were themselves relegated to the rear. I sharpened my wits on them and used their villainy to step forward. I am firmly convinced that opposition and impending disaster frequently draw qualities out of a man that he did not know he possessed; and sometimes as I look at my sixteen-year-old son and feel inclined to shelter him from troubles and from enemies, I wonder whether this is not a complete mistake. Throughout nature, one sees how opposition develops qualities, and I doubt whether man is an exception. I can say with a significant meaning: 'Thank God for my enemies'; they most magnanimously kicked me so far upstairs that I now stand far above them."

How many such significant cases take place continuously! One can always say to the enemies: You will impede and we shall build. You will delay the structure and we shall temper our skill. You will aim all your arrows and we shall uplift our shields. While you will compose subtle strategies, we shall already occupy a new site. And where we shall have but one way, you will have, in persecution, to try hundreds. Your trenches will but point out to us the mountain path. And when we direct our movements, you will have to compile a voluminous book of denials. But we shall be unimpeded by these compilations.

Truly, it is not pleasant for you to enumerate all that is done against your regulations. Your fingers will become numb, as you count upon them all cases of forbiddances and denials. Yet at the end of all actions, the strength will remain with us because we dispelled fear and acquired patience, and we can no longer be disappointed. And we will smile at each of your grimaces, your schemes, and your silences. And this, not because we are specially anointed but because we do not love the dictionaries of negation. And we enter each battle only on a constructive plan.

For the hundredth time we smilingly say: "Thanks to you, enemies and persecutors. You have taught us resourcefulness and indefatigability. Thanks to you, we have found glorious mountains with inexhaustible beds of ore. Thanks to your fury, the hoofs of our horses are shod with pure silver, beyond the means of our persecutors. Thanks to you, our tents glow with a blue light.

You yearn to learn who we are in reality, where are our dwellings, who are our fellow voyagers because you have invented so many slanders about us that you yourselves are hopelessly entangled. Where is the limit?

At the same time, several keen people insist that it is not only useful but highly profitable for you to go our way, and that no one who has walked with us has lost anything but has rather received new possibilities.

Would you know where is our dwelling place? We have many homes in many lands, and vigilant friends guard our dwellings. We will not divulge their names, nor shall we probe into the habitation of your friends. Nor shall we seek to convert them. Many are travelling with us and in all corners of the world, upon the heights flame friendly beacon fires. Around them the benevolent traveler will always find a place. And verily, travelers hasten to them. For besides the printed word and the post, communications are dispatched by invisible forces; and with one sigh, joy, sorrow, and help are transported through the world fleeter than the wind. And like a fiery wall stand the battlements of friends.

This is such a significant time. You need not hope to attract to your cause many youths, for they also are the designated ones. In the most varied countries they also are thinking of one thing—and they easily find the key to the mystery. This mystery leads youth to the glorious beacon fire, and our youth now is aware that the cruel every day can be transformed into a festival of labor, love, and achievement. They have the consciousness that something glorious and radiant is ordained for them. And from that mighty fire, none can repulse them.

We have known those who after their hours of labor, come silently, asking us how to live. And their hands, reddened from toil, nervously twitch over the whole list of necessary, unuttered problems. To these hands one does not give a stone instead of the bread of knowledge.

We remember how in twilight they came, beseeching us not to depart. One could not tell these young friends that it was not away from them that we were departing, but for their sake we were going in order to bring them the treasure casket.

And now you denying ones, you again ask how we can understand each other without disputes. Thus a friend contributes that which is most needed; a friend does not waste time. Thus is the quarrel transformed into a discussion. And the most primitive sense of rhythm and measure is being transformed into the discipline of freedom. And the comprehension of unity, which doubts not but searches for illumination, transforms all life. And then, there is still some word that you can find only yourself, consciously unwavering and righteously striving.

Often you are angry and lose your temper, but you should be just the opposite. You slander and condemn, and, through this, you fill the air with boomerangs that afterward snap your own forehead. "Poor Makar" complains at the cones which painfully strike him, but he has strewn them himself.

You do not object to becoming important and to surrounding yourself with presumption, forgetting that self-importance is the surest sign of vulgarity. Now you speak of science and yet new experiments appear suspicious to you.

Now you laugh about seclusion and you yourself do not realize the most practical usages of the laboratory of life. You yourself are seeking to escape as soon as possible from an overly smoky room.

You often hide yourself and express doubt, while doubt is the most insidious poison invented by vicious beings. Now you doubt and betray, and do not wish to learn that both of these negations are the product of ignorance, which is in no way akin to children—on the contrary, it grows with years into a very ugly garden.

Now you are shocked if you are accused of prejudices, while your entire life is crowded with them. And you will not concede one of your customary habits, which are obscuring the most simple, practical understanding. You fear so much to become ridiculous, that you provoke smiles. And you are shocked at the call: Be new! Be new! Not as on a stage, but in your own life.

You value property as highly as if you were preparing to take it with you to the grave. You do not like to hear the talk of death because it still exists for you, and you have given to cemeteries a great portion of the world. And you carefully outline your ritual of funeral processions as though this procedure was worthy of the greatest attention. And you eschew the word attainment because for you it is linked with conventionalities. According to your ideas it is a strange and improper matter to be occupied in life with these ideals of attainment in service for humanity.

Nor let us even mention your deep reverence for financial matters. It is not only a necessity with you, but a cult is contained for you in the sham formulae of the contemporary world. You dream to gild your rusty shield. But while you will evoke the destruction, we will turn toward creative Lakshmi.

Just now evil is active and the Star of the Mother of the world surrounds the earth with its rays of future creations.

You accuse us of nebulous inconsistencies, but we are occupied with the most practical experiments. And how silently are our friends working, searching for the means of new experiments for good!

In irritation you named our discoveries "panther's leaps." You were ever ready to judge us utterly without knowledge of what we are doing. Although you pretend to condemn those who speak of that which they do not know, yet you yourself are acting so. Where is that justice for which you have sewn such clumsy theatrical togs for yourself? When, to your joy, you believe that we have disappeared, we will be again approaching by a new path. However, let us not quarrel; we must even praise you. Your activity is useful to us, and all your most cunning schemes give us the possibility of continuing the most instructive of chess-games.

And if a constructive goodwill shall be promoted even by you, laudable enemies, let this be so, if only the blessed construction benefits thereby.

Light conquers darkness!

MOLOCH

(Diary Leaves)

IN the autumn of 1929, America presented a horrible spectacle. After a number of prosperous years when prices soared and crowds had flocked to Moloch of the Stock Exchange, the whole structure collapsed and ruin was spread abroad on all hands.

People began to lose millions a day: suicides took place everywhere and a general atmosphere of madness reigned.

Our Institution had been receiving millions in the way of donations; but after the disaster, one of the donors exclaimed: "We have only a hundred and fifty dollars left."

Catastrophes of this sort are supposed to take place every seven years in America, and one can imagine the effect that they are likely to have on the people's character.

It is strange that they do not profit from such warnings. So soon as the *Danse Macabre* is over, they again begin to sacrifice to Moloch.

We had to sell a collection of Old Masters that had been kept for the Museum. It contained excellent primitives, one of which went to the Chicago Museum. Rubens, Van Dyck and the elder Bruegel were some of the pictures in this collection.

In going through life, one has to accustom oneself, I suppose, to all that is terrible, and to the horrible spectacle of a whole country collapsing due to mass madness and to those wolfish appetites that beget calamity.

What then becomes of culture or even civilization? Spontaneous combustion takes place, the undergoers rise in revolt, and one has to pass through a reappraisal of values so as to get some idea of what is relative.

We can only have pity for those innocent victims who because of the sins of their fathers are plunged into the fiery pit of ruin. One can imagine how Armageddon rages and how the adversaries work. There are many horrible spectacles, but the thirty pieces of silver is the worst of all.

We have been told that Rockefeller, when thanked for some philanthropic gift replied: "If this ribbon were merely on account of the money, it would be worth little."

Not many would have said that. Few realize that the dollar is not the king, but that there is another standard, the true one!

Let us hope that after Armageddon, all Molochian calamities will be averted.

THE SELLING OF SOULS

WHAT misery there is in the world today. From all sides comes news of destruction, persecution, and man-made disasters; and this is not all, for there are still other evils in this age of civilization, which can hardly be called an age of culture!

Many shameful proceedings are going on under high-sounding names. We hear of the "adjustment of frontiers" of "union" and, in fact of everything except "annexation." In all this, there is a veritable traffic of human souls.

We rarely hear of war, but the term "pacification" is used with dissimulation and hypocrisy in order to conceal its aggressive character and the fact that it is made to cover the traffic of human souls. Imagine the tragic situation of a citizen who is suddenly told that he belongs to a different nationality, and that if he wishes to save himself he must renounce his ancestry and traditions and adopt an alien way of life. He will be told that his country has ceased to exist and that he now belongs to a conquering newcomer. You will be told that this sort of thing has always gone on, that conquests are inevitable, and people are ready to accuse the past of barbarism and speak of the present as if it were an era of civilization or even culture.

They will tell you that under the influence of philosophy, human nature has at last become refined and that the worst sorts of crime are impossible and that we no longer live according to the law of the jungle. This is by no means true, since people are quite ready today to pervert scientific discovery to the purpose of killing or enslaving.

Men are able to fly, but what do they carry and for what end do they construct huge air fleets? Is it for progress or for criminal ends?

There can be little doubt; all this speeding up, this manufacture of bombs and poison gas is not for mutual goodwill.

It would be hypocritical to speak of savage races today, unless the term be applied to all those who do not wear starched collars. If the soul of civilized man were to be weighed against the soul of so-called savages we might get a surprise.

Under crafty methods there is going on a veritable traffic in human souls, and if it continues we shall have to admit that slave trading is being carried out by civilized countries. This may at first seem exaggerated, but is it? Has humanity renounced violence? No, it has only remained silent or given a hypocritical definition of such invasions. In a street accident, many will steer clear, others become curious, and only a very few will hasten to help. And so we look on at the destruction of valuable treasures, at the horrors of slaughter and the misery of thousands, and say nothing.

The newspapers refrain from commenting on the grounds that should they object, it would only make matters worse. Man has discovered his wings too soon, and they are destined to bring him to violence and infamy rather than to enlightenment. Many a volume has been written to denounce slavery; and in any gathering if you were to ask for those who were its advocates, you would get no answer. Even those engaged in it, at the present time, do not like to admit it, and yet the present traffic is something even worse than open slavery. There have been a thousand societies formed to promote peace, and among the members you will find the owners of munition factories who if they talk much of peace and goodwill are not averse to trading in human souls. With their sharp claws, they mark off fresh boundaries on the map, cutting out all the interests of the soul, which they hold in such contempt.

Scientific research as well as all disinterested efforts tend toward a better future and not toward slave traffic. We often hear of evolution, enlightenment, and a new life, but this will be impossible to achieve through the bartering of souls. Old and young as well as those in their prime are being bartered, and the rising generation already realizes that they have been subject to violence. They will write of this, and the children of the future will learn much about such terrors.

Under hypocritical phases, the traffic in human souls still goes forward. Could there possibly be a greater calamity?

STEADFASTNESS

I RECALL an unforgettable episode from my first exhibition in America. In one of the large cities, a local collector of art and wealthy patron arranged a festive dinner in my honor. Everything was luxurious and on a large scale, and the best people of the city were present. As usual, many speeches were delivered. The host and hostess, both already gray-haired, joyfully and cordially entertained the guests. Everything was magnificently arranged, and the hostess drew my attention to die rooms which were decorated in blue and purple flowers and said: "It is precisely these shades that I adore so much in your paintings."

After dinner one of the lady guests present said to me: "This is indeed a remarkable reception," and added confidentially: "Probably this is the last dinner in this home."

I looked at my neighbor in the greatest amazement, and she, lowering her voice, continued: "Don't you know that our host is absolutely ruined and just yesterday he lost his last three millions?"

Naturally I was shocked, but my neighbor explained: "Of course, it is not easy for him, especially considering his age. He is already seventy-four."

But the apparent steadfastness and calmness of the host and hostess and all the surroundings were in obvious contradiction with this revelation. After this conversation I began to take special interest in the host's fate. Three months after this dinner, they had already moved to their former garage. It seemed that everything was lost; but after three years, this art patron was again a millionaire and again lived in a palatial home.

When I spoke to his friends about my astonishment, asking why his numerous acquaintances and after all the city itself, to which he had donated such huge sums, did not help him, I was told:

"First of all, he would not have accepted any help, and secondly, he is used to such financial storms." This last conversation took place in a large club, where near tall windows in easy chairs were sitting many distinguished members, reading newspapers and talking. My friend, pointing at them, said:

"These are all millionaires. Ask how often every one of them ceased to be a millionaire and then became one again. Just guess who of them is at present on the top of the wave and who is nearing the abyss."

And the club members continued to read quietly and to chat joyfully, as if no troubles ever disturbed them. I asked my friend how he explained such a remarkable state of mind. He shook his shoulder and replied with one word: "Steadfastness."

Verily, the concept of steadfastness should be greatly stressed amid other basic principles of life. Virility is one, goodwill and friendliness is another. Desire to work is a third. Perseverance and inexhaustibility is a fourth. Enthusiasm and optimism is a fifth. But amid all these foundations and many other necessary creative conceptions, steadfastness always remains as a firm cornerstone, giving impulse and success to all progress.

Steadfastness is the result of true equilibrium, which has Libra as its symbol. Such equilibrium is not a heartless calculation, neither despising the surroundings, neither conceit nor selfishness. Steadfastness always stands in relation to responsibility and a sense of duty. Steadfastness will not lose balance, will not slip nor waver. Those who advanced firmly up to the last hour are always steadfast.

In our days of confusion, disillusion, and narrow distrust, the quality of steadfastness is especially blissful. When people so easily become panic-stricken, only a steadfast person can lead with a healthy understanding and can thus save many from the horror of drowning in chaos. When people try to convince themselves of all sorts of prejudice, mirages, and other nonsense, only a firm person can decide in his heart where there is a safe exit. When people become crazy, then even a short squall appears to them like an endless horrible storm. And only steadfastness will remind one of true co-measurement.

Perhaps someone will say that steadfastness is nothing else than common sense. But it will be more correct to say that from common sense, steadfastness is born. The concept of steadfastness is already an expression of reality. Steadfastness is required precisely here on the earthly plane, where there are so many circumstances against which one has to hold out. Therefore, it is so useful, amid many concepts of goodwill, cooperation, and progress to understand the value of steadfastness. Not without reason is it always appreciated how firmly a person stood against certain attacks, strain, and unexpected blows. In such cases vigilance and presence of mind are praiseworthy, but steadfastness will also be acclaimed as something positive and victorious.

As an example of steadfastness, I recall a story that I heard in San Francisco.

A foreigner had arrived. Apparently he was wealthy. He was received everywhere in society. He acquired many friends. He won the reputation of being a good, wealthy, and kindhearted fellow. Once he asked his new friends to lend him ten thousand dollars for a new business. Something curious, though very usual, happened. All of his friends found sufficient reason to refuse his request. More than that, everywhere people showed coldness toward him and some even turned away. Then this foreigner went to visit another person who from the very beginning had been rather formal toward him. He explained his project and asked for a loan of ten thousand. This time the checkbook appeared at once on the table, and the required amount was handed over to him. The next day the foreigner again came to see the same person. The latter asked: "What has happened? Did you miscalculate the amount? Perhaps you need more?" But the foreigner took the check from his pocket and returned it to its previous owner saying:

"No, I need no money. What I need is a partner, and I invite you to join me." And they founded a company that became very prosperous.

And to all other so-called friends, who again smiled most friendly, the foreigner said:

"You have fed me with your dinners. Remember, my table is always served for you."

Dr. J. L. knows this story.

How many instructive experiences are given by life itself! Imagination is nothing else but recollection.

VANDALS

THINGS are beginning to be chaotic and unsettled on this earth. The planet has never been very stable; but at the present moment, there would seem to be, according to the reports, a sort of whirlwind of destruction.

From Europe one of our friends writes: "Today we saw a film, taken in Spain which showed the destruction caused by air raids over Barcelona. The effect was very depressing. Immense buildings were cut in two, as if by a knife; one of these was pulverized, the other still stood with all its rooms open to view and occupied, and one could see the corpses lying everywhere. There was a school that showed how scores of children had been slain, and on the half-demolished platform, the dead body of the teacher. The Spanish Government has arranged an exhibition to show how artistic and historic treasures were destroyed, together with the measures adopted for their preservation. These consist of the exportation of transportable art treasures and the protection of the historic monuments by means of sandbags. No doubt you have also read the plan of "Geneva Refuges" for children and aged people, all of which, however, is only a palliative. Not long ago, at a banquet of the Institute of Higher International Studies, it was agreed that our Pact would be preferable to such measures because of its moral and cultural value. At the same time, everyone agreed that its eventual adversaries, whom we know by their action in Spain, China, and Ethiopia, will not hesitate to violate the Pact or the General Convention of the Red Cross."

In Red Cross circles, they are quite convinced of this.

Thus humanity has so far deviated from the principles of culture and civilization that even the Red Cross is beginning to lose its significance.

And here is another letter. "All the strange discussions in matters of defense that are going on today having nothing in common with our Pact. We are speaking of an international cultural agreement on a humanitarian line while they speak of sandbags."

The idea of burying lofty cathedrals under sandbags is as absurd as to speak of abolishing the Red Cross and wrapping every soldier up in sand bags. The idea of burying national treasures, moreover, has a prehistoric flavor about it. Recently, one of the English ministers, Mr. Eden, foresaw that, in the future, terrified city folk might be obliged to flee to the caves and cellars like the troglodytes of old. Let the worldy-minded, then, adopt such primitive methods and bury their treasures.

All this, however, is so far from the spirit of our Pact that it would be a very easy matter to show our priority and the little value such measures have when compared with a cult for the art treasures of all mankind.

Caricaturists could find matter in these methods, for they might depict a cathedral smothered up to the spires in sandbags, so as to illustrate the biblical warning: "Build not upon the sand."

If humanity is to abandon all its highest principles and stake all its hope on sandbags, then it has come to a very sorry pass.

Everything today justifies us and our friends in issuing a call to defend all national treasures. It is said that when the ostrich gets wind of danger, it thrusts its head beneath its wing or in the sand. Natural history is full of such examples, and we might do worse than study the life of ants and bees who possess superb organization.

In every periodical we look at today we come across illustrations of barbarous destruction. Such documents will continue to live as a shameful witness of what has been done by the humanity of our times, although the whole of mankind is, of course, not necessarily engrossed in such destruction. But such acts are being perpetrated before the eyes of all, and when we figure the percentage of those who raise their voices to protest, it is not overwhelming. In any street accident, you will find four classes of people around you: those who make a genuine effort to help, those who congregate from mere curiosity, those who draw off in fear; and, finally, those who take a pleasure in the misfortune of others. And with vandalism it is all the same. Whether active or passive, they are the same uncultured destroyers. Toleration toward evil differs little from evil itself, and it is high time for humanity to give attention to the passive type of vandal. Before our eyes, all kinds of destruction are going on, either from the bombs of totalitarian warfare or from human poisoning of one sort or another. It is a question of which sort of poison is the more ruinous—that of poison gas or that which aims at the destruction of culture. In the so-called peaceful communities, anticultural processes are now taking place on a large scale, while people remain silent or crowds are divided, as in the case of street accidents. At such times, alas, the number of those who exert themselves on behalf of culture is extremely small, while the crowd of those who are curious or malignant takes on huge proportions.

All these curious or evil-minded people try to excuse their conduct, but they are unwilling to reflect that, in so doing, they range themselves alongside the vandals. All who evade joining in the defense of culture enlist in the ranks of passive vandals. In passivity there is always a kind of activity, which can be very dreadful and repulsive, with consequences that may bring about the disintegration of an entire nation. The passive vandal ought not to imagine that his silence has not effect. On the contrary, history exposes not only the active vandal but also those who stood by idly and looked on while torture and destruction were being committed. How heartless, how cruel are all those who feign deafness and remain silent when they ought to cry out!

We have spoken of defending everything that helps with the evolution of the human race. Defense is one thing, but aggression is quite another. We have issued a call not to bury ourselves under sandbags but to counteract destruction through the power of thought, of culture. Traces of culture are being destroyed, obliterated, and scattered abroad, and, in allowing this, mankind has composed a page of history that will look very black in the future. The doings of such brutal destroyers and tortures will be recorded together with the fact that a vast portion of humanity connived and assisted in such vandalism.

There are many ways of participating in such crimes. One need not launch a bomb oneself from the airplane; there are also those who manufacture bombs and invent arms and engines of destruction. One can stand opposed to cultural undertakings and destruction, distortion of constructive thoughts, bring on a condition of savagery.

From such premeditated schemes, the dispersal, dismemberment, and annihilation of whole groups of accumulated treasures can arise. Everyone who by deed or thought contributes to such destruction must be included with the vandals who play havoc with the human spirit.

Terrible deeds are going on in the world. Devastating wars are no longer known as wars. The most dire destruction goes by the name of "Change of policy" while the vandals strut around in new uniforms and trappings and look upon themselves as the arbiters of destiny. Does it matter which way man rushes to fratricide and self-destruction? Perhaps we shall have a new march composed someday for those who proceed toward criminal vandalism.

Yet there is this enormous majority of curious and malicious onlookers, this odious *tertius gaudens*, who fail to understand that they themselves are furthering all sorts of vandalism.

Toleration in participation is a crime. Man must raise his voice against vandalism: it is horrible to witness that the heirs of Goethe and Schiller have become cruel vandals.

"TERROR ANTIQUUS"

THE historian records as follows the plundering of
Rome by Spaniards and German Landsknechts during
the days of the famous Pope Clementius:

"And what no blockade could stop, were the daily
demoralizing horrible rumors about blasphemous orgies
and vandalism, which took place in Rome, about the
fury of fanatic iconoclasts; St. Peter's Cathedral had been
turned up into stables, the Landsknechts kept their houses
in Raphael's stanzas in the Vatican; the remnants of Pope
Julius had been thrown out of the tomb; the statues of
Apostles were beheaded; the procession of Lutherans
with the spear of St. Longinus, the sacrilege with the
Holy Relic of St. Veronica, the intrusion into the Holy
of Holies; about inhuman cruelties, during night orgies,
about the mock funeral of the cardinal and resurrection
from the coffin, the murder of an abbot for his refusal to
hold mass to a mule. There constantly flows in news even
about a crack in the dome, about processions of priests
and monks led through the streets to be sold, about the
nocturnal conclave of drunken Landsknechts, sacrileging
the holy mass. . . ."

Another eyewitness adds:

"Starvation and pest followed the plundering. The city
was exhausted and soldiers already pillaged not for gold
but bread, searching for it even in the beds of the sick.
A sinister silence, devastation, infection, corpses scattered
everywhere, filled me with horror. Houses were open,
doors broken, shops empty, and in the streets I could see
but brutal soldiers."

We are quoting the above lines describing one of the many plunderings of Rome, because of it in comparison with other invasions, there is usually very little known. In schools one only reads that Pope Clementius had to spend a certain time in the besieged castle of St. Angel, but the real horrors of vandalism and blasphemy are not even mentioned. The Emperor himself and kings did not even consider this state of war. When we study other documents of those times, we find that at some courts this horror was only referred to as an unhappy incident. But when the Spanish representatives arrived to save the city, they could not, even with the help of the generals of the plundering armies, take control of the situation because to such an extent had the vandalism, cruelty, and blasphemy taken hold of the Spaniards and Landsknechts. From where could such terrible cruelty and sacrilege originate? It, of course, originated from everyday hardheartedness. But how could such an atrocity flash up instantly? This evil fire, no doubt, sprang up from habitual rudeness and cursing. We know how the infection of the vulgarity of bad language mischievously creeps into everyday life. Chaos manifests itself everywhere, where even for a minute cultural striving is neglected. One cannot for a moment remain in static condition—either down or up. Much is written in literature, dramas, and tragedies about the nature of cruelty and atrocities. From everyday rudeness, permitted and nurtured, there arises abhorrent blasphemy, vandalism, and other ugly manifestations of ignorance.

The paroxysm of ignorance, as often pointed out, is first of all directed against the Highest. Crass ignorance desires to annihilate something, to cut off someone's head, if even a stone one of a statue; ignorance tries to cut out the child to leave only from the mother's womb, to destroy life, and to leave only an "empty place." Such is the ideal of ignorance. It greets illiteracy, it welcomes pornography. It relishes vulgarity and slander. It is difficult to estimate where one finishes and the other begins. Altogether the scales of ignorance are undefinable.

Since cruelty is created by everyday vulgarity and rudeness, how carefully should one extinguish every form of coarseness. How patiently even the smallest rude expression should be eliminated from every home. Rudeness is absolutely unnecessary. Even wild animals are tamed not by rudeness and cruelty. In education rudeness has long been condemned as giving no useful results and only creating a generation of ruffians.

When we read historical examples of misery and ill-luck that took place owing to everyday vulgarity, when we see that these misfortunes continue also today, then is it not necessary to take definite measures in the schools and in the family to safeguard youth from every form of rudeness? The inexperienced youngster is so easily contaminated with the peril of rudeness. Ugly, bad language is so easily introduced in life. Such language is called improper; in other words, it is not admissible.

In opposition to proper language, there apparently exists dirty language. And if people themselves admit that certain expressions are improper, it means that they themselves consider them dirty. Then why favor dirt in life? No one will pour a pail of slops and garbage on the floor in his room. And if such a thing happens by accident, then even the most primitive people will consider it abominable. But bad language is nothing else but a pail of slops of garbage. Is not bad language just a bad habit? Children are punished for bad habits; but the grownups are not punished and even their dirty expression calls forth encouraging smiles.

The habit of rudeness, ill-language, and blasphemy has spread to such an extent that it is simply not noticed. If people remember all the blasphemous jokes, which cause a roar of laughter, it will be quite natural that today these people go to church as if for prayer and tomorrow they are nurturing their horrible bad language.

It has been said long ago: "Yesterday a small compromise, today another small compromise—tomorrow a great scoundrel." Coarseness surprises not only by its inner cruelty but also by its senselessness.

People like the Pharisees often show such hypocrisy when pretending to regret the loss of purity of language, yet they themselves sometimes sponsor the mutilation of language. Amid rubbish are born horrible microbes and they spread in colossal pernicious epidemics.

It has been asserted that Beauty will save the world. Recently we read an excellent book by the renowned Latvian poet, Richard Rudzitis, *Realization of Beauty will save*. Indeed, everyone will agree with this ardent call. But the very concept of Beauty compels the introduction of refinement into everyday life. Not a senseless luxury, but refined beauty is meant. And such a refined beauty does not depend on material wealth. And, first of all, such refinement should not be abused by any form of rudeness.

We speak of the protection of cultural treasures. And for the realization of this axiom, everyone should free himself from a rude attitude to higher ideals. Besides, let us always remember that when protecting cultural treasures, we must not forget the creators of them and pay tribute to them as to living monuments of culture.

Thus having remembered horrors and cruelty, let us conclude with Love and Beauty as a blissful creative force.

THE MISSION OF WOMANHOOD

WAR is difficult, but still more difficult is post-war reconstruction. When the fundamentals of culture are exposed to danger, when the body and spirit of man is alarmed and suffering from bloody wounds, then above the elements, there is again uplifted some calm miraculous force, the purpose of which is to heal man, harassed in dissonances and unreason, and to lead him to the heart's reason by the gentle contacts of spirituality. This force is the Eternal Feminine. When things are difficult in the home, we turn to woman, who herself has been baptized by the fire of suffering. When it is difficult for the world, we turn to woman, whose heart aches at the wounds to culture and to the spirit.

When we speak about culture, surely we have in mind primarily woman, who widely and irresistibly bears the Banner of refined and exalted Culture at all points, from the cradle to the throne.

Indeed, from the fireside to the government, woman implants the fundamental of Culture. In one form or another the child hears the first word about Culture from its mother. . . . With the utmost selfishness and with no personal egotistical principle, woman introduces cultural bases in the structure, whether in her own small family or of nations.

From the most ancient days, woman has worn a wreath upon her head. With this wreath she is said to have pronounced the most sacred incantations. Is it not the wreath of Unity? And is not this the blessed unity and highest responsibility and beautiful mission of womanhood? From woman, one may learn that we must seek disarmament not in warships and guns but in our spirits. And from where can the young generation hear its first caress of unification? Only from the mother.

To both East and West, the image of the Great Mother—womanhood—is the bridge of ultimate unification. To Raj-Rajeswari, the all-powerful Mother, the Hindu of yesterday and today sings his song. To her the women bring their golden flowers and at her feet they lay the fruits for benediction, carrying them back to their hearths. After glorifying her image, they immerse it in water, lest an impure breath should touch the Beauty of the World. To the Mother is dedicated the site on the Great White Mountain, which has never been climbed. Because, when the hour of extreme need strikes, it is said that there she will stand and will lift up Her Hand for the salvation of the world. And encircled by all whirlwinds and all light, She will rise like a pillar of space, summoning all the forces of the far-off worlds.

In this way it happens that when the West speaks of the "Hundred-armed One" of the Orthodox Church, it is but another facet of the images of the many-armed, all-benevolent Kwan Yin. When the West exalts with reverence the gold, embroidered garment of the Italian Madonna and feels the deep penetration of the paintings of Duccio and Fra Angelico, we are reminded of the symbols of the many-eyed Ominiscient Dukkar. We remember the All-Compassionate. We remember the multitudinous aspects of the All-Bestowing and All-Merciful. We remember how correctly the psychology of the people has conceived the iconography of symbols and what an enormous knowledge lies hidden at present under the dead lines. There, where the conceptions that appear and prejudice is forgotten, appears a smile!

The images of the Mother of the World, of the Madonna, the Mother Kali, the benevolent Dukkar, Ishtar, Kwan-Yin, Miriam, the White Tara, Raj-Rajeswari, Nyuka—all these great images, all these Great Self-sacrificing Beings merge together in one conception, as one Benevolent Unity. And each of these, in spite of the differences of language, comprehensible to all, ordains that there should be, not division but construction. They say that the day of the Mother of the World has come. In the smile of Unity all becomes simple. The Aureole of the Madonna becomes a scientific physical radiation—the aura long since known to humanity.

The symbols of today, so poorly interpreted by a rationalist, instead of being regarded as supernatural, suddenly become subjects for investigation to the sincere research worker. And in this miracle of simplicity and understanding, one distinguishes the breath of the evolution of Truth. A Hindu of today who has graduated from many universities addresses the Great Mother, Raj-Rajeswari Herself, in full reverence.

At the same time, at the other end of the world, people sing: "Let us glorify Thee, Mother of Light."

And the old libraries of China and the ancient Central Asiatic centers preserve, since the most ancient days, many hymns to the same Mother of the World.

Throughout the entire East and in the entire West, there lives the Image of the Mother of the World, and deeply significant salutations are dedicated to this High symbol.

Treasures of the human spirit are so often endangered by destruction, not only during war but also during all kinds of inner unrest. The mission of womanhood is great. When there are difficulties in the home, we turn to the woman. When accounts and calculations are no longer of aid, when enmity and mutual destruction reach their limits, we turn to the woman. When evil forces overcome one, then woman is invoked. When the mechanical mind becomes helpless, then one remembers the woman. Verily, when wrath obscures the judgment of the mind, only the heart finds the saving solution. And where is the heart that can replace the woman's? And where is the courage of the heart-fire that can be compared with the courage of woman at the brink of the insoluble? What hand can replace the calming touch of conviction of a woman's heart? And what eye, having endured the pain of suffering, will respond so self-sacrificingly in the name of Bliss?

Among these great missions of the guidance of Womanhood, adamant-like is the *Cultural Mission* to affirm and propagate the creativeness of mankind. Sponsoring creative thoughts, the consciousness strives toward true progress.

It is you, daughters of the Great Mother of the World, whose hands wave the Banner of Peace, unfurled in the name of the most Beautiful.

Who then if not woman must now rise up and be unified in the name of Culture and the Beautiful? Precisely was it ordained to a woman first to announce the good tidings of the Resurrection.

Under diverse veils, human wisdom nevertheless assumes one face of Beauty, Self-sacrifice, and Endurance. And again on a new mountain must woman go, interpreting the eternal paths to those near her.

Sisters! Fearlessly you shall stand on guard for the improvement of life. You kindle at each hearth a beautiful fire, creative and inspiring. You speak the first word about beauty to the children. You teach them about the blessed hierarchy of knowledge. You relate to the little ones thought about creativeness. You can guard them from dissolution and, from their first days of life, instill the concepts of heroism and achievement. You first tell the little ones about the primacy of cultural values. You pronounce the sacred word "Culture."

Great and beautiful is the work ordained to you women.

Dear sisters, carry on and fear not. Tagore said: "Let me not pray to be sheltered from dangers but to be fearless in facing them. Let me not beg for the stilling of my pain but for the heart to conquer it. Let me not look for allies in life's arena but to my own strength."

CULTURAL UNITY

OUR times are verily difficult because of all the commotions, all non-understanding, and all attacks of darkness against Light. Quite recently there were pictures in magazines showing the *auto-da-fé* of precious books in the streets. It is hard to realize that this could have taken place in the present age, after millions of years of the existence of our planet. But perhaps this terrible tension is the impulse to direct humanity through all storms and over all abysses to peaceful construction and mutual respect. What an epoch-making day might be before us when over all countries, all centers of spirit, beauty, and knowledge could be unfurled the One Banner of Culture! This sign would call everyone to revere the treasures of human genius, to respect culture, and to have a new valuation of labor as the only measure of true values. From childhood people will witness that there exists not only a flag of human health, but there is also a sign of peace and culture for the health of the spirit. This sign, unfurled over all treasures of human genius, will say: "Here are guarded the treasures of all mankind; here above all petty divisions, above illusory frontiers of enmity and hatred is towering the fiery stronghold of love, labor, and all-moving creation.

Real peace, Real Unity is desired by the human heart. It strives to labor creatively and actively. For its labor is a source of joy. It wants to love and expand in the realization of Sublime Beauty. In the highest preception of Beauty and Knowledge all conventional divisions disappear. The heart speaks its own language; it wants to rejoice in that which is common for all, uplifts all and leads to the radiant Future. All symbols and tablets of humanity contain one hieroglyph, the sacred prayer—Peace and Unity.

It is truly beautiful if amid the turmoil of life in the waves of unsolved social problems, we still may hold up before us the eternal Flambeaux (torches) of peace in all ages. It is beautiful, through the inexhaustible well of love and tolerance, to understand the great movements, which connected the highest knowledge with the highest aspirations. Thus in studying and admiring, we are becoming real cooperators with evolution, and out of the brilliant rays of Supreme Light may emerge true knowledge. This refined knowledge is based on real comprehension and tolerance. From this source comes the great understanding, rises the supremely Beautiful, the enlightening and enthusiasm for Unity. Contemporary life is changing rapidly; the signs of a new evolution are knocking all doors. In real unconventional science, we feel the splendid responsibility before the coming generations. We understand gradually the harm of everything negative. We begin to value enlightened positiveness and constructiveness, and in this measure, in merciful tolerance, we can prepare for our next generation a vital happiness, turning vague abstractions into beneficent realities.

On the scrolls of command, it has been inscribed that a spiritual garden is daily in need of the same watering as a garden of flowers. If we still consider the physical flowers the true adornment of our life, then how much more must we remember and prescribe to the creative values of the spirit of the leading place in the life which surrounds us? Let us, then, with untiring eternal vigilance, benevolently mark the manifestations of the workers of culture; and let us strive in every possible way to ease this difficult path of heroic achievement.

Let us also mark and find a place in our lives for the Great Ones, remembering that their name no longer is personal, with all the attributes of the limited ego, but has become the property of pan-human cultures and must be safeguarded and firmly cared for in the most benevolent conditions.

We shall thus continue their self-sacrificing labor and we shall cultivate their creative sowing, which as we see is so often covered with the dirt of non-understanding and overgrown with the seeds of ignorance.

As a daring gardener, the true culture bearer will not forcefully crush those flowers that entered life not from the main road if they belonged to the same precious kinds that he safeguards. The manifestations of culture are just as manifold as are the manifestations of the endless varieties of life itself. They ennoble Be-ness. They are the true branches of the one sacred Tree, whose roots sustain the Universe.

If you shall be asked, of what kind of country and of what a future constitution you dream, you can answer in full dignity: The country of Great Culture will be your noble motto. You will know that in that country will be peace, where knowledge and beauty will be revered.

Everything created by hostility is impractical and perishable. The history of mankind gave us remarkable examples of how necessary just peaceful creativeness was for progress. The hand will tire from the sword, but the creating hand sustained by the might of the Spirit is untiring and unconquerable. No sword can destroy the heritage of Culture. The human mind may temporarily deviate from the primary courses, but at the predestined hour will have to recur to them with the renovated powers of the spirit.

Culture and Peace make man verily invincible, and realizing all spiritual conditions he becomes tolerant and all-embracing. Each intolerance is but a sign of weakness. If we understand that every lie, every fallacy shall be exposed, it means that, first of all, a lie is stupid and impractical. But what has he to hide who has consecrated himself to Peace and Culture? Helping those near, he helps the general welfare, which at all ages was appreciated. Striving to Peace, he becomes a pillar of a progressing State. Not slandering the near, we increase the productiveness.

Not quarreling we shall prove that we possess the knowledge of the foundations. Not wasting time in idleness, we shall prove that we are true coworkers in the plow-field of Culture. Finding joy in everyday's labor, we show that the conception of Infinity is not alien to us. Not harming others, we do not harm ourselves; and eternally giving, we realize that in giving we receive. And this blessed receiving is not a hidden treasure of a miser. We understand how creative is affirmation and how destructive is negation. Amid basic conceptions, those of Peace and Culture are the conceptions that even a complete ignoramus will not dare to attack. There where is culture, is peace. There where is the right solution for difficult social problems is achievement. Culture is the culmination of highest Bliss, of highest Beauty, of highest Knowledge.

We are tired of destruction and negations. Positive creativeness is the fundamental quality of the human spirit. Let us welcome all those who surmounting personal difficulties and casting aside petty selfishness propel their spirits to the task of preserving culture, thus insuring a radiant future. We must not fear enthusiasm. Only the ignorant and the spiritually impotent would scoff at this noble feeling. Such scoffing is but the sign of inspiration for the true Legion of Honor. Nothing can impede us from dedicating ourselves to the service of Culture as long as we believe in it and give to it our most flaming thoughts.

Do not disparage! Only in harmony with evolution can we ascend! And nothing can extinguish the selfless and flaming wings of enthusiasm!

Unity! Unity! Unity!

V

NEW ERA

PANACEA

PLATO ordained in his treatises on statesmanship:
"It is difficult to imagine a better method of education than that that has been discovered and verified and by the experience of centuries it can be expressed 'in two propositions: gymnastics for the body and music for the soul.' In view of this one must consider education in music as the most important; thanks to it Rhythm and Harmony are deeply inrooted into the soul, dominate it, fill it with beauty and transform man into a beautiful thinker. He will partake of the Beautiful and rejoice at it, gladly realize it, become saturated with it and will arrange his life in conformity with it."

Of course, the word "music," in this case, should not be understood as routine musical education, as it is understood now in its narrow sense. Music had in Athens, as a service to all the Muses, a far deeper and broader meaning than today. This conception embraced not only the harmony of sound but the whole domain of poetry, the whole domain of high perceptions, of exquisite forms and creation in general, in its best sense. The great service to the Muses was a real education of taste, which in everything cognizes the great Beautiful. Just to this eternal Beauty in all its vitality, we have to revert, if only the ideas of high constructiveness are not rejected by humanity.

Hippias Maior (beauty) of the dialogue of Plato is not a hazy abstractness but verily the most vital noble conception. The Beautiful in itself! The perceptible and conceivable! In this reality is contained an inspiring, encouraging welcome to the study and inrooting of all ordainments of the Beautiful. "The philosophic moral" of Plato is animated by the sense of the beautiful. And did not Plato himself, who was sold into slavery through the hatred of the tyrant Dionysius and when liberated and dwelling in the gardens of the Academy, prove through his example the vitality of a beautiful path? Of course, Plato's gymnastics were not the coarse football or anticultural breaking of noses of modern prizefights. The gymnastics of Plato were the same gates to the Beautiful—the discipline of harmony and uplifting of the body into the spiritual spheres.

Not once have we spoken about the introduction in school of a chair of ethics of life, a course of the art of thinking. Without the education of the general realization of the beautiful, these two courses will again remain a dead letter. Again, in the course of only a few years, the high vital principles of ethics will turn into a dead dogma if they are not imbued with the Beautiful.

Many vital conceptions of antiquity have become in our household belittled and vulgar instead of the deserved expansion. Thus the all-embracing, wide and lofty service to the Muses turned into a narrow conception of playing one instrument. When you hear nowadays the word music, you imagine first of all a lesson of music often with conventional limitations. When one hears the word "museum," one understands it as a storeroom of any kind of art objects. As every storehouse, this conception creates a certain flavor of deadliness. Such limited conception of the word "museum" as a storage place, so deeply entered our understanding that when one pronounces this conception in its original meaning—*muzeon*—then no one understands what is really meant. Yet every Hellene of even average education would at once know that Muzeon means first of all the Home of the Muses.

Primarily, Muzeon is the abode of all aspects of the Beautiful—not at all in the sense of storing only different kinds of art creations but in the sense of the most vital and creative application of them in life. Thus one hears often nowadays that people express surprise when a Museum, as such, occupies itself with all spheres of Art, occupies itself with the education of good taste and with the spreading of the sense of the Beautiful.

Here we remember the ordainments of Plato. But in the same way, one may also remember Pythagoras with his Laws of the Beautiful, with his adamant foundations of cosmic realizations. The ancient Hellenes went so far as to crown their Pantheon with an altar to the Unknown God. In this exaltation of spirit they came close to the refined inexpressible conception of the ancient Hindus, who pronouncing *"Neti, neti"* by no means wanted to say anything negative, but on the contrary, by saying "not this, not this" manifested thereby the untold greatness of an inexpressible concept.

It is significant that such great conceptions were not abstract, as if living only in the mind and reason: no, they dwelled in the very heart as something living, life-bringing, inalienable and indestructible, as defined so beautifully in the *Bhagavad Gita*. In the heart was aflame that sacred fire, which was at the base of all flaming commandments and also of the hermits of Mt. Sinai. The same sacred fire molded the precious images of St. Theresa, St. Francis, St. Sergius, and all the Fathers of the "Love of the Good," who knew so much and were understood so little.

We speak of the education of good taste, as of a matter of truly basic world significance of every country. When we speak about vital ethics, which should become the favorite school hour of every child, we appeal to the contemporary heart, pleading to it for expansion, if even only to the extent of ancient ordainments.

Can one consider as natural the fact that the conception already so glorified in the time of Pythagoras and Plato has been so narrowed now and lost its actual meaning, after all the ages of so-called progress? Pythagoras even in the fifth century BC symbolized in himself the whole harmonious "Pythagorean Life." It was Pythagoras who affirmed music and astronomy as sisters in science. Pythagoras, who was called by bigots a charlatan, must be horrified to see how, instead of showing a harmonious development, our contemporary life has been broken up and mutilated, and that we do not even understand the meaning of the beautiful hymn to the sun—to Light.

Today very strange formulae sometimes appear in the press. For instance, that the flourishing of the intellect is the sign of degeneration. A very strange formula, if only the author does not attribute to the word "intellect" some special narrow meaning. Of course, if the word "intellect" is only taken as the expression of the conventional withered mind, then to some extent this formula may have its foundation. But it is dangerous in case the author understands intellect as intelligence, which first of all should be connected with the education of good taste as the most vital principle of life.

Quite recently before our eyes, in the West has been adopted a new word—intelligentsia. In the beginning this newcomer was met rather suspiciously, but soon it was adopted in literature. It would be important to determine whether this expression symbolizes the intellect or, according to ancient conceptions, it corresponds to the education of good taste.

If it is a symbol of a refined and expanded consciousness, then we have to greet this innovation, which perhaps will remind us once more of the ancient beautiful principles.

In my letter "Synthesis," the difference of conceptions of Culture and Civilization were discussed. Both these conceptions are sufficiently separated, even in standard dictionaries. Let us not, therefore, return to these two consecutive conceptions, even if someone would be content with the conception of civilization without dreaming about the higher conception of culture.

But remembering about "intelligentsia," it is permissible to ask whether this conception belongs to Civilization, as to the expression of intellect, or whether it does already touch a higher region, that is to say, whether it belongs to the region of Culture, in which the heart and spirit already act. Of course, if we assume that the expression "intelligentsia" should remain only within the limitation of the mind, then there would be no need to burden it with our literary vocabulary. One may permit an innovation only in such cases when something really new is introduced or at least when ancient principles are renewed in present modern circumstances.

Of course, everyone will agree that intelligentsia, this aristocracy of the Spirit, belongs to Culture, and only in this connection could one greet this new literary expression.

In this case, the education of good taste belongs, first of all, of course, to the intelligentsia, and not only does it belong, but it becomes its duty. Without fulfilling this duty, intelligentsia has no right for existence and condemns itself to savagery.

The education of good taste cannot be something abstract, where above all, this is a vital attainment in all spheres of life, for can there be a boundary to the service to the Muses of the ancient Hellenes? If in the old days this service was understood in its full glory and adapted to life in the whole beauty of its principle, then should we not be ashamed, if in superstition and bigotry we cut off the radiant wings of the rising spirits?

When we propose ethics as a course in schools, as a theme most inspiring, limitless, full of constructive principles, we thus, presuppose, at the same time, the transmutation of taste as a defense against vulgarity and ugliness.

Andromeda said: "And I brought thee the Fire!" The ancient Hellene, the follower of Euripides, understood the meaning of this Fire and why this Agni is so precious. We, however, in most cases babble about this inspiring conception as about phosphor matches. We attach the high conception of Phosphor—the bringer of Light—to a match and try to light with it our extinguished hearth in order to prepare the broth for today. But where is Tomorrow, this radiant wonderful Tomorrow?

We have forgotten about it. We have forgotten because

we have lost the ability of searching, have lost the refined taste that urges to betterment, to dreams, to higher consciousness. Dreams have become like dull slumber; but he who does not know how to dream does not belong to the future, does not belong to humanity with its high ideal.

Even the simple truth that dreams about the future are the basic distinction of man from animal has already become a truism. But a truism in itself is no longer a generally accepted truth, as it should be, but has become the synonym of a truth of which one should not think altogether. Nevertheless, disregarding everything, even in times of the greatest difficulties and world crises, let us not defer the thought about the education of taste; let us not put off the thought of life-bringing ethics as of a necessary course of school education. Let us not forget the art of thinking, the art of memory, and let us forever remember the treasure of the heart.

A certain hermit left his retreat and came with the message, saying to everyone: "Thou hast a heart." When he was asked why he does not speak about mercy, patience, devotion, love, and all the other benevolent foundations of life, he replied: "If only they do not forget the heart, the rest will adjust itself." Verily can we appeal for love if it has no place to reside? And where can patience dwell when its abode is closed? Thus in order not to torture ourselves with inapplicable blisses, we must build that garden that will flourish in the realization of the heart. Let us stand firmly on the foundation of the heart, and let us understand that without the heart we are as a lost shell." Thus the Wise Ones ordained. Thus ordains *Agni Yoga*. Thus let us accept and apply.

Without the untiring realization of the Beautiful, without incessant refinement of the heart and consciousness, we would make the laws of earthly existence cruel and deadly in their hatred against humanity. In other words, we would, when killing the Beautiful, assist the most shameful, debased downfall.

The Romans said: *Sub pretextu juris summum jus saepe summa injuria; suaviter in modo fortiter in re.* ("Under the pretext of justice, a strict application of law is often the gravest injury. Be gentle in manner, though resolute in execution.")

Let us be broad and resolute in the realization of the Beautiful!

The very traditions of Art we must safeguard and inroot in contemporary life. Whence else will come the nobleness of spirit? How else will grow the dignity of personality? Whence will descend the realization of broad cooperation and mutual trust? From the very same inexhaustible source of radiant, blessed creativeness. Life is transformed by the achievements of Culture. Difficult as they may be in the time of narrow materialism, we know that these achievements will be the moving force of humanity. Light is one, and the gates to it are verily international and accessible for all who seek light. Darkness is admitted only for the time of sleep, but, verily, it is not for sleep that humanity perfects itself through millions of years.

It is not a truism to think of and invoke Culture. With all means, not restraint in quantity, we must bring into the chalice of Culture all the accumulations of our hearts. It is said that we now approach the epoch of fire. What a wondrous element of nature it is, if we can realize it and apply it benevolently. Kindling the torches of spirit, is it not beautiful to realize that in other countries the very same torches also radiate? This realization of cooperation will strengthen and uplift our quests. Whether we shall behold there friends with the physical eye or feel them in the spirit of our heart, we know not what is more precious. It is important to know that the chalice of the Graal, the chalice of Culture, is interminably being filled and that in hearty cooperation our friends deposit there their best spiritual values.

Leonardo ordained:

"He who despises the art of painting, thus despises a philosophic and refined conception of the universe, because the art of painting is the daughter, or rather grandchild of Nature. Everything that exists was born from Nature and has borne, in its turn, the science of painting. This is why I say that painting is the grandchild of Nature and relative of God. He who blasphemes the art of painting, blasphemes Nature.

"The painter must be all-embracing. O artist, may thy multiformity be as infinite as the manifestations of Nature. Continuing what God has commenced, strive to multiply not the deeds of human hands but the eternal creations of God. Never imitate anyone. And every creation of thine, be a new manifestation of Nature!"

History records the manifold remarkable achievements of Leonardo da Vinci in all domains of life. He left amazing mathematical writings; he investigated the nature of flying; he conducted medical researches and was a distinguished anatomist. He invented musical instruments, studied the chemistry of paint; he loved the wonders of natural history. He adorned cities with magnificent buildings, palaces, schools, libraries; he built large military barracks, constructed one of the best ports in the Adriatic, and planned and built great waterways; he founded mighty forts, constructed war machinery, sketched military plans. Great was his versatility.

But after all these remarkable achievements, he remained in the memory of the world as an artist—as the great artist. Is this not a true victory of Art?

"Verily, verily, Beauty is Brahman. Art is Brahman. Science is Brahman. Every Glory, every Magnificence, every Greatness is Brahman."

Thus exclaimed the Hindu saint coming back from the greatest Samadhi. A new path of beauty and wisdom shall come.

The great Swami Vivekananda tells us:

"Don't you see I am above all a poet?" "That man cannot be truly religious, who has not the faculty of feeling the beauty and grandeur of art." "Non-appreciation of art is crass ignorance."

From former days, perhaps the fifteenth century, in Russia there has come down to us a legend in which Christ is proclaimed as the highest guardian of beauty. According to this legend, when Christ was ascending to heaven, some troubadours approached him and asked:

"Lord Christ, to whom are you leaving us? How can we exist without you?"

And Christ answered:

"My children, I shall give you the golden mountains and silver rivers and beautiful gardens, and you shall be nourished and happy."

But then St. John approached Christ and said:

"O Lord, give them not golden mountains and silver rivers. They do not know how to guard them, and someone rich and powerful will attack them and take away the golden mountains. Give them only your name and your beautiful song, and give the command that all those who appreciate the songs and who care for and guard the singers shall have the open gates to Paradise."

And Christ replied:

"Yes, I shall give them, not golden mountains, but my songs; and all who appreciate them shall find the open gates to Paradise."

Rabindranath Tagore finishes his book *What Is Art* with such words:

"In Art the person in us is sending its answer to the Supreme Person, who reveals Himself to us in a world of endless beauty across the lightless world of facts."

There is no other way, O friends scattered! May my call penetrate to you. Let us join ourselves by the invisible threads of the Beautiful. I turn to you, I call to you; in the name of Beauty and Wisdom, let us combine for struggle and work.

During the days of Armageddon, let us ponder on Eternal Values, which are the cornerstone of Evolution.

BOOKCASE

ONE recalls an incident: In the office of a certain president are two visitors. The walls of the old room are decorated with massive oak bookcases. Through the glass panels temptingly glow the backs with their rich bindings. Although the bindings are not old, they are heavily gold-leaved. Apparently, here is a lover of books. How splendid that at the head of this undertaking, there is a collector who has not spared money in his tempting bindings.

One of the visitors yields to the temptation of turning the leaves and holding in his hands this treasure of the spirit. The bookcase is apparently unlocked and raising his hand, the booklover attempts to take one of the volumes. But oh, the horror! The entire shelf falls on his head, revealing that these are false bindings without any sign of a book. His most sensitive wish violated, the booklover with trembling hands, replaces upon its shelf, this unworthy imitation: "Let us get away from here soon. Can one expect anything decent from such a clown!" The other visitor smiles: "Here one is punished for loving books because it is a happiness not only to read a good book but even to hold it in one's hands."

How many such false libraries are spread all over the world: and whom do their owners presume to cheat—their own friends or themselves? In this falsification lies hidden an unusually subtle disdain of knowledge and a refined insult toward the book as the witness of human achievement. And not only are the contents of the book being violated but in such falsifications, objectively as well as in words, is being assaulted the very significance of the creation of the spirit.

"Tell me who are your enemies and I will tell you who you are," said the ancients. One may say, "Show me your bookcase and I will tell you who you are."

One of the most exhausting tasks is the search for a new apartment. But through this involuntary intrusion into numerous dwellings, you undoubtedly discover observations about the facts of life. You pass through numerous apartments of approximate wealth that are filled with furniture. But where is the bookcase? Where is the writing desk? Why are the rooms sometimes overcrowded with such strange, ugly objects, yet these two friends of existence—a writing desk and a bookcase—are lacking? Is there a place to put them? It appears upon examination that a small desk could still be placed somewhere, but the walls are all so figured out that there is no place for a bookcase.

The landlady, noticing your disappointment, points out a small inside closet and with a smile of condescension, indulging your demand, says: "If you have so many books, you can use this closet instead of using it for other domestic things." Thereby you see that the minute measures of the closet appear to be regal for such a luxury as books.

In this regrettably patronizing attitude toward the book you recall the priceless libraries that are apparently thrown out on the street markets. And you once more sorrowfully recall all the stories of how herrings and cucumbers were wrapped in the priceless pages torn from the rarest editions. Then, when you look upon the small bookcase that is being offered to you, and you calculate that only with difficulty could even a hundred volumes fit there, you again hear the "worldly" sages ask you: "Why, then, keep so many books at home?" And they will be only repeating the words of the famous Muslim conquerer who ordered the most priceless libraries to be destroyed as useless, since it is said that the one Koran comprises everything which is necessary for a human being.

The absence of a writing desk is explained quite

definitely by the reminder that a writing desk is supposed to stand in an office. Herein is apparent a definite suggestion that outside the office, there should be no mental occupations and evening relaxations are meant for a hilarious time that should not burden the brain. And thus the so-called relaxations, which should be most priceless hours of accumulation and refinement of consciousness, are dissipated like pearls thrown in the dust of the street.

And thus the book in contemporary usage becomes an object of luxury. The "sane" mind categorizes bibliophiles as luxurious maniacs. The mediocre consciousness altogether unlearns to read, as he even good-naturedly confesses. "I cannot read long books," "I cannot concentrate," "I haven't got the time," says a man on his way to a boxing match or to throw balls into the air or simply too busy himself gossiping about his neighbor.

And there is both time and money to possess houses that are a treasury of knowledge, but the thought about these treasures simply leaves our daily habit. By what do people live? Through many objects. But the realization of this, as well as the beauty of the book itself as a creation, passes out of the life.

So also can one observe the character and the essence of a friend according to the condition in which they return the books loaned to them. It is true that very often you meet with a most careful, a most honorable attitude toward the book, and then you understand why certain volumes remained from the seventeenth and fifteenth centuries. But to one's sorrow more often the books are returned in an irreparably harmed way so that one's soul aches for the desecrated author. To burn a book with something, to turn down the leaves, perhaps to tear away the corner, and sometimes even to cut out the illustration that one likes is not considered a sacrilege. Every librarian will tell you about his grievances not only regarding lost books but also editions mutilated forever.

He who destroys a book reveals the low condition of his consciousness. Truism though this be, let whoever reads it be afraid to soil or tear a book. In the midst of universal crises, material as well as spiritual, the general latitude toward books will be one of the convincing circumstances. Yes, when we will again learn to love a book disinterestedly, as a pure creation of art, and heartily to safeguard it, will be also when also some of the most difficult of life's problems will solve themselves—without discussions, without evil thoughts and clashes. And in our dwellings we will also find a place for a bookcase and for a writing desk as well as for the sacred images, which by their presence remind us about the Highest, the Beautiful, and the Infinite.

Someone may say, "I knew this long ago, this is not new to me." How good it is if he says so; maybe on the strength of that, he will read one more book and his attitude toward these true friends of every home will be more solicitous; and in turn, he will say that which is so known to him and to others. Because it is often about that, which they do not apply, that people say: "I knew that long ago." One must say to them again, "The worse for you."

The books of recent editions have become very meager— both in measure and in their specific contents. The author is seemingly afraid to bore because the publisher dins into his ears about the peculiar demands of the reader.

And suddenly you discover that most of the books are being read by poor people, and the desire of true realizations lives in people who with difficulty earn for themselves the bread of tomorrow. Looking over the almanac of world information, you will, with keen interest, follow the statistic of literacy as well as the number of volumes in public libraries of the world. How inconsistent with many official presentations are distributed the number of books in these National Treasuries. Let us not quote these instructive numbers because *The World Almanac*, a yearly book, is in reach of those who desire to get acquainted with the consistency of these acquisitions. For many people, the figures will contain great surprises.

Because of that, let us not forget that literacy, although

undoubtedly a step to culture, is of itself not yet a guarantee of those reading books or their sane cultural application. If one could take another census, namely as to how many of the literate people do not read books, the results would be very instructive. Then also, if from the number of readers would be eliminated the readers of cheap fiction, we would see that the entire number of serious books and editions is supported by a comparatively minute amount of people out of the entire population of the world.

This condition still further demands a careful attitude not only toward serious editions, but also toward those individuals who make out of them a wise and proper application.

Some touching episodes about the loving care of books are not forgotten. Unforgettable is the story of one poor writer who wanted to give to his bride, as a wedding present, what to him was the most valuable thing, a monograph on the creation of an artist who most inspired him. It is also unforgettable when this touching love toward books is kindled independently in the most early youth. A small girl, in a very rich home, carries with difficulty the Bible with illustrations by Doré, too heavy for the child's strength. She is not permitted to take this book, but she takes advantage of the absence of her elders—not for mischief and play but in order again to utilize this moment of freedom to commune with the great Images.

Dear to us are these children, the bearers of the best Images, who, directed by their hearts, independently seek the bookcase in their search for this unchangeable friend of true happiness.

Because Edison spontaneously sought the bookcase, from early childhood he realized how he could benefit humanity. In the community instinct of newspaper work is also expressed a hearty striving toward the spreading of the useful.

Let us also remember the great mind, Ruskin, who so touchingly contributed his first efforts and inspirations toward the great Biblical Epos. Let us remember many glorious ones. Long ago the power of thought was already spoken about as well as the art of thinking. But every art must be developed and nurtured, and shall not the hearth of this sacred art be near a bookcase?

Let us turn to the bookcase not only as to a comforter and guardian but also as to a leader and vitalizer. Do not the consistently creative minds of great thinkers emanate from it? Or vitality? Or does not the resistance to all evil and to all the unprecedented obstacles of existence come from it? And does not creative joy come from it?

WAY SIGNS

HOW many milestones are there on every path and how little attention do we pay to them! To a friend of mine an acquaintance complained: "My whole life I have been awaiting a Sign. I send my best thoughts but I have no reply. Is this just?"

My friend asked her to tell him about her life. And she told him the following: "I was very rich, and this gave me the possibility to help people and to support a great many. Then, not of my fault, there came ruin. It is true, I do not starve. But, I no longer have the possibility to help as I did before. And this is my constant sorrow. I fail to understand why it was necessary to ruin me and thus place me under eternal complaints for not being able to help."

My friend explained to her: "Don't you see? Your expected answer had already been given, but you did not understand it. You mistook the good advice for a misfortune. For you unfortunately imagined that help should only be financial. Thus you destroyed the most precious realization that spiritual help achieves far greater results than a financial one. Admit it, you took pleasure in giving away from your surplus, not submitting yourself to any privation, nor to danger, nor to difficulties. And even now, not everything has been taken away from you. You do not starve, and it seems that you could help others all the more with your own worldly experience. How many new and useful advices you could give? From your own experience, you could prove to others the insignificance of material means, if they can be destroyed so easily. But if you will consider your present position as a misfortune, then what further reply can you expect? Only when you shall realize the usefulness of your present state, when you understand that the conception of money was perverted in your own mind, only then will you be ready for the next step."

The same friend has also narrated another case. He was told to show to a certain lady in Chicago a portrait. The lady was greatly moved upon seeing this portrait, and said: "How do you know the drama of my life? Once we were in Paris with some American friends and were sitting in a small cafe. Unexpectedly the same person entered whose portrait you have just shown me, and having seated himself not far from the door, began looking at me attentively. I understood within my heart that I should approach him and that in this would lie the future of my life. On the other hand, the conventionalities of behavior whispered to me that it would be inadmissible in the eyes of my friend to leave them and go to the stranger. A great struggle took place within me, and he continued looking at me, expecting me to choose my path. Some more time passed, the conventionalities, keeping me to my seat, and the stranger got up and went out. I understood that I failed to answer the call and had decided my fate according to conventionalities. In this lies the drama of my life."

On a later occasion, my friend told me of another remarkable way sign. He was told to open in a certain city an educational institution. After investigating many possibilities, he decided to talk over matters with a certain lady who had come to this city. She made an appointment to meet him in the morning at the local museum. Reaching there with expectations, my friend noticed a tall stranger, who passed him several times. Then the stranger stopped next to him and pointing to a tapestry hanging on the wall, he said: "They knew the style of living. We have lost it." My friend replied accordingly, and the stranger invited him to sit down on a nearby bench; and placing his finger upon my friend's forehead, he said: "You came here to talk about a certain matter known to you. Do not talk about it. For another three months, nothing can yet be done along this line. And then everything will come to you of itself." Whereupon the stranger, having given a few more important advices, quickly got up and waving his hand in a friendly manner, said "Good luck," and went out. My friend, of course, took the advice, never mentioned anything to the lady about what he expected, and in three months everything took place as predicted. My friend still cannot comprehend how it was that he never asked the name of this remarkable stranger, of whom he has never heard from since and never met him again. And this is precisely how things happen.

One more sign. A friend—an artist—was telling me that at the time his exhibition was held at a seaside city, he was in great need of a definite sum of money. But despite all the outer success of the exhibition, the sales were not progressing. It seemed that the more the friend was inwardly anxious the more difficult the situation became. The more so, since he did not want to make his need of money known in public. As if all kinds of unforeseen circumstances had come up against him, someone got sick, someone went away and had not as yet returned. The exhibition was coming to an end, and the friend was in a very sad mental state. A few days prior to the closing of the exhibition, in the morning, it was not yet eight o'clock when the telephone bell rang and the voice of a young lady said nervously and hurriedly: "I have only fifteen minutes before my boat leaves. I am at the door of your exhibition and I must have one of your paintings. Please come immediately to advise me which to select." Needless to say, my friend hurried to get there and found at the door a very nice young lady from Honolulu, who with a check in hand was waiting to decide about the picture. Having made her decision, she took the painting off the wall and, disregarding the protest of the man in charge of the exhibition, hurried to the automobile that was waiting for her. Of course, you will not doubt that the check was exactly the amount that my friend needed. Likewise, you will not doubt that the young lady did not know, nor could she know, the sum needed by my friend; but that is just how it happens.

I remember another very significant episode. My friends decided to visit a certain country, whereas another part of the world had been indicated to them. With good motives my friends yet persisted and had even bought tickets for the mentioned country. Yet the indication had to be fulfilled, and something unusual took place. All means prepared for that trip suddenly vanished in two or three days, and thus my friends had no other choice but to fulfill the indication. Such signs clearly point out what measures must be applied in order to safeguard the predestined.

And yet another sign. One of my friends had to see a man who was very dangerous for him. Of course, all thoughts were directed to avoiding this fateful meeting. By strange circumstances several times this meeting did not take place, some unexpected impediments suddenly arose. But in the end, apparently, it could no longer be avoided. Probably the power of the thoughts sent could not help any longer. And thus my friend, having come to the meeting place awaited the appointment. The time had arrived. But the dangerous man had not as yet appeared. And suddenly a great excitement arose, and it appeared that, in the end, this evil man could not turn up—for his heart had failed. Such measures also take place when there is no other alternative.

And here is another sign of long memories. The aunt of my wife with her husband and son went in a cold winter to visit a far-off estate. They lost their way. Night came. The storm increased. And they had to think of some kind of shelter. All of a sudden they noticed a manor unknown to them. They drove up to the gate. It appeared that the owners had not lived there for a long time, but the watchman agreed to open the house for shelter. As soon as their sleighs stopped at the door, the aunt of my wife, who had never been in this place before exclaimed in horror: "No, I shall never enter this place. Some terrible drama has taken place here." When her husband and her son began to persuade her, she said: "Go in and see for yourself." And then she described all the interior of the house and mentioned in detail a large painting of a lady in white. When the worried travelers entered the house, they were amazed to recognize that which was described to them; and when they reached the room with the portrait, they themselves were so upset that they immediately left this unhappy house. Many such signs can be met if we but find within ourselves enough attentiveness to discern them.

And one more sign of an answer. Our friends moved into a new house. The luggage had already been brought in. And among these was an old clock that was broken and could not be wound up any longer. The lady was thinking how long they would live in this new house. And all of a sudden, the old unwound clock struck loudly ten times. And this was the exact number of years that they stayed at this place. But many, perhaps, would not have paid attention to the mere striking of a clock.

Another sign. It had been indicated that a very valuable packet would be received. Time passed. Our friends had almost forgotten about it, having reached Paris on their travel, when all of a sudden a message was brought from the bank, Bankers Trust, to the effect that a packet had arrived. And it appeared that in this most usual way, the most unusual sending was delivered. As you see, it may also happen thus.

And how many letters from unknown places of origin have been received! How many necessary books were pointed out as if by chance, and how many remarkable dates may be heard by an attentive ear! How many benevolent signs are given in life! If these signs are given for the good, if their sole object is to help humanity, then verily they will be truly good signs. Some light-minded people fear whether they are good and do not know how to interpret them. But look heartily through the magnifying glass of the future and listen to the megaphone of coming events, and you shall see what is the purpose of these benevolent signs.

If a sign is given for the upliftment of the heart, for the purposes of healing, for the overcoming of difficulties, for faith and perfection, it means this sign is useful and one must know how to discern it. And let us again repeat, that one must not expect that those signs that would be dictated by our selfishness and limited egoism is already evil and limited. One must find within oneself sufficient benevolence, in order to accept the signs in that form, in that expression, that the Highest has ordained as the best.

When people pray for protection against nightmares and ghosts, this will be one of the very necessary prayers. Truly, one must protect oneself against all kinds of dark phantoms, from everything that tends to plunge us into the darkness, and first of all, one must guard against ignorance. The lack of desire to know and to accept—will this not already be a succumbing to the power of evil spirits? The man who leaves this earth and does not think about the future will be like the one who received a most valuable book but who did not open it beyond its binding.

Attentiveness in life will not be conventional and a morbid abstraction. On the contrary, the more attentive is man, the more beauty will open up for him. Every minute of concentration and silence, he will consider as one more merging into the beautiful height. He will think over and guard more carefully that which has been accumulated by him earlier. And the accumulated is not phantom-like, but of the spirit-eternal.

I remember a reliable story of the sea. A certain captain of a steamer fell ill and because of the incurable disease was taken to the hospital, thus having to leave forever his beloved ship. The new captain who was just as experienced, on passing a rocky island some distance away, decided to lie down to rest. At this moment, through his dream he heard a voice: "Take to the right." But he did not get up. Then the second time he heard the same command. And finally a thundering voice shouted for the third time: "Take to the right." Then the captain got up and ran up to the bridge, repeating the order, "Take to the right." And it was high time, for the ship was heading straight to the reefs. At the same time, in the faraway hospital, the former captain of the ship threw himself out of the window with the same command on his lips. Admiral T. will substantiate this true story.

Some people consider all such signs as Christmas fairy tales or as coincidences not worth of attention. The majority of these would-be skeptics are very timid themselves and, therefore, are even afraid to think that above their everyday life, besides their backyard weeds, there may be something that makes it worthwhile to think and pay more attention to life. The spasmodic attitude toward faith or the accidental reading of related books helps but little because everything is required in persistent, careful, and attentive striving. It is not yet sufficient if man now and then shows signs of attentiveness on his part. One must always be attentive. One must penetrate into the surrounding conditions as if it were a profound and beautiful book given for everyday application. Again, certain thoughtless people will call this way of thinking abstract philosophy. They understand high expressions in a narrow meaning. But is it not from love for sane pondering that the most solid and irrefutable facts are formed? The same thinking will safeguard from cruelty and coarseness. For why should not refinement and upliftment of our consciousness go hand in hand?

What a wonderful impression is made by a person of whom one may be certain that he will not admit cruelty nor coarseness; it is a guarantee against savagery. If you meet a person who has retrograded and relapsed into savagery, one may be sure that originally he did not try hard for the Common Good, nor try to improve himself.

Along the vast snowy plains, one may sometimes notice withered twigs, which have been placed there by someone to indicate a hidden road. Sometimes a traveler will attentively watch for them and will direct his steed along these signs. But there are also conceited travelers, who, surprised at the seemingly unreasonable windings of the road, continue their way without paying heed to these indications. How many unexpected difficulties and dangers they may call upon themselves amid the hidden hillocks and ravines! An experienced coachman when noticing the tracks of those deviating from the signs will regretfully wave his hand and exclaim: "Look how the devil lured them away!"

Precisely an evil force, precisely ignorance and conceit distract the attention of the unwise from the signs that had been so carefully safeguarded for them. The lessons in attentiveness will also be experiments in benevolence, and on these paths is already prepared a true protection. And along these way signs, travelers will proceed.

SPACE IS CRYING

IT was recently reported that in a certain city in Europe such a powerful radio station was built that it suffocated many other stations. It may seem that there is nothing extraordinary in this because radio stations may be built of various degrees of power. But this news is significant because it indicated that a new kind of warfare in space is taking place. Humanity has used the latest inventions mostly for murderous purposes. The crying of the radio can thunder across the world and draw attention to various inhuman cruelties. But somebody wants to stifle such spatial complaints. Apparently someone is trying to take space itself by the throat and prevent news that is undesirable for himself. Such violence against space is most significant. It is difficult to imagine what can take place if humanity is to become accustomed to such a form of violence. Fools will pretend that against a powerful station one can build a far stronger one, but then where would such a marathon of mutual strangling end? It would be wrong to imagine that space can contain an unlimited amount of energy. But no one can say that these doses of energy can be unlimited. It is apparent that stronger energies swallow up the weaker ones. Let us extend this idea and in progression we shall witness a horrible war in space. No one can foretell the consequences of such a war. No one can know to what an extent space can be violated and poisoned. One thing is clear—that people in mutual hatred can evoke the most horrible, destructive energies. If at the moment no terrible explosion and no pernicious epidemics take place it does not mean that they may not occur later. People again accuse solar spots as being the cause of all of their own follies. Science is ahead of human psychology. Science has already plunged itself into an ocean of new dangers arising from the misuse of energies. Light-mindedly people try to poison and violate the beneficial life-giving space. Whither will such progress lead?

In the times of Akbar the Great, it was forbidden under grave penalty to sell unstable colors. And ancient Sastras also insisted on the high quality of paints. It would seem that since then, world civilization should have improved the quality of materials. But it seems civilization pursues some other aims. It has forgotten the humanitarian sciences and rejected the ideas of stability of materials. It is strange but true that some new models of machinery are far less stable than previous models. As regards artists' materials, they have many new enemies created by the same "civilization." Thus, for example, many colors do not withstand sulfur, vapor and other chemical emanations, with which the atmosphere of modern cities is saturated. Instead of protecting health, we can witness an inadmissible waste. On Paris avenues certain kinds of trees perished from gasoline fumes. One can imagine how similar chemical gases react badly upon the health and articles of human production, especially delicate masterpieces of art. King Louis of France became immortal by the cynicism of his utterance: *Aprés nous, le deluge!* ("After us, the flood!") Unfortunately this principle is applied in many domains of modern life. With hypocritical modesty you may be told: "It is not for us to worry about the stableness of our creations; let time itself be the judge." Yet those who say so understand very well that the bad quality of material, of which they are aware, deprives the next generation of its just heritage. Not from egotism, but in the name of wise care should we safeguard what belongs to the youth, for we work for the future. Archaeology often gives remarkable examples of the stability of materials. We are grateful to unknown builders who have left for us a beautiful heritage that humanity can enjoy throughout millenniums. It may be said that it is not known how long our planet will exist altogether. Among astronomical and cosmical considerations, there seems no place for the question of the stability of earthly materials. But as long as our old earth exists, it is necessary to think how it is possible to improve materials and avoid the poisoning of space.

RECORDS OF THOUGHTS

A newspaper reports: "Record of human thought—Experiment of two Cambridge Professors."—"Two Professors of the Cambridge University have succeeded in making cinema photographs of human thought. One of them is Dr. Adrian, Professor of Physiology and a distinguished Member of the Royal Society, the other is Prof. Mathews. Adrian, who has dedicated his whole life to the investigation of the mysteries of the nervous system, in 1932 received the Nobel Prize and only a few days back was awarded the Gold Medal of the Royal Society."

"When a person sits quietly in a chair with closed eyes and his thought is not occupied with anything serious, then his brain matter produces regular electrical discharges at the rate of about ten discharges per second. With the help of very complicated and ingenuous apparati and a photo-electric camera, Prof. Adrian succeeded in registering these discharges on a cinema-film. He likewise observed that as soon as his patient opens his eyes and begins to concentrate his attention on something, the frequency of discharges increases considerably and reaches usually about 2,000 per sec."

"The rhythmic impulses continue also during deep sleep and also when the person (or animal) is subjected to the influence of narcotics. The professor proved by experimental methods the similarity of vibrations in different persons of the sight of the same object or manifestation. Different thoughts, which arise as a consequence of the action of the visual nerves, give different impressions upon the film.

"Prof. Adrian confined his experiments mainly to that part of the human brain which controls vision. He proved that this region of the brain is extraordinarily small. And Prof. Adrian established the fact with the help of his apparati, that the greater part of the human brain does not participate in any mental process.

"Prof. Adrian carried his experiments to such a degree of perfection that he can now easily change his photographic records of thought into sound and can broadcast it over the radio for the public. During a public demonstration the audience heard a great variety of sounds, varying with the visual impressions of the patient, who sat upon the stage and opened his eyes at the direction of the professor."

Thus something quite natural and perhaps long ago known is already being recorded already by crude mechanical apparati. Long before these mechanical records were achieved, the great Indian scholar Sir Jagadis Bose in similar experiments recorded the pulse of plants and demonstrated even for a casual observer, how plants react to pain and light and how the appearance of even a distant cloud reacts upon the pulse. Graphically he showed on a screen the agony of a plant's death, poisoned or transfixed. At the same time, he recorded the influence of human energy upon the life of the same plants, which not long ago were in the eyes of civilized people regarded to be but mere lower growths, devoid of any senses.

By the movement of the needle, which records the pulse of the plant, one can notice the influence of human energy of thought. A kind thought, a sympathetic thought could protect the plant from the action of poison. In the same degree, a hostile thought would increase the fatal action.

If only quicker, as quickly as possible, the realization of the importance and power of thought would penetrate into the minds of even the uneducated masses! It is ridiculous and humiliating to subject that lofty experiment upon human thought to the action of coarse mechanical apparatuses. But for a coarse consciousness, similar methods of investigation are necessary. The realization alone of the significance of thought would already considerably transform our earthly existence.

In the realm of television, important, purely mechanical improvements take place. It has just been reported that during the current year, this transmission of vision at a distance will receive new possibilities. This is quite possible since once the field has been entered, the results in this direction will no doubt accumulate shortly. Gradually the reflection of the quality of thought will also become apparent through television, when images of persons are transmitted.

Even some observant photographers point out that the difference of photographs depends not only on purely external conditions but also on the inner state of the subject. Thus also in this case we arrive at the concept of the reflection of thought.

Discussions about hypnotism and suggestion, that is to say about the trained methods of influence, have already become common. But the limited consciousness as yet but feebly admits that not only in cases of trained mental influences but absolutely cases of more or less clear thinking, powerful reactions upon the surroundings take place.

This consideration will once more remind us of the concept of responsibility, about which we recently had several evidences. What lofty beauty is contained in the idea of responsibility and service! And there is no such spot on earth where man would not be subject to these two great predestinations.

When we evoke from space words and sounds, are they not also followed by the ever-present properties of the energy of thought? Along tremendous distances the human voice, directed by thought, clearly resounds.

No doubt, across vast space together with the outer Sound are also stretched the inner strings of a mighty energy. Some will sense them quite clearly; another, though feeling them, will deny. And in such a negation there will be again present the element of fear. For the fearing consciousness shudders at the very hint that it is surrounded by influences and energies. Precisely that which should uplift people casts the weak- willed into fear. Precisely into fear, which is the consequence of something indefinite and chaotic. But fear will not save us from chaos. Fears are the very gates to chaos!

It is beautiful, being clad in valor, to realize the grandeur of thought and of all the energies that it sets into action. Though through mechanical means, nevertheless let people hurriedly approach the thoughts about thought in all its mighty significance. And instead of a chaotic fear, many seemingly complicated problems of life will become illumined by the realization of all the possibilities of thought. Not without reason was it said: "Act not only in body, but also in thought!"

What a beautiful concept:
—*"Thought in Infinity."*

FROM BEYOND

THERE is a particular kind of people who call themselves skeptics and who require "material proofs," and yet in this, for each proof they will find some disproof of their own. If a witness to something appears, they will say that it simply seemed so to him. If a great number of witnesses come forward, it will very likely be declared that mass psychosis took place. If they see the impression of something on a material film, they will probably suspect some cleverly fabricated falsification. In this they lose sight of the fact that a man who is too suspicious of others bears within himself the germs of that very thing which he is so ready to impute to others.

Among all the forms of evidence, the most striking ones for skeptics will be signs that have appeared on material objects. If something appears upon a film that was not in front of the camera at the moment of exposure, then even a sworn doubter will be shaken in his confirmed skepticism, that is to say, in his ignorance. So many times each one has had occasion to meet with people who have solemnly declared that if proofs should be manifested to them, they would proclaim far and wide that of which they had been convinced. But when these proofs that they were awaiting appeared before their very eyes, not only did none of them proclaim anything publicly, but they continued quite coolly to wear the same mantle of skeptical complacence. Does one need to cite examples of this?

Let us leave for a while the matter of personal observation and for the time being disregard the great number of witnesses, while we recall several episodes in the field of photography. A large amount of literature has grown up regarding the question of photographing forms "from beyond." In a book by Kautz can be found a whole series of prints that it is difficult to suspect of any falsification. Likewise it is just as impossible to regard as spurious those accidental prints that the photographers themselves consider due simply to defective films. I recall how, once in India, a photograph was taken of a deceased person, and on the print beside the body appeared a whole row of figures, which those intimate with the deceased conclusively recognized as relatives of his who had preceded him in death. Likewise we have had occasion to see simple passport photographs upon which in the most unusual places appeared faces which could not be accounted for. Photographers have been chagrined at deteriorated films, but such "deterioration" can take place far oftener than may be supposed.

Quite recently there was communicated to us the following "mysterious" episode, which took place during the filming of a motion picture:

This amazing story which occurred on the set in one of the Hollywood studios was related by the distinguished American cinema artist, Warner Baxter. During the making of the picture sequences, in the course of the action, he was to represent a man mourning over the death of his wife. The actor was in great form, and the director remarked that never before in his life had he played his role with such verisimilitude.

That evening the film taken was run off in the projection room at the studio in the presence of the director. After several minutes he rushed to the telephone and called Baxter.

"Come immediately," he said in a trembling voice, "something absolutely unbelievable has happened."

Baxter hastened to the studio in an automobile. The director led him into the projection room and told the operator to return the film taken that morning.

That which Baxter saw on the screen stunned him also.

He saw himself seated in an armchair in an attitude of despair. Suddenly behind his back appeared quite perceptible lineaments of a woman's figure. Neither Baxter nor the director could find any explanation for this astonishing manifestation. The possibility of the unobserved appearance of an outsider before the camera during the filming was absolutely excluded. Likewise there could be no question of a technical trick. The cameraman affirmed on oath that he had used an absolutely immaculate roll of film.

The next day the taking of this same scene was repeated, with all measures of precaution being taken. When this second film was run off, the amazed spectators again saw this mysterious apparition behind the actor's back.

In the words of Warner Baxter, to this day he has not succeeded in accounting for this astonishing manifestation. Some of the cinema artists who believe in the occult sciences affirm that in the case cited there took place a manifestation of some particular spirit. Others affirm that the thoughts of the actor, attaining a high degree of tension, took on a material form. The fact that the mysterious specter appeared in both the successive exposures excludes any possibility of fraud or trick.

Let us set aside for a while carrying out to conclusion arguments as to precisely how to explain the unexpected appearance of the figure on the film. On those themes it is possible to discuss at great length, and for skeptics such conjectures will still be unconvincing. But the very appearance of the figure on the film, which was testified to by the many who saw this registration, remains indisputable. It is especially characteristic that the episode occurred twice. It is entirely impossible to form conjectures and conclusions about precisely what attendant circumstances could contribute to such a manifestation. Obviously there exist such conditions, complicated as viewed by human thinking, which do not as yet yield to formulation.

We have had occasion to hear in what unexpected conditions the most remarkable prints have resulted. Yet at the same time, when according to human reasoning, the "best" conditions were arranged, no results were obtained. Precisely the unexpectedness of manifestations especially arrests the attention. In this very unexpectedness vanishes any suggestion of fraud. And again, what falsification could be looked for in those cases, when people not only do not rejoice at the manifestations but on the contrary consider them simply deterioration of the films?

It has been related to us, how a friend of ours obtained from a photographer's studio a so-called unsuccessful photograph, upon which in different positions there had come out some strange unaccounted for faces. The photographer was extremely apologetic for such strangely spoiled film and did not even want to give away a negative, which in his opinion as unsuccessful. In this it is characteristic that the apartment itself of the photographer was quite the usual type, in which there were made numerous exposures every day. And our friend himself was in a most ordinary and worldly frame of mind, being completely removed from thought about anything extraordinary. Many times we have happened to hear that surprising manifestations occur not when they are expected by the human reason but precisely in the most unexpected circumstances. We have happened to see the furniture of rooms where remarkable prints had been made, and it was amazing that in such a drab atmosphere, anything unusual could take place. Evidently there exist especially subtle conditions that for the present elude human thinking.

Likewise by their own premature conclusions, people frequently destroy the possibilities of significant manifestations. The grossest judgments during the subtlest manifestations can only be harmful. Before making any arbitrary conclusions, one should, without prejudice, collect all the available facts. In this matter, let people call you materialists—it is unimportant how they shall define your methods. But first of all it is important to display impartiality in relationships. The film is a material object. No one will suspect the film and the photographic apparatus of anything "supernatural." But if these material objects note down something most subtle, it is all the same by what path and what method, provided the new facts penetrate into the human consciousness. Everything that broadens and bestows new possibilities must be accepted with gratitude. If a noteworthy fact comes out, not in a specially constructed laboratory but amid the most worldly surroundings, then certainly this detail in no way belittles its true significance. It is possible to call to mind so many of the most useful discoveries made not by specialists in the particular field but sometimes, as it were, by casual workers. From the domain of metallurgy, we have had occasion to hear how specialists have paid attention to the particular methods employed by certain experienced workmen. Precisely these "casual" methods subsequently proved especially useful in the hands of specialists, forming them into an integral and significant improvement.

Specialists divide themselves into two camps. Some, even those who are serious scholars, arrogantly pass by the most interesting facts if they are not arrayed in scientific garb. Whereas the others, amid the most ordinary surroundings, know how to observe and to work out the most important improvements. Of course it is well known that there has been inspected only the most insignificant portion of brain activity. Not without reason has attention frequently been turned to the fact that human natural relationships have been studied least of all. Call these domains psychology or, circumstantially, reflexology; give them any names that can assist your experiments, but guard these most precious fields against light-minded outrage.

It is highly indicative that such books as Alexis Carrel's *Man, the Unknown* have reached ten editions and are considered the most widely circulated in the international market. Man is still striving for cognition. Apart from epidemics of dances and newly devised games, people in all countries are striving for enlightenment. News has reached us that at present in Moscow upon suggestion of the late Maxim Gorky, a colossal block of buildings covering 450 hectares is being erected, dedicated to the study of man. The central place is occupied by the All-Union Institute of Experimental Medicine. Research with goodwill is the first factor in advancement.

ESSENCE

THE essential nature of people is fundamentally good. The first time this realization was fortified in me was during an experiment long ago with the extrusion of the subtle body.

My friend, a physician, had put to sleep a certain G.; and drawing out his subtle body, ordered him to send it into a house where he had never been before. By means of following his subtle body, the sleeper pointed out a series of characteristic details. Then he was directed to rise up to a certain floor of the house and to enter a certain door. The sleeping man outlined the details of the hallway, saying that there was before him a door. Again he was directed to go further and to tell what he saw. He described the room and said that a man was seated at a table reading. Then he was directed to "approach and frighten him."

Silence followed.

"I direct you to go near him and frighten him." Again silence, and then, in a timid voice:

"I cannot."

"Explain why you cannot."

"Impossible, he has a weak heart."

"Then do not frighten him, but as much as you can without harm, make your influence felt. What do you see?"

"He has turned and lit a second lamp."

"If it is not dangerous, increase your influence. What do you see?"

"He jumped up and went into the adjoining room where a woman is sitting."

At the conclusion of the experiment, we telephoned our

acquaintance, and without telling him about the matter, indirectly led him to relate his sensations. He said:

"Today I had a strange experience. A little while ago, I was seated with a book, and suddenly I felt some inexplicable presence. I am ashamed to tell you that this sensation was so sharp in its effect that I had a desire for more light. Nevertheless, the feeling became so strong that I went to tell my wife about it and to sit with her."

Apart from the experiment itself, which so clearly demonstrates the causes of many of our sensations, one detail had in it for me personally an unforgettable significance. In earthly circumstances the man would not take account of whether someone had a weak heart. He would frighten, abuse, cause him evil, without considering any such thing. But the subtle body, that about which the Apostle Paul speaks so clearly, in its essence is inclined toward good. As you see, before carrying out the order to frighten, there was manifested the consideration of sensing the condition of the heart. The essence of good whispered here that it would be dangerous to do harm to an already weak heart.

One such experiment, in the most ordinary everyday circumstances, already leads one beyond the boundaries of the bodily-limited. There resulted not only the extrusion of the subtle body, but a remarkable testing of the good of the essential nature. How much dark burden must weight down luminous subtle essence for people to reach such misanthropy as they do. Again, as St. Anthony has said: "Hell is ignorance." Of course, the whole dark burden is primarily from ignorance. In such a situation, how needful are good thoughts, which with their unseen wings touch the oppressed beclouded forehead.

When in their ignorance, people say: "Why these concentrations of thought, why these hermits withdrawing from the world? Why, they are egoists, and they think only of their own salvation." There is a great mistake in such a judgment. If even in the most ordinary experiment we could convince ourselves of the good and noble essence of the subtle body, if we saw that a thought of good transcended all commands, usually so unquestioned in such cases, then so needful are these thoughts of good. What simple yet touching solicitude is told in the simple reply about the weak heart. And right now there are not a few weak hearts, and who has the right to overburden them? Right now there are many mortally smitten hearts which could no longer hold up under a careless impact. And this will be murder just as precisely as killing with a dagger, bullet, or poison. Does not poison penetrate into the heart through an attack of malice? What an enormous number of murders—actual, intentional, malicious in their prolongation—takes place outside the reach of any courts or penalties! To poison a man is inadmissible; this is right. But then why is it possible to gnaw and tear the heart of a man? Surely if people would even sometimes, though briefly, reflect in the morning hours about something good, apart from their own selfish interests, this would be a great offering to the world.

Of course, ignorant cynics will probably sneer, considering that in any case this thought is nothing more than a blade of grass in the wind. Any cynicism about thought, about the spirit, about intangible possibilities will be a clear example of the grossest ignorance. When these ignorant ones, grinning maliciously, say: "Whither should we, of small culture, plunge into an ocean of thoughts"—this will be said not at all in humility or timidity but will be the expression of the ugliest arrogance.

Often people dream in secret of encountering something, as they say in popular language, supernatural. Precisely as if in the greatness of nature, there can be the natural and, as an antithesis, the supernatural. Of course, this ordinary expression, found in popular usage, does not lead to a true cognition. But the root of the matter is this, that as soon as people have chanced to come in contact with even the beginning of such an unusual manifestation, they have fallen into such unrestrained heart palpitation that the manifestation stopped short. It was suspended for the very same reason as in the case of the experiment related above. It has been clearly established that the uncultivated heart and the inexperienced consciousness cannot endure anything loftier than their trivial routine.

Very often certain inexplicable heart palpitations are spoken about. People attribute them to the category of sex, or to inordinate work, or to some other excesses. But among these manifestations not a few cases would be found, when some beautiful wings have already touched someone expectant or unexpectant, yet he at the first proximity to them would suffer a mortal trembling. This too will so often be from the incompatible distinction between earthly language and the Heavenly tongue.

So much good and compassion is contained in the simple consideration about the weak heart. If people, even in their everyday life would admit to themselves more often this humane thought about a neighbor's pain, about over-fatigue and weakness of his heart, then surely in this way, they would become in many cases more humane.

Manifestations of the dead have been recounted in all sorts of narratives. They are entirely beyond question. Among them it is undoubtedly true that many times, though with a highly needful goal in view, departed relatives and friend could not tell them their good news solely because of that same animal terror on the part of those to whom they appeared. Cases are known that when desiring to save a person from peril, departed ones have had to undertake a whole series of gradual approaches in order to free the person first of all from fear. Precisely fear so often prevents receiving the best news.

These manifestations, such good news and wishes to help, have been written about so much, that it is impossible to go into an enumeration of the individual episodes. Beginning with theological and on through many philosophical, historical, and poetic narratives, it is everywhere affirmed that there is no death as such, and that the proximity of the worlds can be sensed even amid everyday life. All this is past doubting. But malice and hatred, which have so taken possession of humanity in our time, make it imperative to recall once more that the essential nature of man is good, and that everything evil and hideously harmful will be first of all an additional effect of ignorance.

The very dark ones, those creatures that have fallen very low, exert their influence first of all on the ignorant. Their favorite expedient is intimidation in many ways. They try so hard to obscure and to lower the consciousness of their victim, that he feels himself isolated, alone; and finally, he can see his fortune in communion with the dark ones. And these, likewise, try to deprive the victim of all true joys, imposing upon him all the shameful surrogates of self-indulgence.

Man wishes to forget himself. Instead of wishing it possible to reflect more clearly and to take up arms in the spiritual battle, he is compelled to forget himself. In the delirious desire of forgetfulness, it is easier to take possession of him and make him an obedient instrument, cajoling him into ignorance. Whereas, only the thought of good, which lies in the foundation, can impel one to a thirst for knowledge. And then man does not lose a day or hour in order to learn, to make better, and to make beautiful everything possible. In this process, thought of good will also be a thought of beauty.

PARAPSYCHOLOGY

NEW upward flights of thought bring to life new words. Not so long ago the concept of psychology won for itself the right of acceptance—we need not repeat the significance of this Greek word, for it is sufficiently well known to everyone. Psychology has gradually conquered new fields and penetrated into the depths of the human consciousness. It has been linked with neurology and dealt with in the "Institutes of the Brain"; it has touched upon the domain of the heart and concentrated upon the study of energy and thought.

Long ago, Plato asserted that Ideas rule the world, but only comparatively recently has a science of thought been constituted. It is quite natural that this broadest of provinces should require a new and refined designation. Thus there has resulted the significant superstructure upon the concept of psychology; there was born parapsychology. Radio waves, sensitive photographic films, and many new paths of science have become allied with the fields of parapsychology, and not by chance has man's attention been drawn to this higher domain, which must transform many of the basic features of life.

In the dark period of the Middle Ages, any investigations into the region of parapsychology would surely have been terminated by the inquisition with torture and the stake. And even now our contemporary "inquisitors" are not above accusing learned investigators of sorcery or insanity. We recall how our friend, the late Professor Bechterev, was not only subjected to official persecutions for his research into the study of thought, but in the devious turns of public opinion, there were more than once heard whispers about a nervous malady of the scholar himself. We likewise know that for their research in the domain of thought, serious scientists have been visited with all sorts of official annoyance, and sometimes have even been deprived of university appointments. This has happened both in Europe and in America. But evolution flows on over any human obstructions and calumnies. Evolution is unyieldingly resistant to dark ignorance, and life itself displays the brilliant advancement of that which even in the recent past would have aroused the scoffing of the ignorant. Surely we cannot forget that even in our own time one scientific Academy pronounced Edison's phonograph the trick of a charlatan. Not so long ago a certain physician asserted that since microorganisms required such great magnification for study of them, they could have absolutely no significance or application in medical practice! You may see statements of this kind being circulated right now by the printed word. But since stagnation has an ossifying effect, all the live portions of humanity will be irresistibly impelled to true broad cognition.

We know that in America alone some forty scholars are occupied with the study of thought energy. Before us lie copies of the journal *Parapsychology*, published under the editorship of Professor Rhine (Duke University, South Carolina) and his books *Extra-Sensory Perception* and *New Frontiers of the Mind*. Professors Rhine and McDougall have worked for many years upon thought transmission at a distance. We have already had occasion to make note of their brilliant results in this field. Now Professor Rhine has taken into collaboration an entire large group of intelligent students and together with them has carried out a series of most instructive experiments.

At first the transmission of thoughts was effected at the shortest intervals and in the simplest formulas; after this the experiments passed on to involve greater distances and were made complicated in the thought content. In the course of several years, it became established that thought can undoubtedly be transmitted at a distance, and that for this, people do not at all have to become some sort of devotees of the supernatural, but they can operate within the limits of the mind and the will. It is unquestionable that the domain of thought, the field of disclosure of the subtlest primary energy, has been ordained for the immediately forthcoming days of humanity. Thus, precisely science, call it material science or positive or as you please, but precisely scientific cognition will reveal to mankind those domains to which the most ancient symbols have alluded.

If world thought be directed along a definite path, a great number of unexpected auxiliaries can be discerned by the observant mind of the investigator. People have appeared, sometimes most ordinary ones, who can detect radio waves without a receiver or can see through dense objects, thus confirming the fact that the senses can act outside the limits of physical conditions.

There is a young girl in Latvia who reads thoughts, doing this under the surveillance of physicians and scholars. Medical supervision excludes any sort of charlatanism or self-interested exploitation. In the last analysis, such phenomenon ceases to be supernatural since through training, the students of the University in South Carolina can attain very significant results by perfectly natural means.

Likewise, extremely remarkable are experiments with a recently devised apparatus that records the most subtle pulsations of the heart, which have hitherto been undetected. Recently Dr. Anita Muhl described to us the most interesting experiments performed by her. These showed that lofty thought heightened tension enormously and refined the vibrations; whereas ordinary thought, not to mention that of a low order, immediately lowered the vibrations. Moreover, it was noticed that the unified thought of a group of people constituting a chain augmented tension extraordinarily. Doctor Muhl brought back observations made during her recent visit to Iceland and Denmark, and now India, where she is sojourning, will undoubtedly provide her with new impulses.

Of course, any such considerations, even though confirmed by mechanical apparatus, will continue to remain *terra incognita* for the majority of people. But fortunately evolution has never been brought about by the majority but has been realized by an unselfish minority who are ready to subject themselves to the thrusts of the ignorant. But the right judgment of history is inevitable. The names of ignorant opponents of knowledge become symbols of infamous retrogression. The name of Herostratus, who destroyed works of art, has remained in schoolbooks, but not at all in connection with the matters that this madman had in mind. The names of the ignoramuses who voted for the expulsion of the great Aristides from Athens have recently been discovered in the course of excavations upon the Acropolis and added to the dark roster of the ignorant and the deniers. Surely we cannot forget the man who could detect radio waves without apparatus and who, in our civilized days, was immured in an insane asylum because physicians of a certain type could not admit the existence of this faculty. In general many human capacities confound people of a sluggish, retrogressive nature, and they will have to pass through many shameful hours, when all the things which they have denied shall occupy a place in the precise sciences.

Even at present, certain obscurantists regard the transmission of thought at a distance as verging on witchcraft. We can cite examples when this field, already established by scores of scientists, provokes gross ridicule and mocking cries about the reception of news out "of the blue sky." Without speaking of the examples recorded in the literature of all ages and peoples, it is permissible to remind the ignorant that the radio waves, which have already become a part of their everyday life, are received precisely out of the blue sky. It is sad to reflect that people give no thought to many obvious manifestations and to the cosmic fundamentals or laws that lie behind them. Sometimes the ignorant are not averse to repeating parrot-like certain truisms without understanding their significance. Thus, those who jeer at news from the blue sky do not suspect that they are speaking about what has already been established by scientific investigations and recorded by machines.

So much has been said and written about the subtlest energies, which are so gradually being apprehended by humanity! The absurd prohibitions created by the inertia of stagnant deniers are beginning to fall away. Only yesterday we read about the establishment of a special governmental committee for the investigation of Hindu popular medicine. The ordinances of the Ayurveda, so recently ridiculed, are coming to life again under the hand of enlightened scholars. In Moscow has been founded an Institute for the Study of Tibetan Medicine; western scientists have found to be of vast significance the indications given in ancient Chinese annals, which are entirely conformable to the latest European scientific discoveries. And the ancient medicine man who brewed a potion from toads has found his justification in contemporary science, which has revealed the large quantity of adrenalin in these amphibians; moreover, there has been found in these creatures a new substance, buffonin, which is closely akin to digitalis. One might cite a multitude of similar examples among latest discoveries. The ass hide of Chinese medicine has also been justified in the matter of vitamin content by the latest researches of Doctor Reed.

Another scientist, Doctor Reele, has determined under the most ancient symbols the existence of indications, the significance of which has now been understood and thus advanced by science. In such manner, in different branches of science, the ancient elements of knowledge are making their appearance under a new and entirely modern aspect. If these parallels be collected, there results a voluminous treatise. But the crowning dome of all these quests will be that fundamental domain which now goes under the name of parapsychology because in its basis lies everywhere that same great primary or psychic energy. The visionary dream of thought has already been formulated in the science of thought. Human thought that anticipates all discoveries is borne into space and reaches the human consciousness precisely "out of the blue sky." The brain activity of man is comparable to electrical phenomena; recently the biologist G. Lakhovsky asserted that all ethical teachings have a definitely biological foundation. Thus in its turn Lakhovsky's work confirms the experiments of Doctor Muhl with electrical apparatus that records graphically the significance of qualities of thought. Even the myth about the cap of invisibility receives scientific confirmation in the discovery of rays that make objects invisible. Thus there arises everywhere new and boundless knowledge replacing recent negations and mockery. To all deniers can only be given the advice: "Know more, and stop not your ears with the wadding of criminal ignorance." In remote antiquity it was said that ignorance is the forefather of all crimes and offenses, of all miseries and calamities.

Call it parapsychology or science of thought, be it revealed as psychic or primary energy, it is alone clear that evolution imperatively directs mankind to the discovery of the subtlest energies. Unprejudiced science is striving in quests for new energies in space, that infinite source of all forces and all cognition. Our age is the epoch of a world outlook based on Energetics.

SIGNS OF OUR ERA

(Diary Leaves)

THE Institute of Psychosynthesis in Rome, under the directorship of Dr. Robert Assagioli; several institutes of parapsychology in Germany; metapsychical institutes in France; courses of psychology at Duke University in North Carolina conducted by Prof. Rhine; the Psychoneurological Institute in Russia; the Institute of Physiology, in the name of Pavlov; courses in psychology held by Professor Jung in Zurich; The Eranos Foundation in Ascona in Switzerland; The Yoga Institute in Bombay. The Institute for Research in Evolutionary Biology in London; interesting researches of the Lister Institute in England; experiments of the Icelandian Professor Kohlman in thought-photography; a special chair for Psychic Research at the University in Stockholm, and the innumerable Societies for Psychic Research spread throughout the world. One can quote endlessly such and similar hearths of living thought, which strive toward expansion of new limits in science. If even these wonderful achievements are as yet not united and are often under the pressure of hypocrisy and conventionality, still every unprejudiced observer can convince himself that lately, as true signs of our epoch, the paths of liberated science are victoriously widened.

In the ocean of printed matter, it is difficult to summarize qualitatively and quantitatively the entire scope of what takes place. Besides, not all ways of communication are accessible to the self-sacrificing worker, who in most cases does not possess wealth and riches. Usually means are subsidized only in the case of obviously utilitarian experiments. Similarly in the Middle Ages, it was easier to find means for experiments in transmutation of baser metals into gold; and now the great leading might of thought is hardly ever appreciated by the narrow utilitarian and mechanical consciousness.

Of course, all sorts of conventions, congresses, and correspondence serve the purpose; but in these casual contacts, there is much unsaid and misunderstood, and thus contemplated deductions are again delayed. Yet one thing is clear—that the so-called spiritualization of science is gradually introduced everywhere. The hysterical shoutings of ignoramuses and all those who harbor evil intentions remain isolated in their destructive hatefulness. It is true, these thundering attacks of ignorance are still deafening, but public opinion, however, expresses a persistent desire to combat ignorance. In encyclopedias one can find instructive examples of how recently severely criticized researches of daring pioneers are already now evaluated more cautiously. Thus all devotees of knowledge, being ready to combat ignorance, can compile encouraging records of what has been attained recently.

Yet to fight ignorance is imperative and undeferrable. No one should lull himself in the erroneous idea that there is already sufficient knowledge. In infinity, cognizance never suffices. The more efforts there will be toward realization of knowledge, the madder and uglier will be the convulsions of ignorance. Was not Paracelsus, so highly venerated today, killed by enviers, who hated his attainments? Even we witnessed how the great Mendeleev was not elected to the Academy of Science, and yet he established the periodic table of atoms. There are further numerous examples when achievements have been appreciated far away from the birthplace of the discoverer. One remembers the significant words of Rabindranath Tagore after the bestowal of the Nobel Prize. The great poet and thinker said to a delegation that had come to congratulate him: "Why do you congratulate me today and not before?"

In the saving box of life, one can find many examples that are quite out of place and which in the future should not be repeated. The organized combat of ignorance, the self-sacrificing crusade for Culture, the defense of science against all destructive attempts should become the significant seal of our age. The beautiful might of thought! The realization of psychic energy.

Let us cordially meet every scientific movement. Let us find strength to liberate ourselves from personal habits and superstitions. Let us not think that it is easy to conquer atavism, for the physical strata carry in themselves the prejudices of many ages. But if we shall firmly realize the burden of such sediments, then already one of the most difficult locks will be opened. Later we shall also unlock the next, when we shall understand why we have to apply in the earthly world full action. Only in this way shall we reach the third entrance, where we shall understand the treasure of the basic energy entrusted to mankind. He who will teach to acknowledge it will be the true teacher. Man does not reach the realization of his might without a teacher. There are various traps on the path of man. Every hidden or manifested asp hopes to conceal from man the most precious. He as a lost traveler does not know in what element to search for progress, but the treasure is within himself. The wisdom of all ages ordains "Know thyself." This advice turns the attention to the most sacred, which is predestined to manifest itself. The fiery might, temporarily called psychic energy, will give man the path to his future happiness. We cannot hope that humanity will easily cognize its own heritage; they will invent all convictions to defile every discovery of the energy. They will pass in silence over the predestined quality of their advance, but yet, the path is one.

We shall never deny that we watch with the greatest enthusiasm the attainments of science. Be this in the Society of Psychic Research, or in the cause of thought transference at Duke University, or in the matter of photography of the invisible world—absolutely to all scientific experiments every cultural person should be well-wishingly open. The diary leaves "Combating Ignorance" give, as it were, a reply to uncultural conspiracies. The aims of the Society of Psychic Research, its highest form, and also all experiments concerning psychic energy should be met with welcome open-mindedness and thorough scientific control.

Only ignoramuses are not aware of how many most useful institutions and university courses for investigation of psychic phenomena have been started lately in many countries. Only ignoramuses do not want to know how many scientific books have been published in this connection by such eminent scientists, as for example. Dr. Alexis Carrel's *Man, the Unknown,* etc. Thus, let every uncultural attack upon science meet with a definite well-founded resistance; may the silly, militant ignoramuses remain in their own hole, as they deserve.

We shall always remain well-wishers toward all sincere seekers and pioneers. The psychic researchers, physiologists to whatever camp they may belong, are true pioneers of the science of the future. Subtle manifestations, the power of thought, as the basis of human creativeness and progress will find a deserved place of honor amid the attainments of evolution. "Study all surroundings," "Cognise untiringly!" "The Heart is infinite," "Winged is thought."

From the depths of the ages come many encouraging calls. The human-cooperator receives support from all strongholds of the ancient and new knowledge. The study of the progression of collective energy can prove that unity is not only a moral concept but a mighty psychic moving power. When we reiterate about unity, we wish to suggest the cognizance of the great force that is at the disposal of every human being. It is impossible for an inexperienced research worker to imagine how collective energy increases. One should prepare the consciousness for such a manifestation. The success of the experiment depends on the striving of all participants. If even a single person does not wish to cooperate wholeheartedly then it is better not even to experiment. The power of united force was already known in antiquity. Solitary observers sometimes united for joint research with the result that a whole chain was obtained, and the observers placed their hands on the shoulder of the predecessors. One could witness the most extraordinary fluctuation of energy; when the striving was uniform the intensification of energy was enormous. Thus when I speak of unity, I have in view a real force. May all those who should know it, remember this.

Psychic energy in antiquity was sometimes called the "air of the heart." This was meant to indicate that the heart lives by psychic energy. Truly, as man cannot live long without air, so does the heart cease to live without psychic energy. Many ancient definitions should be benevolently reconsidered. People long ago understood a manifestation that now has been neglected

The magnetization of water placed near a sleeping person is already proof of the emanation of his radiations and of the deposit of energy on objects. One should carefully study such deposits, for they can remind of the duty of man to saturate the surroundings with beautiful sediments. Every sleep is not only a study for the subtle body but also a nursery for psychic accumulations.

Experiments with the expansion of depository forces are also most instructive. One can notice that energy evaporates in different degrees. Some powerful radiations can last decidedly longer when they are sent by pure thinking. Hence pure thinking is not only also a moral concept but the real multiplication of power. The ability to conceive the true meaning of moral concepts pertains to the domain of science. One cannot light-mindedly divide science into materialistic and spiritual—there is no borderline.

One should conduct observations not only of concordant manifestations but also of disuniting ones. An experiment is valuable when manifold. One cannot at the beginning of an experiment preclude what irradients will be needed for the intensification of the reaction. One can enlist the cooperation of most unexpected objects, for the faculties of subtle energies cannot be limited. Such an infinity of possibilities does not interfere with the scientific methods of research. One can apply individual methods and accept such new manifestations courageously. No one can indicate where human power is at an end. And precisely not a superman but every healthy person can become winged by happy achievements. In every household psychic energy can be studied. No special expensive laboratories are needed to educate the consciousness. Every age brings its own message to humanity. Psychic energy has the aim to help humanity amid its unsolvable problems.

Knowing how to patiently study war conditions are most favorable for the experiment. There may be cosmic conditions or bright color schemes or experiments with minerals or observations of animal life. One can observe how the presence of a person in an adjoining room reacts upon the current of energy. Man does not realize in what mood he is at a given moment. One may see that man will affirm his best mood, but the apparatus will show irritation or other bad feelings. Man will not hide his inner feeling because of a desire to lie, but more often because he is incapable of defining his perceptions.

Besides the investigation of psychic energy with regard to color, tests are also on sound and fragrance. One can obtain the convincing effects of music; noting the distance and the musical harmonies themselves. Much is spoken about the influence of music upon people, but practical experiments are seldom conducted. One may study the influence of music upon the mood of a person, but this is commonplace. Of course, it is presumed that gay music imbues with joy and sad music with sorrow, but such conclusions are not sufficient. One should ascertain what harmonies are nearest to the psychic energy of man. What symphony can most powerfully induce rest or inspiration in man? One must try out various musical compositions. The very quality of harmonization will give the best indications about the path of sound in human life. Similarly one should investigate the influence of fragrances. One should keep close aromatic flowers and various ingredients that can excite or decrease psychic energy. And finally one can unite color, sound and fragrance and study the cooperation of these three moving forces.

People will, after all, understand what mighty influences surround them. They will understand that the entire routine of their life manifests a great influence upon their fate. People will learn to pay more attention to every object. They will surround themselves by true friends and will escape destructive influences. Thus the salutary energy will help in the reorganization of life.

Usually least attention is given to the most important. But we shall not be tired to reiterate what is most needed for humanity. Amid such seeming repetitions, we shall affirm the desire for knowledge. People have become accustomed to somebody else thinking for them and that it is the duty of the world to look after them. But everyone should bring his own cooperation. The ability to apply one's psychic energy will gradually educate the consciousness.

In the family, in schools, in public life, there will be affirmed the cognizance of subtle energies. The art of thinking in all its beauty will again become the beloved sport—the true wings of humanity.

COMBATING IGNORANCE

THE extermination of ignorance should be carried out on a world scale. No nation can boast that it is sufficiently educated. Nobody has sufficient strength to conquer ignorance single-handedly. Knowledge should be universal and should be supported in full cooperation. Ways of communication know no limitations. Thus also the path of knowledge should flourish through exchange of opinion. One should not think that somewhere enough has already been done for education. Knowledge spreads to such an extent that a constant renewal of methods is required. It is horrible to witness fossilized brains, which do not admit new achievements. No denier can ever be a true scientist. Science is free, honest, and fearless. Science can change instantaneously and can enlighten upon world problems. Science is beautiful and, therefore, is infinite. Science does not tolerate prohibition, prejudice, and superstition. Science can find the great even in the quest of the small. Ask great scientists how often the most astonishing discoveries took place during ordinary research. The eye was open and the brain was not dusty. The path of those who know how to investigate without limitations is the Path of the Future. Verily the struggle against ignorance is undeferrable, as against decomposition and decay. Combating evil ignorance is not easy, for it has many henchmen. It lurks in many countries and is clothed in various garments. One has to apply courage and patience, for the battle with ignorance is the conquest of chaos.

Already five centuries before our era, there came from the East the blessed words: "Ignorance is the worst crime." Later on the great hermits of the first centuries of Christianity also ordained that "Ignorance is hell." Truly all fratricidal crimes have their origin in this dark abyss. The same evil source pollutes the world with lies and darkness, which create the most ugly, the most cruel, and abhorrent evildoings.

To swallow food does not yet mean to live. In the same way to be literate does not mean to be educated. Literacy is a natural food, but we see that as food it may be either useful or harmful because it can serve both good and bad. Education and culture are synonymous. In both is contained readiness for infinite cognizance. In the furnace of such a constant rejuvenation of consciousness, the very essence of man is being purified. Through the honest and unlimited labor of knowledge, people are ennobled and begin to understand the concept of service to humanity. The true scholar has an open eye and is moved by freedom of thought. But as everything in life, the eye and thought must also be educated. From the first steps of education an enlightened admission and broadening of the horizon should be laid at the foundation of primary schools. Knowledge should be freed from conventional limitations. Knowledge is the path to joy, but joy is a special wisdom.

The scientist and the artist know the meaning of the word inspiration. They know, what is realization, which opens to them new refined forms and reveals subtle energies previously unnoticed or perhaps forgotten. From antiquity there came the realization that thought is an energy, that thought is light-bearing. For ages certain people knew that thought can be transmitted. But even such an old axiom has only lately entered the scientific minds before the very eyes of our present generation. We all were witness, how quite recently the ignoramuses scoffed at so-called magnetism and hypnotism.

It went so far that the same force under various names was accepted differently. Mesmerism was ridiculed and condemned, but the same force under the name of hypnotism received a certain right for existence. There are peculiar reasons why some pills have to be gilded and medicine phials have to be adorned with special attractive labels. And one can understand why some chemicals, which are now fully recognized, had to be veiled by the alchemists under the names of the eagle and the phoenix, and many other symbols.

We all remember how at the foundation by Prof. Bekhterev of the Neurological Institute, every skeptic ridiculed his experiments of thought transmission. The fact that the name of Bekhterev was widely revered and renowned did not save him from derision and not even from most formidable suspicions. Ignoramuses organized a whispering campaign, stating that a whole institution could not be devoted to the research of the nervous system and thought alone. They whispered of some political intrigues, about some love affairs, and even that Bekhterev had become insane. Such were the colossal allegations invented by ignorance. I remember how during this whispering campaign we painfully remembered the book by Gaston Tissandé Martyrs of Science. Verily, where are the limits when during our present generation a certain academy called the great Edison a charlatan for his invention of the phonograph, and certain universities did not admit women to higher education. I repeat that this happened not during the medieval ages but before our very eyes, and such shameful actions were committed not by illiterate savages but by people bearing the conventional official label of a scientist. Let us not enumerate the endless row of true martyrs of science in all countries; but since we quoted the persecution of education for women, let us also recall the case of the mathematician genius, Sophie Kovalevskaya, who was not admitted to any university and yet received world recognition for her work on higher mathematics. And there are not a few excellent scholars and physicians, who being persecuted by their colleagues were compelled to leave their own country.

The world is proud of the name of the great physiologist Pavlov; everywhere are being affirmed and admired his formulae of reflexes and other ingenious solutions of biological problems. But even this glorious international achievement crowned by the Nobel Prize, calls forth in certain circles a contemptuous shrugging of the shoulders. Amid the latter one, one will also discover ignorance. Verily no uniforms and robes, no dead scholastic labels can cover human hatred, envy, and bigotry. It is far easier to combat illiteracy than to annihilate the sinister hydra of hatred, with all of its many heads of jealousy, doubt, slander, and all hidden campaigns, which the forces of darkness so cunningly manipulate. The forces of darkness, the forces of ignorance—these shameful synonyms—are closely united. Of all feelings, love and hatred are the most powerful and unifying.

Of course, in spite of all ferocious attempts of ignorance, enlightened knowledge progresses in the whole world. Let us remember the recent achievements that made the world rejoice. Let us remember the remarkable discovery of the great biologist Sir Jagadis Bose concerning the life of plants. Professor A. H. Compton states that human thought is the most important factor of the world. Prof. S. Metalnikoff of the Pasteur Institute makes most important research in the field of immunity and immortality of protozoa. Dr. Kotick investigates the transfer of sensitiveness. Dr. Walter Stempell of Müenster University proves the existence of invisible radiation of all living organisms. Dr. Paul Dobler of Heilbronn University affirms the existence of earthly radiation and its relation to the diving rod, which has till recently been ridiculed. Prof. Harry M. Johnson of Virginia University arrives at interesting conclusions regarding insanity. Dr. Otrian, in charge of a meteorological station in Germany investigates extraordinary cosmic influences. L'Abbe More, the French astronomer, makes the most interesting conclusions about sunspots. The American biologist Bernard Proctor investigates special life conditions on heights. The French scientist Dr. Levy Valency warns of possible epidemics of insanity. Dr. Riese experiments with the effect of rhythm.

Dr. Bernard Reid, a British scientist, draws a parallel between ancient medicine and modern vitamin research. A Hungarian scientist discovers rays for invisibility. Everyone knows of the experiments of Professors Richet and Gilley and the research of Sir Oliver Lodge. Prof. V. van Haas of the Leiden University proves the impossibility of absolute zero. Dr. Kennon of Harvard speaks of the element of luck in scientific research. The chemist Mingley gives a bold prognosis of future discoveries. Prof. J. B. Rhine of Harvard and Prof. William McDougall have reached astonishing results at Duke University in the field of extrasensory perception and thought-transference. How many wonderful achievements! In every country there are enlightened scholars, who untiringly and fearlessly pioneer in the field of science. And still such great men remain solitary, and everyone in his field is subject to undeserved obstacles.

One can quote pages of research conducted lately that widen the frame of conventional thinking. Nature itself comes to aid every thinker. Sunspots, with all the deductions around them, of which the greatest authorities such as Sir James Jeans of Cambridge and Dr. C. G. Abbott of the Smithsonian Institute, remind us that the time is not far when ridiculed Astrology will turn out to be nothing less than a formula of Astrochemistry, and thus yet another branch of science will no longer be denied. People will understand that they are surrounded in life by powerful chemism and that they themselves represent the most refined and mighty chemical laboratory.

Everyone has read of the recently conducted experiments with the chemism of human secretions and radiation from the fingertips; some of these radiations are so powerful that they can kill harmful bacteria. Let us also remember the experiment of Prof. Yurevitch that proved that the energy radiated by man is a conductor and a connection that enables the combination of certain elements. And did not the famous experiments of Keally, which were so unjustly persecuted, prove the same?

Thus the investigation of human radiation and psychic energy imperatively calls humanity toward an amazing transfiguration of life.

Ignoramuses like to scoff at the yogi of India. For them, walking on fire, sitting on water, the consumption of terrible poisons without effect, the stopping or acceleration of the pulse at will, the burial alive and return to life after several weeks—are but skillful tricks and charlatanism. But in the last issue of the *Modern Review*, there is an article, supported by photographs, on fire-walking in Mysore. The journal quotes this in connection with the demonstration in London of the Kashmiri Khuda Bux, widely announced through the press of the whole world. Sitting on the water of the Ganges was regarded as charlatanism, and even people who had witnessed it whispered carefully: "Who knows, perhaps they were supported under the water." But quite recently, the British press reported the case of a woman, who lost weight to such an extent that this manifestation on the water was quite easy for her. The whole world was amazed to read about the striking phenomena of Theresa Neumann of Bavaria, and now the newspapers were filled with astounding accounts of Shanti Devi in Delhi, a girl of nine. This unforgettable case was verified by many reliable people.

From Latvia there comes news of the extraordinary ability of a girl of eight to read thoughts. There has also been registered a case of the reception of radio waves by a person without a receiver, and the astonishing faculty of two Italian boys to see through walls and other opaque objects. No doubt during the time of the Inquisition all these unfortunate persons, owing to their abilities, would have been burned at the stake. But even nowadays, the man who could catch radio waves mentally, had to go through a lunatic asylum! Let us also not forget the remarkable prevision and clairaudience of St. Joan of Arc, who saved France, but who for her abilities was burned on the pyre by the contemporary evil ignoramuses.

But not only the persons themselves who owned these

extraordinary faculties but also those who conducted research in these fields have been subjected by ignoramuses up to now to endless persecution. Let us also remember the unjust scoffing to which the Society of Psychic Research was so often subjected, whereas the aims of the Society deserve full support. Every nucleus of a new unprejudiced scientific conquest is attacked. This creates an ugly sight. On one part, there are new educational institutions being opened, which by their very appearance seem to invite new research; yet on the other part, every unusual manifestation that did not enter into the elementary textbooks is not only ridiculed but also prosecuted. It means that the hydra of ignorance dwells not only in illiteracy but also in fossilized perception and in human hatred.

"Every denial of Truth is ignorance and is harmful not only to the negator himself but to space as a whole. Opposition to Truth poisons space. But there exists a still more abhorrent action, when people who have also cognized Truth later turn away from it. Such shameful retreat into darkness is insane. One can find in the history of humanity that sometimes particles of Truth were realized, but afterward because of crass ignorance, certain pseudo-teachers tried again to conceal from people these immutable facts. And actions resulted that in the future will be regarded as the most shameful pages of history. And without any proof of their inaccuracy, it was ordered to deny the obvious facts. As if a disbelief in the existence of the sun was commanded, because due to weak eyesight, somebody could not look at the sun. Thus owing to ignorance and egotism, someone forbade others to cognize reality. Let people remember how many apostates reveal themselves at various epochs. Perhaps such remembrances will lead humanity to honesty and justice."

Thus everyone, for whom Education and Culture are not empty words, should, in his field as far as he can, fight ignorance. Let no one say that he has no possibility to do so—this would be untrue. *Helas*, open and hidden ignorance in all its cunningness exists everywhere. In every household a clear mind can discern where dust and rubbish have to be removed. And today when in the world there thunder guns and poisonous gases compete with each other, now the combating of ignorance is imperative. A defense of the best, most beautiful and most enlightened will be needed.

If anyone does succeed in his noble efforts, still it will be a heroic attempt and not an abstract intention. Besides, in every effort there is already a vital element of action. Therefore, every effort is already beneficial. No doubt some servitors of ignorance will whisper that precisely now words about culture and enlightenment are out of place. This is their typical trick—to find at every moment of life a reason why exactly at that hour a striving to culture and education are untimely. By this formula, the henchmen of ignorance betray themselves. "Mine" always reveals himself. But Good, Culture, and Education are needed at every hour.

There can be no such a state of consciousness in which it is untimely to be humane. And only human hatred could whisper denying this Truth; hatred—this horrible monster, in the darkness of its cave, always dreams of transforming mankind into beasts that should devour each other.

Verily, from small to great, everyone can, and it is the duty of everyone to bring his might to the cause of combating ignorance. Uniting in groups and by himself, everyone somewhere can stop the evil doings of the monster of ignorance. Every labor already contains the striving to perfection and enlightenment. Only ignorance can belittle labor as such and can shamelessly scoff at the quest of science. In just indignation against every grimace of ignorance, the worker for Culture will find a vital thought and thundering word and will record by beautiful deeds the victorious path of enlightenment.

Glory to the Knights of Culture! Glory to the heroes of labor! Glory to the Courageous!

www.ingramcontent.com/pod-product-compliance
Lightning Source LLC
Chambersburg PA
CBHW070727030726
47601CB00002B/161